The Roots of Nationalism:
Studies in Northern Europe

The Roots of Nationalism:
Studies in Northern Europe

Edited by
ROSALIND MITCHISON

Papers of a Conference
held in September 1979
at the University of Wales Conference Centre,
Gregynog Hall, under the auspices of
the Social Science Research Council,
organised by Professor T. C. Smout
of the University of Edinburgh
and Professor I. G. Jones
of University College, Aberystwyth

JOHN DONALD PUBLISHERS LTD
EDINBURGH

Printed in Great Britain by Bell & Bain Ltd., Glasgow.

Contents

6. WALES

7. SCOTLAND

Contributors

Alan Butt Philip, D.Phil., lecturer at the Centre for European Industrial Studies, University of Bath

Alf Kaartvedt, professor at the University of Bergen

Kjell Haugland, cand. philol., Oppdal, Norway

A. Pontoppidan Thyssen, docent, dr. theol., at the Institute of Church History, University of Aarhus

Lorenz Rerup, professor at the University of Roskilde

Yrjö Blomstedt, professor at the University of Helsinki

Matti Klinge, professor at the University of Helsinki

Gunnar Karlsson, dr. phil., lecturer at the Institute of History, University of Iceland

L. M. Cullen, professor of Modern Irish History, Trinity College, Dublin

Colin Baber, lecturer at University College, Cardiff

Glanmor Williams, professor of History, University College, Swansea

Rosalind Mitchison, reader in Economic History, University of Edinburgh

R. H. Campbell, professor of Economic History, University of Stirling

European Nationalism in the Nineteenth and Twentieth Centuries

Alan Butt Philip

NATIONALISM is one of the great, if not the greatest, forces in modern European history. Historians often point to the nineteenth century as the age of national movements and self-determination, and I would not wish to deny the importance of the ideas of Fichte or Herder or Mazzini, or the significance of the unification of Germany and Italy. But the twentieth century has an even stronger claim to be called the age of nationalism when all the power and the paradoxes, the sentiment and brutality of nationalist ideas came to be unleashed upon European nations and societies like some unguided missile. Respect for national identity and the principle of self-determination was one of the guiding principles underlying the Versailles Treaty in 1919. Nationalism not only destroyed the Ottoman and Austro-Hungarian empires (but, interestingly, not the Russian Empire); it was also the harbinger of the ambitions of the Third Reich; and it has launched a large number of twentieth century autonomist movements, some of which have succeeded in their aims as in Iceland; the majority of which, however, remain today in national and international politics as elements that cannot be ignored economically, culturally or politically.

Nationalism has for a very long time defied both logic and definition. Its appeal is to the emotional part of human nature, frequently playing upon what is imprecisely described by nationalists as 'natural' or 'moral' or 'right'. The main body of nationalist beliefs can be summarised as follows. There is a natural division of mankind into nations. Every nation has its own personality or character (sometimes even a mission to the world) which is the product of its history and culture. In addition all nations have the right to run their own affairs, and only by so doing can a nation realise its full potential. Finally the first loyalty of the citizen, of each individual, is to the nation state.

One of the fascinations of the study of nationalism is to try and assess why different emphases are placed upon different parts of this set of typical nationalist beliefs by different nations and by the same nations at different periods in their history. One of the many difficulties in studying nationalism — apart from the very large number of examples scattered across the world — is that to study it adequately requires a multidisciplinary approach including history, geography, economics, political science, sociology, psychology and literature.

Political nationalism is the active solidarity of a group of people who share a common culture or history and a sense of nationhood and who seek to give this common experience a political reality whether by means of self-government or some other kind of political recognition, if not autonomy. This definition of political nationalism includes several concepts which are essential to the understanding of the phenomenon. Activity distinguishes nationalism from national consciousness and suggests the assertive qualities which are so characteristic of nationalisms across the globe. Solidarity stresses the binding together of different social classes and individuals in support of common national aims. Nationalism is of course without significance unless it activates a group of people who are prepared to a greater or lesser extent to submerge their individual identities in a larger national identity which they consciously hold in common. The common history or culture which provides such a vital background for the growth of nationalism is effectively the means by which individuals can share and articulate their separate national identity and thus acquire a common experience and a common idiom which reinforces their consciousness of being part of a definable nation.

Many historians and political scientists have written in disparaging terms about nationalism; often their reactions have been profoundly conditioned by the growth of national socialism and fascism in the Europe of the 1930s, and the appalling uses to which the nationalist appeal was put.

The experience of Europe in the first half of the twentieth century as regards nationalism shows us how dangerous any ideology can be when pursued to extreme logical conclusions regardless of reality or basic human feeling for one's fellow men. Nationalism moves like the wind through human society, sometimes resembling an invigorating sea breeze, sometimes like the whirlwind that destroys all that comes into contact with it. To condemn nationalism is as pointless as condemning the wind. Nationalism has become one of the basic elements of political societies all over the world. It must be treated as a fact of political existence, not as a necessary force for good or evil.

Not that we should be complacent about the extent to which nationalism has permeated the consciousness of those who take an interest in the community and in political issues across the world. It is not only those nations which have yet to establish themselves or which seek to recreate separate institutions which display nationalist qualities. Nationalism is alive and flourishing in many of Europe's older nation-states and is an important factor in assessing the diplomatic and political behaviour of these states. Leaders such as Winston Churchill and General de Gaulle channelled the force of nationalism to serve their political ends in time of war and peace. Those who have tried to advance the integration of western European countries since 1945, through supranational institutions such as the European Community and NATO, have too easily discounted the strength of national identities to which the people tenaciously hold. The interdependent world has proved unable to replace the old habits, old loyalties and old attitudes which sustain modern nationalism. Nationalism has also enjoyed close and complex links with imperialism, which was both a product of the developing economic demands of the European countries, their rivalry and need for national self-expression as well as the key activator of modern Asian and African nationalist movements striving to disengage themselves from the white man's economic and political yoke.

In my own study of contemporary Welsh nationalism there appeared a striking contrast between the expression of Welsh nationalist sentiment in the first decades of the twentieth century and the post-1945 nationalist movement. The former aligned itself fully with British imperialism, claiming a special Celtic contribution to the achievements of the British empire. Modern nationalist thinking in Wales dissociates itself completely from imperial aspirations and claims that Wales, like other more distant outposts of empire, has suffered from the exploitation of her labour and her natural resources by capitalist outsiders who have taken their profits away with them. The United Kingdom whose success abroad was earlier celebrated by its constituent countries is now pilloried as an imperial relic, unable to compete in world markets and unable to meet the needs of its Celtic dependencies.

Public attention to the issues of Scottish and Welsh nationalism has been seriously sustained only during the 1970s. Yet Welsh and Scottish nationalism are not flashes in the pan but enduring social, political and cultural forces which the political community in Britain ignores at its peril. Welsh and Scottish claims for political autonomy enjoy a long historical tradition which English conquests and dynastic alliances have dulled but never completely removed. Nationalist attitudes in Scotland and Wales are not the exclusive preserve of the nationalist parties and their supporters. All the inhabitants of these two countries are influenced by and affected by their nationalism. In Wales a special dimension to the nationalist issue arises from the struggle the Welsh language is having simply to survive. Nationalism when linked with a minority language can be extremely divisive, where the national community is itself split along language lines. But if the language issue is ignored or treated with benign neglect by those in authority this may only serve to heighten the sense of grievance that the linguistic minority has against the state and its government and thus the linguistic cleavage in that community is intensified. Such has been the experience of modern Wales. Yet it is extremely difficult for governments and the public administration to respond to minority linguistic demands without alienating the majority, as events in Canada and Wales have shown, especially when powerful long-term economic and cultural forces appear to be stacked against the minority culture whatever action is taken by legislators.

A feature of almost every nationalist movement in Europe has been the common pattern according to which it has developed. The first stage in this process is the revival of interest in a nation's past, a taste for antiquarianism and the discovery of local history, acquired perhaps by members of the gentry and indulged in as a hobby with no ulterior political motive in view. The second stage reflects the transformation of this aristocratic interest into an intellectual movement with a nationalist perspective. The researches of the antiquarians are synthesised and built upon. The history of the nation is transcribed, revived and reinterpreted: its culture is analysed and exalted, its language purified and standardised. The third stage sees the transfer of this new perspective, as a result of education, literature and social changes, to the civic and political leaders. The nationalist idea offers a new analysis of the condition of their country, one that not only explains at a stroke the source of their discontents but which often carries revolutionary implications for the system of government. The fourth stage in this nationalist paradigm occurs when the new leaders of the country seek to communicate their nationalist ideas to the population at large and to invoke these ideas as the basis for social, cultural, economic and political change. The nationalist élite call in the bourgeoisie and the masses to redress the balance of the ancient régime, and if their appeal is heard, then major political changes result. Such is the experience, in general terms, of many nations. This paradigm does not fit exactly all known nationalist movements, nor does it predict the timescale required for their development. We cannot even be sure that nationalist ideas are the cause of the development of such nationalist movements rather than symptoms of other more subtle and fundamental social changes. At the very least nationalism is a major catalyst in bringing such changes about.

Nationalism has many different facets which stand in the way of a rigorous and complete analysis of it as a political phenomenon. Historians have seen in nationalism an influence for good by virtue of stimulus it has provided for popular democracy and cultural enrichment as well as a force for evil, as ideological ally of racism and provoker of continental war. Nationalism can give encouragement to those leaders and states which wish to deprive others of what territory or riches they already hold. Equally it may develop as the defensive reaction of a people threatened with economic, cultural or political changes by outside influences. The popular image of nationalism today likens it to the amoeba in that its main feature seems to be the capacity to divide and thus to multiply the number of states. But nationalism in the light of history is a political force that can build a nation-state, maintain it, and be responsible for its break-up.

The simplicity of nationalist ideas should never be underestimated. It means that they can be easily transmitted and understood by a mass electorate, whether literate or uneducated. Nationalism is thus able to be the great political mobiliser, providing an all-purpose framework into which popular grievances can easily be fitted. Hence part of the appeal of nationalism for youth. At the same time nationalism fulfils a psychological need for the young in search of an identity in a grouping larger than the family which they are outgrowing. Nor is nationalism an exclusive political ideology. It can change its colour like the chameleon according to the political and social landscape. Liberals were nationalists in the nineteenth century, Leninists in the twentieth. Nationalism thus has a remarkable fly-paper quality which guarantees its continuation as a major influence in world affairs.

Yet however much historians and political scientists have been able to research into and understand European nationalism, there is much that has yet to be explained, and many issues to be resolved. Our explanations have so far concentrated upon the subjective attractions of nationalist ideas for individuals, but are there not circumstances in a country's development when nationalism may become an objective necessity if its economic and political organisation is to be transformed? There has been little attempt to analyse systematically whether nationalism in Europe today is the same phenomenon as nineteenth century nationalism, produced by analogous conditions and voicing the same demands. If historic and contemporary nationalism are different, what are their distinguishing features? Are these features simply reflections of the defining qualities of nineteenth century society and culture? The nineteenth century saw the triumph of two unifying national movements in Germany and Italy. Twentieth century European nationalism has been characterised by national movements which have sought to divide existing states, although there are examples of this from the nineteenth century too.

In this century governments and political observers continue to wrestle with the problem of meeting the claims for autonomy made by minority nationalist movements without succumbing to separatism. We need to know a great deal more about political and administrative relations in those countries which already have experience of devolution and federalism. Nor should we be blind to the fact that nationalism can be a strong ideological tool in the hands of an existing government as well as being a social movement for political change. For General de Gaulle in France, nationalist ideology was the great consolidating force upon which he shaped and sustained the Fifth Republic. While in Norway in 1972, when the government of that country sought to strengthen its links with Europe by joining the European Community, an *ad hoc* popular movement successfully tapped the wellsprings of Norwegian nationalism and brought about the rejection of this initiative in a national referendum. Nationalism has never been without international dimensions, especially for those who have sought to maintain a balance of power in Europe. But the international aspects of nationalism have acquired new clothes in the form of the parallel development of supranational institutions such as the European Community which experience the interplay of national and governmental interests, as well as the export of new nationalist guerilla and terrorist activities (such as hi-jacks) beyond national frontiers.

It is an accepted wisdom that nationalism needs to be buttressed by certain key factors which distinguish one nation from another. Among these factors are counted a common territory, a common language, a common culture, a common history, and a common religion. Not all these factors are present in every national movement but no nationalism worthy of the name can thrive if they are all absent.

The existence of a definable national territory is one of the most helpful and typical determinants of nationalism. Images of 'fatherland' and 'motherland' suggest the transfer of the national territory from generation to generation and the durability, the security, and the inalienability of the link between the land and the people who inhabit it. Yet the absence of a national land did not prevent the Jews from surviving as a nation, nor does the existence of a national territory prevent it from being claimed by rival nations. The physical separation of one people from another may also encourage a distinctive national feeling: contrast the relations between the English and the Welsh with those obtaining between the English and the Irish. Yet this factor is not conclusive because every Ireland and Iceland adduced in support can be countered by a Sicily and Sardinia in opposition. Population movements are also complicating the distinctiveness of national territories. Inward migration in particular can dilute the claims of a nation to its territory or even its nationality; examples of this include the anglicisation of South East Wales and the problematic relations between Navarre and the rest of the Basque country.

A national language is often considered one of the most important building-blocks for nationalism. Yet it is not an essential element as the cases of the U.S.A. and the Republic of Ireland show: Bernard Shaw once remarked that England and Ireland were two nations divided by a common language. The linguistic nationalists of Wales who adopted in the 1960s the adage *cenedl heb iaith cenedl heb galon* [a nation without a language is a nation without a heart] were unconsciously condemning a large number of healthy nations to death. Yet the existence of a national language does provide a tangible differentiating mark between social groups and has in many cases proved a source of nationalist grievances which governments often find hard, if not impossible, to rectify. Bureaucracies are peculiarly resistant to the claims of multi-lingual communities. The language issue has several times in the history of Europe been used as a symbol for more general complaints by social groups concerning their lack of status or economic power within a wider community. Yet the case of Wales shows too how an appeal to linguistic nationalism can divide rather than unite a nation, if the national language is not in fact spoken by a large majority of its population. The unanswered question, however, remains: why is linguistic nationalism such a feature of twentieth century European nationalism? Is it that groups in the peripheral regions of the larger nation-states are seeking an identity or self-consciously trying to renew an old identity? Or are these regions only now being fully assimilated into the larger linguistic communities and this is their reaction to the dominance of the mass media and the mass culture associated with the most widely used languages?

The links between nationalism and religion are among the most intriguing sociological aspects of nationalism. Nationalism can certainly be a substitute religion rising up in a society as the hold of religion upon it declines. Such a view links the rise of nationalism to the secularisation of society, with new belief systems replacing traditional beliefs which have broken down as a result of social and economic change. Yet there are many examples in Europe where nationalism has found allies amongst the clergy, especially where a national culture seems to be in danger, and the nineteenth century nationalist movement in Wales became closely linked with the demands of the nonconformists for full civil and political rights.

Language and religion are themselves basic ingredients in national culture, a concept which however is particularly difficult to define. Are we to identify such a culture as a literary tradition, a form of social behaviour or set of social relationships, or as a way of thinking — a national idiom? A distinctive culture however defined has played a major part in many nationalist movements. The translation of the Bible into vernacular languages has incidentally sustained and standardised minority languages all over Europe. Most of us are all too aware how broadcasting and the mass media in the contemporary world influence our individual perspectives, vocabulary and thought processes, albeit imprecisely. We do not know how great the consequences of such influences are upon the cultural development of our own societies but we suspect they are considerable. There would appear to be much truth in the view that nationalist movements often contain a cultural reaction to social and economic changes.

During the twentieth century it has become an inevitable task for historians to assess the economic aspects of nationalism and nationalist movements. The massive improvement in communications in the nineteenth century with the associated urbanisation and industrialisation of the population of European states created the social and economic conditions in which nationalism could be successfully launched, and effected the unification of many countries linking industries to markets, governments to governed. From the 1960s a different economic analysis has been advanced in regard to modern minority nationalisms. These are seen as reflecting the uneven economic development obtaining within a given nation-state, or expressing the sense of 'relative deprivation' between one region and another. The concept of 'internal colonialism' has been introduced in order to define the particularly dependent economic relations obtaining between the core and the periphery of some states. Different economic analyses are now plentiful but solid empirical testing of the theories propounded is hard to find. Nationalism as a means of correcting the uneven development between core and periphery may prove to be dysfunctional, as was for decades the case in Ireland. Relative deprivation does not adequately describe the position of Basque and Catalan nationalism which survives in two of the wealthier parts of modern Spain. The extent to which external capital and enterprise has exploited the economies of Scotland and Wales is frequently misrepresented by adherents of the internal colonialism thesis.

Another argument advanced is that in contemporary Europe minority nationalisms have become more credible to the public because our conceptions of what is an economically viable state have changed as a result of collective military and economic arrangements such as NATO and the EEC. The viability of small states such as Luxembourg and Iceland despite international industrial competition suggests that breakaway states may well be able to survive as economically independent entities. This argument assumes that the viability issue was not a serious one for earlier generations of nationalism. Economic issues certainly did play a part in many nationalist movements, for example the concern of German nationalists to break down the artificial barriers to trade within Germany produced by the immense political subdivision of the country. For small countries such as Iceland and Ireland in the last century the question of economic viability had to be and was faced by their nationalist movements.

The main problem facing scholars in regard to the phenomenon of nationalism is that so many studies of nationalism have related only to one country. The greatest need for future research lies in the comparative field. Three particular areas suggest themselves for further study. Economic and social historians have raised the question whether nationalism is a necessary ideological force to enable major or rapid economic development to take place. This thesis deserves to be tested in the light of the history of all the nation-states of Europe. Secondly, many of the minority nationalisms of Europe since 1945 have erupted in a period which is characterised by increased international and regional economic interdependence. Economic forces seem to be pulling in international and centralist directions at the same time as cultural and political forces are pushing towards more autonomy, even separatism. Are such divergent trends reconcilable or are they recipes for future instability? Finally, there is the apparent paradox at a political level of the internationalisation of much of the world's decision-making at the same time as peripheral and minority nationalisms are becoming so strident. Are these phenomena related in some way, the centralisation on the one hand perhaps provoking in reaction the particularist identity on the other? Perhaps we should even be preparing to close a chapter of European history as the large nation-states begin to dismantle themselves: first Italy and Spain, possibly to be followed soon by Britain, and later still by Germany and France? If this were to happen, we would either be returning to an earlier European position in which the nation and the state were not coterminous entities, or we would have discovered that nations can change their size and definition over time.

There is no set formula which, if applied to a group of people, will inspire amongst them a sense of nationhood. It is not an easy thing to create a nation or a national community. Factors or circumstances which in one country can be used as a springboard for national consciousness and regeneration can so easily in other countries be factors which divide a people from each other: language and religion are two examples. Nations develop over the course of centuries, reacting to events and environment, and from this shared experience they unconsciously evolve individual characteristics, ways of life and idioms, which are transferred through succeeding generations. National tradition of this kind can contain both laudable qualities — tolerance, piety, enterprise — and others that are undesirable — racism and chauvinism. In different generations particular facets of this tradition can be stressed, which others ignore: a good example is the part played by the Irish language in Irish nationalism. But the national tradition can never be entirely abandoned, even in countries which are beholden to other ideologies, without losing at the same time a sense of belonging to a particular place or community, which is both the cement that binds peoples together, enabling them to act in concert, and a real psychological need shared by most individuals. This sense of community is most easily developed at a local level. But with the expansion of modern mass communications, especially transport, the press and broadcasting, the mobility of people and their exposure to a common culture and experience have been enormously increased. It is much easier for individuals who are separated by long distances from each other to consider themselves members of the same nation, and this becomes one of the justifications of larger states. This trend does not however invalidate the personal need individuals feel to belong to a national community. Indeed the speed of economic and industrial changes, and the upset to individuals' relations with each other caused by the erosion of religious belief and the break-up of close family ties which are the hallmarks of modern society, provide an urgent need for some simple and ineradicable set of social relationships which the national community and national consciousness can supply. Thus is cast the essential setting for appeals to nationalism, and it is no surprise that nationalism continues in its many diverse forms to exert a powerful hold over the minds of mankind. Even so the principle of national self-determination is not infinitely applicable and, if it were so applied, the resulting fragmentation of the political and economic communities of the world would be counterproductive in terms of satisfying the needs and aspirations of individuals.

The Economic Basis of Norwegian Nationalism in the Nineteenth Century

Alf Kaartvedt

1. The End of the Dano-Norwegian Union and the New Union with Sweden

THE present political institutions of Norway were created in 1814. For more than 400 years Norway had been part of the joint Dano-Norwegian monarchy, but by the Treaty of Kiel (14 January 1814) the Allies forced the Danish King, who had loyally stood by Napoleon, to cede Norway to the King of Sweden in compensation for the latter's active role in the struggle against Bonaparte. But this *diktat* of the Great Powers roused the Norwegians to resistance; they refused to accept the provisions of the treaty, declared their country independent, gave themselves a free constitution and chose as their king the Danish Crown Prince Christian Frederik. However, after a short war with Sweden in defence of their newly won freedom, the Norwegians were forced to capitulate and accept the union with Sweden. This union was to last until 1905 when the country united finally to break it. But the free constitution of 1814 was from the beginning preserved within the Union, which was formally established as between two equal states.

Thus under the new union — and in contrast to the earlier union with Denmark — Norway was not subordinate to Sweden; in the words of the Constitution, and these described a reality, Norway was 'a free, sovereign, indivisible and independent kingdom, united with Sweden under one king'. The Union consisted of little else than the joint monarchy and a common foreign policy; it can thus be categorised as a personal union. Norway had its own parliament and government with a separate budget; it maintained its own national bank and monetary system, and it operated its own customs policy, so that agreements between the two countries on customs matters had the character of an international treaty. Thus 'the Norwegian King' signed treaties with 'the Swedish King'. Moreover Norway maintained its own defence forces which were not integrated with those of Sweden. The Norwegian army was divided into regular and territorial units; of these the first could, with the Storting's (Parliament's) permission, be sent abroad, but the latter could not under any circumstances leave the country. And, to growing Swedish irritation, the Storting was free to reduce the regular units and increase the territorials, which it did as the nationalist movement gained strength in the country. Just how little co-ordination there was in defence — the Union's *raison d'être* — can be shown by events in the 1890s; in these years the Norwegian King, Oscar II, was obliged to authorise a Norwegian programme of re-armament, which among other things included the building of a chain of forts along the border with Sweden, at the same time that he, as King of Sweden, was working to strengthen Swedish defences for fear of an eventual war with Norway.

In one area of common interest, however, a practical, if not constitutional, union was established which was to have great significance for the future: a development in which Sweden clearly emerged as *primus inter pares*. This was foreign affairs. In 1814 the Swedish Foreign Ministry had taken over responsibility for the Union's foreign policy. This meant that the foreign policy of the two states was conducted by a Swedish Government department and that, constitutionally, the foreign minister answered only to the Swedish authorities. Despite the fact that Norwegian influence on foreign affairs grew markedly throughout the years of the Union, this issue led to unending wrangles between the two countries and became a factor in the break-up of the Union in 1905.

2. Nationalism and Historical Research

Norwegian nationalism in the nineteenth and early twentieth centuries was built upon the same general elements as nationalism elsewhere: an emphasis upon the national culture, linguistic self-identity and national self-assertion, both political and economic. But nationalism in Norway naturally also had its specific characteristics, which are of especial interest in our context. Its specific character was the result of a tension arising from Norway's two unions, long-term influences derived from the over 400-year old union with Denmark and the consequences of the new reality after 1814, the enforced union with Sweden. Those internal social, economic, cultural and political conflicts that would have in any event arisen as democracy emerged during the nineteenth century were coloured and sharpened by the legacy of the Danish union and the Norwegian attitude towards that with Sweden.

Historians in the Union period enthusiastically devoted their energies to the problem of national identity and to the question as to which political party most authentically represented national aspirations. In the process they provided historical and constitutional arguments to be used by the conflicting political parties and by the nation as a whole. Precisely because these arguments ran so deeply through the national life in this period, they survived both in historical writings and political debates long after the dissolution in 1905. Party historians continued to feel the need to defend and explain the policies of the past because these policies were still a subject of debate and controversy up until the Second World War. Just as the legacy of the revolution of 1789 influenced all sides of French politics throughout the nineteenth century and beyond, so nationalism in relation to both the old and new unions has coloured Norwegian political thought. A recent example was the great debate on Norwegian membership of the European Economic Community that began in the 1960s and culminated in the referendum of 1972, when a majority of the voters rejected membership. The debate was in effect a restatement of arguments from the period of the Union, and there is little doubt that the legacy of those arguments concerning national sovereignty and values served to weaken the pro-EEC forces.

Despite the overwhelming preoccupation with the question of national identity, Norwegian historians have never systematically adopted the approach which is the theme of this seminar, namely the economic basis of nationalism. We know a great deal about the political, social and cultural aspects, but few historians have addressed themselves to the question to what extent nationalism in Norway was based on economic grievances, either real or fancied. Occasional discussions have appeared but in general this aspect has been neglected.

3. The Main Political Trends, 1814-1905

Before discussing the economic basis of Norwegian nationalism, it is necessary to sketch in the main developments within party politics in the period 1814 to 1905.

In the following discussion, I distinguish between two profound and pervasive tendencies, namely *patriotism* and *nationalism*. This distinction, which is far from semantic, can be traced back to the 1860s when the two trends discussed below came forth into political expression, to join again in 1905 in a national movement finally committed to ending the Union.

A. The patriotic conservative tradition

By the Constitution of 1814, political power was vested in the following social groups: (1) those who were or had been senior civil servants (*embetsmenn*, directly appointed by the king-in-council), (2) those in towns who had citizenship (mainly tradesmen and artisans), or who owned a house or a site above a certain value, and (3) those in country districts who owned or leased taxable land. Thus in a European context the suffrage was quite liberal. In theory, because they constituted about 90% of the population, the farmers could control the organs of power. But the reality was otherwise. In the absence of a nobility, the dominant political classes between 1814 and c. 1870 were the senior civil servants (the bureaucracy) and the upper middle classes. These social groups had emerged as a result of administrative and economic developments under Dano-Norwegian absolutism and were strongly influenced by Danish culture. It was this élitist alliance of bureaucrats and businessmen which had led the Norwegian Revolution in 1814 against the Treaty of Kiel, and which was the architect of the liberal constitution of that year. The same élite, in the following decades, systematically and stubbornly defended both the constitution and national integrity against Swedish attempts to tighten the union by strengthening the king's power in Norway. Its overwhelming dominance in Norwegian politics in the first half of the nineteenth century has been summed up by a Norwegian historian (Jens Arup Seip) thus: 'It controlled both the government and Storting and at its strongest rode both like two horses in tandem.' Although these groups lost control of the Storting in the 1860s, they continued to be entrenched in the government, which became and was proclaimed as the conservative element within the constitution. As a consequence the government became animated by an anti-parliamentarian spirit. The regime, described by Seip as the 'Bureaucrat's state', broke down in 1884, when the opposition, newly organised as a political party, the Liberals (*Venstre*), successfully impeached the whole Government and took power themselves, a move which marked a breakthrough for the parliamentary system in Norway. Thenceforward, the conservative elements, the bureaucrats and bourgeois together with moderate forces within rural society, had to defend their interests through an organised political party, the Conservatives (*Høyre*), which was established in August 1884. The party was both patriotic and loyal to the Union, a dualism which was perfectly natural and acceptable to its members. It maintained the bureaucratic-bourgeois patriotic tradition of the first years of the Union and worked for Norwegian equality in the conduct of foreign policy. At the same time, since the Union was no longer felt to be a threat to Norwegian integrity, it accepted it as a shield for national political freedom and sovereignty because it served as a guarantee for peace within the Scandinavian peninsula. Furthermore, the Union was felt by this party to have brought in its train great economic advantages to Norway. Moreover, the monarchical union of the two countries was a dam against the floodtide of radical republicanism. The Union was, in sum, a good thing, but it could and indeed should be better, not least by giving Norway an equal say in foreign affairs through peaceful negotiations with the Swedes.

B. The national-liberal tradition

Until the end of the 1860s, the farmers, the great mass of the Norwegian electorate, played a secondary if restraining role in Norwegian politics in alliance with urban liberals. Opposition between farmer and bureaucrat was fundamental in Norwegian society: for the former, the latter represented an alien urban culture. As the representative of a centralising, undemocratic and expensive administration, the bureaucrat sought to burden the farmer with demands and taxes that were contrary to his needs and interests. Furthermore, the farmers not merely saw no economic benefit from the Union, but feared it as an uncontrollable vehicle of Swedish militarism. Thus from the 1870s they came to form, in conjunction with the urban nationalist liberals, a parliamentary opposition which found its formal expression in the Liberal Party in 1884. As a result of economic transformation (urbanisation and industrialisation) and the extension of the suffrage to all adult men in 1898, the Liberal Party after the breakthrough of parliamentarism also recruited into its ranks the lower middle class and labour and, to a limited degree, business circles. Because of the variety of social interests within this party, it was politically very heterogeneous. One wing comprised conservative and religious farmers opposed to any far-reaching social reform, to excessive extension of the suffrage and to 'unnecessary' expenditure by state or municipality; by contrast, the other wing, the progressive lower middle class and labourers, worked for general male suffrage and progressive taxation to finance a social reform policy. It was to the latter wing, naturally, that radical and often atheist intellectuals were attracted. But despite this heterogeneity the Liberal Party held together, with occasional splits in 1888 and 1903, because the majority of the electorate persisted in regarding it as the authentic voice of Norwegian nationalism.

This liberal nationalism can be measured by its increasingly aggressive stance towards the Union. Its development falls into two periods, a defensive phase from the 1860s up to about 1890, and an active phase thereafter until 1905. In the first period, the Liberal nationalists opposed any and every move to strengthen the Union even if it brought momentary gain to Norway, for example more extensive influence on the conduct of foreign policy. Swedish concessions were never to be paid for by a closer union. In the second phase, the majority came to the opinion that Norway had the legal right to establish its own consular service and the greater moral as well as legal right to conduct its own foreign affairs, and that if Sweden could not accept this, then the Union should be abandoned.

In the nationalist debates, both democratic/political and economic/financial arguments were employed. Thus it was argued that a closer union implied living together with a state where the conservative forces were much stronger and more powerful (for example in Sweden there was a nobility) than in Norway. In the great debate of 1880-84 on the question of the constitutional veto, the king explicitly opposed the Liberal opposition with the argument that an absolute veto in the hands of the king was the cornerstone of the Union. Without the veto, the monarchy would be powerless to defend the Union. This argument had a profound and negative effect on the Liberal attitude to the Union: the Union was felt to be an obstacle to Norwegian democratic aspirations. Thus was Norwegian anti-union republicanism born. In a speech to thousands of party members in 1882, the poet Bjørnstjerne Bjørnson proclaimed,

> Your king is a Swede, but when his Norwegian Government asserts for him an absolute veto over the Constitution — in violation of both its letter and spirit — let that cost that government and all who claim the same dear. If the monarchy asserts that the absolute veto cannot be surrendered, you must openly reply, 'If that is so, then must the Norwegian People surrender the monarchy' — it is good to be the second in a union, but to be first alone is better.

In point of fact, the constitution was unclear on this important question. Thus when the Liberal majority rejected the Government's contention that the king had an absolute constitutional veto, it was admitted that if the king had been king of Norway alone, then the question might have been decided in a different fashion. But to allow such a prerogative to a king who was also king of Sweden was incompatible with the national interest.

The socio-economic basis of the nationalist movement was a rural society in the process of transforming itself from a subsistence to a cash economy, lacking any

significant foreign export markets, and a lower middle class pre-occupied with
local economic problems. For these groups the Union could have little economic
appeal. When in 1890, during the debate on the revision of the Interstate Treaty,
the Conservatives lauded the Union's economic benefits, the ironic commentary
from the nationalist quarter on the alleged benefits was, 'A little eau de cologne
and some doubtful sweets'. For purely political reasons the Liberals preferred to
emphasise the alleged harm caused to Norwegian shipping interests by the
continuance of a common consular service, claiming that it would necessarily tend
to favour Swedish interests before those of Norway when these conflicted. This
bias was conceivable, in view of the two countries' differing customs policies and
the enormous growth in the Norwegian economy, especially shipping; it rarely
occurred in fact.

Perhaps the most useful way to uncover the economic basis — or rather, the
economic dimension — of Norwegian nationalism is to ask the question, why were
the patriots by 1904-5 willing to join the nationalists to bring down the Union?

4. Economic Basis of Nationalism

In the first critical years Carl Johan tried in different ways to undermine the
union arrangements established in the years 1814-15. These arrangements were
cemented by the Union Treaty of 1815 (Riksakten), which being based upon the
principle of equality between the two nations and the constitutional integrity of
each, sought primarily to secure the monarchical succession to the personal union.
To obtain a closer union than the one he had been obliged hastily to accept in 1814,
when his presence was needed on the battlefields against Napoleon, Carl Johan,
especially in the years 1818-1824 with 1821 as the dénouement, used his personal
power as king of Norway in order to merge Norway with Sweden. One line of
attack was political: through a series of royal proposals he tried to strengthen
conservative monarchy, one could almost say, to 'Carl-Johanize' the Norwegian
constitution. Another line of attack was more subtle and was based on economic
issues, namely to undermine and sabotage the attempts of the Norwegian
government and Storting to bring into order the chaotic and impoverished
financial and monetary system of the young Norwegian state. Indeed he went so
far as by means of secret agents to provoke riots among the farmers against the
economic policy of the government. His manipulations behind the scenes were
naturally enough known only to limited government circles, which fought back
vigorously. But in some cases he had openly to fight for his cause, for instance in
the Repayment question with Denmark and in the Bodø Affair, both of which
were to arouse a vehement Norwegian reaction.

Under the Treaty of Kiel Norway had inherited an obligation to pay a share of
the common Dano-Norwegian national debt incurred before 1814. The king tried
to press Norway to accept responsibility for a share much larger than the
Norwegians felt — correctly — that they were able to bear under the prevailing
difficult economic conditions. In our context it matters little that the king's policy

was quite comprehensible; he was a French *parvenu* upon the Swedish throne under pressure from the Holy Alliance which at the Conference of Aachen in 1818 had, in the name of legitimacy, endorsed Denmark's claims upon Norway. The Norwegians reacted fiercely, but there was more to come, namely the Bodø Affair of 1819.

The Bodø Affair reads like a crime novel, wherein reality outweighs even the most fanciful imagination. In essence, the affair concerned an attempt by powerful British trading interests to smuggle into Norway through the northern port of Bodø great quantities of goods to make a financial killing on the Norwegian market. Following the discovery and seizure of their goods by the Norwegian authorities, the smugglers sought and secured official assistance from the British Government. In consequence they regained their goods and then had the effrontery to demand and obtain a large sum from Norway in compensation for the alleged injustice they had suffered. The affair was partly settled over the heads of the Norwegian Government by Carl Johan and his Foreign Ministry, who because of current trade negotiations with Britain felt that they could not afford to alienate her. The king forced the Norwegians to give in. In vain did the Norwegian Storting attempt to re-open the affair, in 1827, 1833, 1836 and again in 1839. The Bodø Affair became a touchstone of nationalist sentiment: so long as foreign policy was made in Stockholm so long would Norwegian economic interests suffer. The affair thus served as a powerful impulse in the struggle for control over foreign policy, where from the 1830s onwards the Norwegians indeed succeeded in obtaining a considerable say.

The attitude of the upper classes in Norway towards the Union depended not only on how the latter functioned politically but also economically. It soon became apparent that the Union was not only satisfactory in the sense that it did not hamper national capitalist development and growth, but even more that it directly benefited the Norwegian economy. For the first time, economic relations between the two countries were systematically regulated by the Interstate Treaty of 1827, which was later renewed and liberalised. This gave both partners equal customs rights and at the same time regulated imports from third countries and the transit of foreign manufactured or semi-manufactured goods.

At first Swedish business, both in regard to industry and handicrafts, as the more advanced and active, profited the most from the customs agreement. Both because of this and because of a marked political will towards greater integration, Sweden sought up to the 1860s to establish a straightforward customs union on the German model. But the Norwegians rejected the proposal on political and economic grounds. Instead, from the mid-nineteenth century, the Norwegians showed an increasing interest in an expanded Interstate Treaty. Two factors contributed to this; early on it had become evident that the Union was of the greatest benefit to Norwegian shipping since Great Britain under its Navigation Laws treated the united states as one state and granted Norwegian shipping the same benefits as Swedish. As a result Norwegian shipping increasingly took over the carriage of Swedish goods — primarily wood and iron exports. This contributed to the remarkable growth in the Norwegian mercantile marine throughout the nineteenth century. At the same time, Norwegian industry competed more and more with its Swedish rivals, winning a large share of the latter's home market. It was thus not surprising that Norway accepted a renewed revision of the Interstate Treaty in 1874 in which, except for some revenue-bearing items, a free market for the products of the two countries became the basic principle. When the law was revised in 1890, the Conservatives emphasised its great value for Norwegian trade and industry.

Because of this Scandinavian economic co-operation, it is understandable that Norwegian trading, industrial and shipping circles were not militantly nationalist. These influential groups were reconciled to the Union; they were at one and the same time both patriots and loyal to the Union. But that loyalty was to be undermined by the turn of the century by two concurrent economic trends, so that by 1905 the Conservatives had become nationalist.

First, by the end of the 1890s the Union had lost its economic *raison d'être*. From about this time Norwegian and Swedish customs policies went their separate ways, the Norwegians continuing to be freetraders, and the Swedish protectionists. As a consequence Sweden's attitude towards the Interstate Treaty changed, since a joint custom system could operate only when both countries followed more or less the same policies. In 1895 Sweden, in its own well-understood economic interests, cancelled the Interstate Treaty with effect from 1897. But from the point of view of Union politics this was a major blunder; the economic umbilical cord of the Union had been cut. Thenceforth, Norway had little to gain from the Union economically. Moreover, Swedish unwillingness to accept both a separate Norwegian consular service and an equal voice in foreign policy matters led from 1895 to a growing danger of war between the two partners to the Union.

Under these circumstances the business community in Norway saw two possible solutions to the problem of the Union which was distracting national opinion from economic policy and growth, and which might even result in war, disastrous to trade, shipping and industry. There could be either — and primarily — a *détente* based upon absolute equality within the Union, or separation. Dissolution of the Union once achieved — and it was hoped peacefully — it would be possible to direct national energies towards economic development and the exploitation of the country's resources.

A second economic factor (the term used in a broad sense) that helped to bring down the union was 'the bourgeois policy of internal collaboration' (Rolf Danielsen), a policy which came to be expressed towards the turn of the century. This policy had its roots in a growing desire in Conservative and Liberal party circles jointly to protect the establishment against Liberal and Socialist extremism, an extremism becoming more threatening with the extension of the suffrage towards the end of the 1890s. In 1903 the Liberal party split. Moderate Liberals, primarily representing business interests, joined the Conservatives and the Moderates, winning the parliamentary elections of that year and forming a coalition government. The coalition partners agreed that the existing party system was not suited to the new socio-economic realities. These parties had grown out of the bygone constitutional and Union struggles of the 1880s and early '90s, but no longer reflected the 'natural' (a catchword of the times) class divisions of society. Party divisions should be drawn up upon other criteria, namely along 'natural' social lines, bourgeois opposing socialist and semi-socialist. 'The danger now threatening the country is of an economic and social kind, and it is in this arena that future electoral campaigns will be fought out . . . The old Conservative party will die, as the old Liberal party is doing. But from their ashes new parties will arise, those of the bourgeoisie and the socialists.' This prophecy comes from *Morgenavisen,* the 'old liberal' Christian Michelsen's mouthpiece. It was considered that since the bulk of the Norwegian voters were at heart 'sound, sensible and moderate', the majority of the Liberal voters could be won over to a new United bourgeois party. A prerequisite for such a coalitition was the removal of the Union issue from Norwegian internal politics one way or the other, because it was considered that the nationalist enthusiasm produced by the Union struggle was the sole force binding together the different elements — moderate farmers and business circles on the one hand, and radicals on the other — in the Liberal Party. There were but two ways to remove the Union issue, either negotiations with Sweden leading to a satisfactory readjustment of Norway's position or a clean break. How to tackle this dilemma became the crucial question for the Conservative party by the turn of the century. It could no longer afford to endanger its future as a party and thereby the political defence of its vital economic interests by a policy of Union that threatened to make it a permanent minority party. Its patience towards Sweden served to inspire a nationalist militancy among the voters in favour of the Liberals. The Union had in fact become too costly for the Conservative party. In order to cement the alliance with the moderate Liberals and engineer the break-up of the old nationalist Liberal party, this party remodelled its Union policy, accepting separation if negotiations failed to produce the right result. A decisive ideological turn in the party's Union policy from patriotism to nationalism can be registered towards the beginning of 1905, when it became apparent that Sweden was not willing to give up its *primus inter pares* position in a revised Union. So the Conservative party joined with the other nationalist forces in Norway under the leadership of the 'old liberal' Christian Michelsen, a Bergen shipowner, to break up the Union in June 1905.

The end of the Union aroused enormous expectations in business circles — they felt they were breathing a fresher and freer air, that a new economic era was opening before them.

An Outline Of Norwegian Cultural Nationalism in the Second Half of the Nineteenth Century

Kjell Haugland

FROM the 1860s and up to 1905, when the Swedish-Norwegian union was dissolved, Norwegian politics were pervaded by an active nationalism. We know that this political phenomenon was a characteristic feature in the development of many European countries in the nineteenth century, so Norwegian history in this field is in harmony with a general trend. Political nationalism in Europe had — almost without exception — a cultural dimension. Here also Norwegian history followed the general European pattern. The policy of self-assertion towards Sweden was paralleled by a strong national cultural movement. Political and cultural nationalism stimulated each other and were so interwoven that it is quite impossible to study either phenomenon separately.

The main element of the cultural nationalism was the language question, but it also pervaded other aspects of Norwegian cultural life. The most conspicuous consequence of the national cultural movement in this period was the development of two written languages. But the cultural movement also had lasting effects on social development and the relations between the regions of Norway. In the following I will try to outline the historical and contemporary background of the cultural nationalism, its aims and ways of working, and its social consequences. The survey will be concentrated on the language question.

To understand cultural nationalism in general and the language revival in particular, it is necessary to understand the historical background. The starting point is the political union between Norway and Denmark, which had lasted for over 400 years when it was dissolved in 1814. From the early sixteenth century Norway had the status of a Danish territory, governed from Copenhagen through the king's bureaucracy. This position as a dependent province strongly contrasts with the situation in the High Middle Ages, when Norway had possessed an effective government which had also controlled areas outside the Scandinavian peninsula. The loss of political identity was paralleled by a linguistic decay. The old Norwegian-Icelandic written language of the Middle Ages, which was the bearer of a considerable literature (the Sagas), completely disappeared in Norway. In the sixteenth century Danish reigned supreme as a written language. The old Norwegian language lived on in the rural dialects, but it was of course much changed during the centuries by linguistic developments. Danish to some extent influenced the spoken language in the towns, because it was used by the upper classes there. The king's bureaucracy was mainly recruited from Denmark, and Danish accordingly was the spoken language of this social group. The peasant language had a low social status, and persons who intended to climb the social ladder had to change their speech. The political liberation of 1814 did not change this situation. For political reasons the written language of Norway was named Norwegian in the constitution, but this did not change the realities. The cultural union with Denmark continued after political ties were cut. It was said that the Norwegian upper classes spoke a better Danish than the Danes themselves, because they used a more literal pronunciation, without any influence of dialect.

It is not difficult to find parallels to the political-cultural development outlined here in other parts of Europe. But the situation in Norway had a specific feature which must be kept in mind when making comparisons: Danish and Norwegian are closely related languages, and therefore mutually intelligible. Both belong to the Nordic branch of Indo-European. Accordingly the languages could influence each other; there was no impassable linguistic barrier. The Norwegian peasant understood his Danish-speaking minister, and the ambitious townsman could adjust his speech to the Danish high-status language.

We should also keep in mind the fact that Norwegian dialects vary greatly in different parts of the country, both lexically and grammatically. This is an old linguistic phenomenon. The Nordic languages have two main branches: West- and East-Nordic, and the dividing line roughly follows the mountainous districts between West and East Norway. While the dialects in the Western parts of the country belong to the same branch as Icelandic and Faroese, the spoken dialects of East Norway are more closely related to Swedish and Danish. Accordingly it was easier to accept the Danish written language in East Norway than in the Western districts.

Finally it is important to bear in mind the strong regionalism which has played an important role in Norwegian history. Both politically and culturally the regions have different patterns, and to some extent there have always been tensions between them — especially between East and West Norway. It is obvious that the barrier which natural conditions created for communication led to isolation, but the tension between the regions must also be viewed in a social context. Farming conditions are much better in the Eastern parts of the country than in the Western fjord and mountain districts. Therefore the farming communities in East Norway achieved a marked social stratification, with well-to-do farmers at the top and a numerous proletariat at the bottom. In the Western districts there was a much more even social structure, with a population which consisted mainly of fishermen and peasants. In combination with the linguistic differences such social factors gave the regions different cultural-social identities. Norwegian cultural nationalism was to be strongly marked by this.

The idea of creating a specific Norwegian written language was put forward for discussion as early as the 1830s. But it was not until two or three decades later that proposals of this kind began to gain ground outside academic circles. The growth of the idea of linguistic revival which took place in the second half of the century was closely connected with the development of political nationalism, which from the 1860s grew because of increasing tension between Norway and Sweden over the union.

From the beginning the national language reformers were confronted with a complicated question of principle: should the new written language be based wholly on Norwegian dialects, or was it better to Norwegianise the existing Danish language with elements from the dialects? In other words, should Norway choose the path of linguistic revolution or that of evolution?

From these principal positions two groupings and two specific languages developed. The adherents of 'Norwegianising' gave their support to the written language which at that time frequently was named Dano-Norwegian, but which is today called *Bokmål* ('the language of the book'). This language, which originally was Danish, acquired during the second half of the nineteenth century a steadily increasing Norwegian character. A breakthrough for this development was the activity in collecting and publishing oral traditional material from the rural societies, especially folktales and legends. The compilers were obliged to use Norwegian linguistic elements to display the distinctive quality of this material. The path to 'Norwegianising' seemed to be practicable. But the adherents of linguistic revolution did not accept it, and they united around *Landsmål* (later on called *Nynorsk*, i.e. New-Norwegian). This was a wholly new written language, based on the scientific work of a peasant's son, Ivar Aasen. Throughout a long life he studied the Norwegian dialects and published grammars and dictionaries which became the foundation of *Landsmål*. It must be noted that the new language had a strong West Nordic and archaic character.

When the promoters of *Landsmål* rejected the alternative of Norwegianisation, they had two main arguments for their view. Firstly, they argued that compromise was unacceptable from a national point of view. Since language was the essence of a national culture, it must be based wholly on national roots. It was impossible to compromise. Secondly they were of the opinion that mixing languages was contrary to linguistic laws. A language was a living organism with its own identity, bound to the history of the country, and a policy of linguistic mixing would simply lead to a form of bastard language. This view had its origin in a Romantic concept of language and the combination of language and *volksgeist* which was typical of this period of European cultural life.

Popular support for the two languages shows a marked geographical-social-political pattern. The supporters of *Bokmål* were mainly people from the middle and upper classes in the towns. Also in the rural communities in the 'flat country' of East Norway and in North Norway it seemed impossible to obtain popular support for *Landsmål*. It was mostly people living in the Western fjord and mountain districts who supported this linguistic alternative. Politically the *Landsmål* movement was associated with the nationalist-democratic Liberal Party (*Venstre*), while the interests of *Bokmål* were looked after by the Conservative Party (*Høyre*). The language question became an important divisive issue within the party system. This was demonstrated in 1885 when the national assembly decided to place *Landsmål* on an equal footing with *Bokmål* as an official language, and thus sanctioned a linguistic partition of the country. The debate and the

C

voting on the so-called equality proposal followed the party lines. The same situation could be observed in the districts. To a great extent it was the same persons who were at the head of the *Landsmål* movement and who led the local Liberal associations. In summary: the *Landsmål* movement was the core of the cultural nationalism which was an aspect of the general nationalist current. It was centred in the *Venstre* party.

It was national considerations in the widest sense that constituted the ideological base of the language revival:

> What is it that finally, i.e. morally, gives a people the right to lead an independent life amongst the nations? — It is its *spiritual independence*, its originality, that it has national power and self-respect, that it has the courage to be itself and live fully on its own conditions, and that it also manages to *maintain* its nationality, måke it objective and obvious as such. Therefore it has been said: *The language boundary is the boundary of nationality*, the people are recognised and judged according to their language, their spiritual independence, their originality, their moral power, in one word: *their right to exist*.

In this manner did the *Landsmål* leader Arne Garborg express one essential point in the ideology which had been built around Norwegian language reform, and the aims of which were acknowledged in Garborg's book *Den ny-norske sprog- og nationalitetsbevaegelse* (1877) — from which the above quotation is taken. The *Landsmål* supporters constantly pointed out that language was the main expression of national identity — and without a specific identity a people could not exist. They often referred to contemporary European language revival movements in order to relate their own efforts to a wider reality and to show that they worked in harmony with the spirit of the times: a general European search to make national awareness a reality.

Behind the national arguments we perceive the political realities of the time — Norway's position as the weaker partner in a union. The activities to promote *Landsmål* were presented as part of a national mobilisation to defend Norway's integrity and to hinder political and cultural integration. A typical example of this way of thinking was the arrangement of combined courses of *Landsmål* and rifle shooting in the border areas. The fear of cultural infiltration from Sweden increased considerably at the turn of the century. Leaders of the *Landsmål* movement argued that the growing immigration of Swedish labour and the distribution of Swedish literature would give the language a new 'non-Norwegian' element.

From time to time we can observe socialist groupings in the *Landsmål* movement, but they never grew strong. During the whole period the movement was dominated by Liberals. The Socialists who were favourably inclined to *Landsmål* viewed the question of language in the perspective of class struggle. *Bokmål* was the language of the upper classes, and activities to create a new written language from the rural dialects must be regarded as part of the process of social liberation of the workers and the peasants. From a tactical point of view it was probably not opportune to combine the question of language reform and

Socialism. Socialist ideology had — and still has — a weak position within Norwegian peasant society.

But even though the proponents of *Landsmål* did not present their movement with a Socialist terminology, it was obvious that their national argument had important social implications. In reality it reversed the whole of the traditional pattern of values and prestige within Norwegian society. The language of the upper classes was branded as inferior from a national point of view, while the despised peasant language was raised up as the only acceptable national tongue. This was the most important consequence of the *Landsmål* movement.

The peasant in the nationalist areas received this message from the *Landsmål* proponents, and actively utilised the social striking power inherent in a national re-evaluation of society, so that social differences and conflicts between peripheral and central areas became at an early stage the strongest under-current in the Norwegian linguistic controversy. The expression 'the Danish bigwig language', used by the proponent O.J. Fjørtoft in the lampoon *Nokre or te bondevenne og målmenn* (Some words to peasant friends and *Landsmål* proponents) (1871), shows in a nutshell how the national and social values could be tied together. This integrated argument for national and social self-assertion is found in the innumerable and extended parliamentary debates on language policy. The farmer-representative Lars Liestøl expressed it in the following manner in the great debate of 1885 on the principle of *Landsmål* in the schools:

> In this country we have an old and excellent literature in Old Norse, which has been the written language of the country through some of the greatest and most glorious periods, until we came under Danish rule and had forced upon us a language which was not our own. When we got rid of the tie, we started to establish the old family traditions in our country, and we started establishing the old language, which has a literature — the equal of which is not to be found in many countries. This is it, what we will attach ourselves to, and that language, which is being spoken out in the country, is a heritage from the great time. — Yes, we agree to that, we want peace and quiet in school, we do not want a school director to come into a school and say: that language, which the farmers speak, that must not be read in this school, it has no right to be here. But we farmers want it so that the children should have the same right to read their mother tongue in school as they have to read the ordinary *Bokmål*, which they should know; that their mother tongue from which they obtained the basis for their awakening intellectual life is so respected and so good that it has the same right to be read in school as that spoken by the minister's children. This is a great cause for popular education, it is a great national cause, a real people's cause, one of the biggest that has been discussed since 1814, and if this cause is correctly instituted, it will be strong enough to lift the whole farming community and the so-called simple community up to a level equal to that which is called the educated society. The farming community would have a more powerful expression of their thoughts, their view of life and the true basic thoughts would influence more strongly social conditions.

Towards the end of the nineteenth century the Norwegian farming community was in a difficult situation resulting from inner structural changes and increasing outside pressure. The keywords in the understanding of this crisis are industrialisation, urbanisation, emigration, and the change from a barter to a cash economy. The farming community had a great need for political and cultural reinforcement to withstand the pressure, and the language movement became an important part of the defence line. It is important to note that the language movement did not catch on throughout the whole of the farming community, but was limited roughly to the fjord and mountain areas in southern Norway. These were districts with limited resources, and they were hard hit by partial depopulation. The geographic pattern of support for the language movement was, however, probably the result of several factors: language conditions, social structures, the local propaganda effort by the *Landsmål* proponents; it also seems to have involved old regional clashes of interest.

Political commitment and function became a characteristic feature of the *Landsmål* movement. Several factors were responsible for this. First, it was necessary to put pressure on various political agencies and decision-making bodies to have resolutions passed that would secure the position of *Landsmål* alongside the established language. The educational system was, for example, a key position which had to be won by constant pressure on local and central authorities. Secondly, the language movement ideology had, as we have seen, a marked political character. But to some extent this activity in the political field represented a predicament which was difficult to resolve. As spokesmen for a national movement, the *Landsmål* adherents were in principle prepared to pose as a national movement and remain outside — or rather, above — party politics and the prosaic everyday struggle. A party political commitment might create splits in the movement and restrict its freedom of action.

But even though the adherents of *Landsmål* tried to present the language revival movement as a national cause above party politics, the movement in actual fact was closely linked to the national democratic Liberal Party (*Venstre*). It acted as a pressure group within the party. When the *Landsmål* adherents founded a central organisation for the movement in 1906, called *Norigs Mållag*, its first meeting set forth a programme (a compulsory essay in *Landsmål* in the University Entrance Examination) intended for the Liberal Party platform. Marius Haegstad, the first chairman, said in his introductory speech that the language movement was not attached to any political party: 'It is as Norwegians that we make our demands. Otherwise we are at home in all parties. What we agree upon here, the individual will work for in his party.' But some years later Haegstad said, regarding the background for the political programme in 1906, that he had been in touch with the editor of the *Landsmål* movement's chief organ some time before the meeting and 'we soon agreed that we ought to try to get a *Landsmål* essay in the University Entrance Examination as part of the programme of the Liberal Party.'

As characteristic of its aversion towards the central areas and the upper classes was the strong republican current in parts of the *Landsmål* movement in 1905, after the union between Norway and Sweden had been dissolved and the question of the constitution — whether monarchy or republic — was being debated. Many leading *Landsmål* adherents worked energetically for a republic. Fear that a

Norwegian royal house and court would strengthen the capital and increase cultural centralisation was behind this attitude.

A characteristic feature of the *Landsmål* movement during the first fifty years of its existence was the lack of a comprehensive organisation. The first *Landsmål* organisations were established in 1868: *Det Norske Samlaget* in Oslo and *Vestmannalaget* in Bergen. But it was not until the turn of the century that the organisational process speeded up. At that time a number of country organisations were established which in 1906 joined the central organisation, *Norigs Mållag*. But even at that time the local organisational basis of the movement was strikingly weak: barely fifty local *Landsmål* associations were actively working.

Weak organisation is a feature of the *Landsmål* movement which gives it a special position when we compare it with other contemporary popular movements. It is important to bear in mind that during the second half of the nineteenth century the growth of a variety of movements took place in Norway: religious movements, social ones (among others the temperance movement, which had a very broad popular support and a comprehensive organisation), and political movements. A general feature of these movements was the development of local and central organisations. For several reasons the *Landsmål* adherents did not display the same organisational sense; from its beginning the *Landsmål* movement was hampered by internal debates and struggles on the question of the form of the new language. *Landsmål* adherents in the Western districts at an early stage took a conservative position in the debate on the question of form, and the debate was gradually marked by a certain antagonism between West Norway and the other parts of the country. Internal tension of this kind made it difficult and dangerous to try to unite the *Landsmål* adherents under one leadership.

The weak organisational activity must also be viewed in connection with the ideology on which the *Landsmål* movement was based. It had a strong aversion to centralisation and supported the peripheral districts and the values of the peasant communities there against the various centres and their culture. It was quite natural that this dislike of dominating centres was reflected in the structure of the movement; it was to a great extent adapted to individual, unorganised work. But the main reason for the rather primitive organisational structure of the *Landsmål* movement seems to be the fact that the language revival was to a great extent channelled through the organisation and institutions of other movements and groups.

The most important institution in the efforts to promote *Landsmål* were the Folk High Schools (*folkehögskolane*). These schools, which originated in the work of the Danish nationalist and cultural philosopher Nikolai Grundtvig, are specifically Scandinavian. In the 1860s and 1870s a number of Folk High Schools were established in Norway. Their programme may be summed up thus: protection of the national elements of language and way of life, the awakening of the sense of national history, support of the rural communities, a pedagogical method based upon 'the living word'. The Folk High Schools had a strong aversion to the traditional 'learned' schools, because in these the way of teaching was characterised by much uninspired learning by heart of classical languages and because they did not stimulate the personality of the pupils. The Folk High Schools had thus a marked social function. They were established in rural communities and recruited their pupils from the peasant society, while the traditional academic schools were largely tied to towns and the upper social strata. This is another example of how cultural nationalism in Norway was part of the social struggle.

A great number of the teachers of the Folk High Schools had important positions in the promotion of *Landsmål*. Many of them were also prominent Liberal politicians and played an important role when the language question was debated in the national assembly. But the greatest effort for the cause of *Landsmål* came from the Folk High Schools through their influence on thousands of young pupils. When the boys and girls returned home from these schools, many had become keen *Landsmål* adherents. This was the basis for a new popular movement, which emerged and was organised in the 1890s: the Liberal Youth Movement (*den frilynde ungdomsrörsla*). It set up its central organisation in 1896, called *Norigs ungdomslag*, and at the turn of the century it comprised about 20,000 members. Like the Folk High Schools, the Liberal Youth organisations worked for a national cultural programme where the central aim was the protection of the values of the rural communities. This programme was realised through many different activities, for example afforestation, the teaching of *Landsmål*, and a campaign to obtain a flag for the National Day. An important element in the activities of the youth associations were the annual summer conventions, which normally were held out in the open and which had a marked national programme. They were often arranged in connection with St. Olaf's Day (July 29th), the memorial day of the Norwegian Saint, King Olaf.

In the local youth associations and in the work to promote *Landsmål* the teachers in the primary schools played an important role. Normally they were recruited from the rural society. There was a marked tension between this group of teachers and those with an academic background who worked in the secondary schools. The teachers in the rural primary schools generally represented the national cultural view which was based on the values of the peasant society.

If we sum up the consequences of the national cultural revival during the period which we have concentrated on here, we can without doubt use the words comprehensive and profound. First the unity of literary language was broken. After the so-called equality resolution was passed by the national assembly in 1885 it was politically impossible to prevent *Landsmål* from having an equal footing with *Bokmål* in the school system. At the turn of the century the interpretation of the concept of equality was extended from 'the right to use' to 'the duty to know'. This meant that all candidates at two of the important public examinations had to write an essay in each of the two languages. This indicates how strong the political position of the *Landsmål* movement had grown, but it embittered the language dispute.

The most profound consequences of Norwegian cultural nationalism generally and of the promotion of *Landsmål* especially are to be found in the social field. By giving first priority to the values of the peasant society, it strengthened the self-respect and vitality of the rural communities which were seriously endangered by the extensive process of socio-economic transition which Norway entered upon in the middle of the nineteenth century. The cultural movement became a strong counterbalance to the forces of centralisation and contributed to preserving the balance between centre and periphery.

A SHORT BIBLIOGRAPHY

Burgun, Achille: *Le développement linguistique en Norvège depuis 1814.* Kra. (Oslo 1919-21).
Det Norske Samlaget 1868-1968. (Oslo 1968).
Haugen, Einar: *Language Conflict and Language Planning. The Case of Modern Norwegian.* (Harvard University Press 1966).
Haugland, Kjell: *Striden kring sidemålsstilen.* (Oslo 1971).
Hovdan, Peder: *Frå folkemål til riksmål. Blad or Noregs nyaste målsoga.* (Oslo 1928).
Lothe, Anders: *Målreisingssoga i Sogn og Fjordane.* (Florø 1950).
Midttun, Olav: *Mål og menn.* 2. utg. (Oslo 1968).
Nygaard, Rolf: *Fra dansk-norsk til norsk riksmål. Rettskrivningsstrevet i bokmålet inntil 1907.* (Oslo 1945).
Skard, Vemund: *Frå Dølen til Fedraheimen. Målstriden 1870-1877.* (Oslo 1949).
Vestmannalaget i femti aar. 1868-1918. (Bergen 1918).

The Rise of Nationalism in the Danish Monarchy 1800-1864, with Special Reference to its Socio-economic and Cultural Aspects

A. Pontoppidan Thyssen

THE year 1864 ranks as a watershed in recent Danish history, particularly from the point of view to be adopted in the present paper. After 1864 Denmark was a small homogeneous nation-state, whereas before 1864 the Danish Monarchy comprised a number of regions, each with a character, language and civil service of its own. The Kingdom of Denmark proper comprised only North Jutland and the Danish islands between Jutland and Sweden. To this were added, till 1864, the Duchies of Schleswig and Holstein, till 1814 the Kingdom of Norway (ceded to Sweden in 1814), between 1815 and 1864 the small Duchy of Lauenburg, south of Holstein, and, for various periods, Iceland, Greenland, the Faroe Islands and some small Indian and West Indian colonies.

However, the national development to be traced in this paper mainly concerns the Kingdom and the Duchies of Schleswig and Holstein, which, around the year 1800, were three integrated 'states'. As such they were looked upon and referred to by contemporaries, and after the loss of Norway these three regions in particular were collectively referred to as the Danish United Monarchy (*Gesamtstaat*). The boundary between the Kingdom and the Duchy of Schleswig was formed by a line south of the town of Kolding along the Konge River to its estuary in the tidal flats of the North Sea, and the boundary between the two Duchies ran north of Kiel along the River Eider to its estuary in the North Sea.

Since 811 the Eider had been the recognised frontier between the Carolingian Empire and the Kingdom of Denmark. Between the Eider and the town of Schleswig, the *Dannevirke*, a large system of fortifications (cf. Antoninus' turf wall from Forth to Clyde) had been erected in several sections between the ninth and twelfth centuries. The Duchy of Schleswig was in fact a Danish earldom with an aboriginal Danish population and an original Danish designation, viz. South Jutland. Only in the fourteenth century was it named after the town of Schleswig. The Danish name was revived by Danish national circles in the 1840s, but is now mostly used of the northern part, re-united with the mother country in 1920.

Holstein, on the contrary, was a German dukedom comprising the area between the rivers Eider and Elbe. But this distinction and the Eider frontier had lost their importance in several respects. From the thirteenth century the Duchy of

31

Schleswig was partitioned among collateral branches of the Danish royal house, who aspired to independence and married into families belonging to the high nobility of Holstein. By this process and by war these families acquired landed property in Schleswig, at times large parts of Denmark too, and dominated both Duchies from 1326 to 1459, so that from then onwards German became the official language also of Schleswig. In 1460 both Duchies were united to the Kingdom, but not as a Danish conquest. On the contrary, a descendant of and heir to the reigning Holstein princely house, Christian of Oldenburg, first became King of Denmark and was then recognised as Duke of both Schleswig and Holstein with the express obligation to maintain the interdependence of the Duchies and their independence from the Kingdom.

New partitions followed, but in the eighteenth century (particularly in 1721 and 1773) Schleswig and Holstein were again united under the Danish kings of the House of Oldenburg. They were, however, still an independent unity with a German administrative body of their own, the so-called German Chancellery in Copenhagen. But the Duchy of Schleswig had retained a certain character of its own: its old legislation was Danish in origin, the vernacular of the majority, as also the language in church and school in the northern rural districts (approximately north of the present frontier), was Danish. Moreover, some of these districts were crown land (so-called royal enclaves). But more significant were the German language and culture of the upper classes and the civil service, and the administrative links between the Duchy and Holstein. At the beginning of the nineteenth century, therefore, Schleswig was reckoned among the King's German duchies.

Denmark proper was administered in Danish by the analogous 'Danish Chancellery', but even the Kingdom was strongly influenced by German language and culture. After the Reformation church and theology became closely tied to Lutheran Germany. Until c. 1800 the Royal House was mainly German-speaking, and on the introduction of absolute monarchy (1660) surrounded itself chiefly with aristocrats from Holstein and other German areas, and until 1772 the army was commanded in German. In Copenhagen there was a big German colony, which, headed by Schleswig-Holstein nobles, the officials of the German Chancellery and four German vicars, still led fashion at the end of the eighteenth century. At that time educated Danes were expected to have a working knowledge of German, and Danish families sent their children to German educational establishments or employed German private teachers. To this must be added a prolonged occupational influence from the south, among other things by a steady influx of artisans and other skilled people from the Duchies and from Germany. In this Denmark drew on the more advanced agricultural and industrial skills of the Duchies. The Kingdom had one large city only, Copenhagen, with 100,000 inhabitants around the year 1800, but the Duchies had several towns of middling size, and these grew more rapidly than those of the Kingdom, which in 1840 had a total population of about 1.3 million. At this date the population of the two Duchies amounted to 800,000 (Schleswig 350,000 and Holstein rather more than 450,000; Lauenburg 45,000). In the Kingdom the urban population amounted to

20.3 per cent, in the Duchies as a whole to 24.1 per cent, and in Holstein alone to 27.1 per cent.

There was thus a strong German element in the Danish-German United Monarchy, but only in the 1830s and 1840s did seriously conflicting national movements arise. However, mention should first be made of some precursors before 1830, as these throw light on the genesis of nationalism, the main theme of this paper.

1800-1830. The Age of Patriotism

Strictly speaking the age of patriotism began well before 1800. The word patriotism was applied to the approved attitude towards the State and towards tasks of nation-wide importance. This was the period of the Enlightenment, which can be considered to have started in Denmark about the year 1750, and which reached its peak of influence just before 1800. In fact, patriotism can be defined as the practical aspect of the Enlightenment, and showed a gradual shift from a static to a more dynamic conception of society. The theory of the religious foundation of monarchy was superseded by ideas derived from natural law; absolutism became enlightened despotism, assumed to exist for the sake of the inhabitants and expected to work for the common good. And, properly speaking, the same applied to all subjects, who were also expected to prove their patriotism by devoting their lives to the service of these ideals.

In literature the new ideas manifested themselves chiefly in a profusion of pamphlets and periodicals. No fewer than 116 periodicals were started between 1770 and 1800, informative, argumentative and moralising, animated by progressive ideas and reforming zeal. They concerned themselves with a wide spectrum of social problems: school reform and cultural tasks, sanitary and social measures, agriculture and urban trades. There was a proliferation of patriotic societies. Mention may be made of the Society for Promoting Danish Language and History (1746) and the Royal Agricultural Society of Denmark (1769) which aimed to encourage both 'the agriculturist, the artist and the tradesman', but especially to promote agriculture. There was also the Patriotic Society of Schleswig-Holstein, established in 1786, and after a period of languor reinvigorated in 1812. It was associated with 33 similar societies for the common weal in 'the Danish states'. Generally speaking, its aim was to promote 'the intellectual, moral and commercial forces' of the Duchies.

Thus, the patriotic endeavours were of a cultural, economic and social nature. In the main they manifested themselves not as a political opposition, but rather with strong emphasis on their loyalty to Crown and Government. Towards the end of the eighteenth century when Liberty, Equality and the Rights of Man became catchwords turned against privilege of rank and feudal oppression, censures of the government were sometimes heard. But till then the patriotic activists met with sympathetic response from the Government, which allowed considerable freedom of the press and which carried through numerous reforms inspired by the public debate.

Of the greatest importance were a succession of agricultural reforms aiming at larger productivity by the emancipation of the peasantry. In 1750, the land of the peasants had mostly been in the hands of great landowners, cultivated under the open-field system. The peasant had been obliged to work on his lord's domain for so many days in the year without pay, as well as to pay rent to his lord, and legally he was highly dependent on him. On the manors of South Schleswig and Holstein he had been a serf. But this picture was completely changed by the agricultural reforms. In 1815, nearly three quarters of the strip holdings had been exchanged, two thirds of the farms now being freeholds. The obligation to work on the lord's domain had been abolished or reduced and the legal status of the farmers much improved. A comprehensive programme of school reforms with schools run by local authorities and with compulsory education for all had been set up, humanisation of the administration of justice, improvement of poor relief and health services, liberalisation of trade, equal status for the Jews, and restrictions on the slave trade, had all been carried through.

These reforms are part of the picture of patriotism. Typically, in the age of patriotism, it manifested itself not only as patriotic feelings, but as reforming zeal. It was based on the current European idea of the Enlightenment, but also, in the Danish United Monarchy, on a socio-economic development giving rise to a strong middle class of 'enlightened citizens', government officials and intellectuals of middle-class extraction, well-to-do merchants, manufacturers and other captains of industry. It was these particularly who took the lead, even if patriotic civic-mindedness was not lacking in higher circles.

The official class was favoured by the interest taken by absolutism in efficient and uniform administration, and this in its turn required a specialised education. A law degree at two levels was instituted in 1736 at the University of Copenhagen, and the annual number of graduates grew to one hundred or more in the years after 1800. Until the 1770s the heads of the administration were recruited from the nobility, but after that time commoners also might reach the top of the ladder, and from 1821 a law degree was a requirement for all offices of a legal nature. Both at the University of Copenhagen and at that of the Duchies at Kiel the number of law students at the end of the eighteenth century was on a par with that of theological students, the dominating group in the past. But theologians and clergymen also played a prominent and many-sided rôle in the reform movement, especially in the reform of the schools.

The prosperity of the upper middle classes was due to general economic growth after 1750, particularly to expanding demand for agricultural products. This demand stimulated production, which is estimated to have doubled between 1750 and 1800, while the price of corn rose by 50 per cent between 1788 and 1805. The affluence arising from this spread to other social groups in both town and country. Agricultural reform was a strong incitement to the reform movement as a whole.

However, when the depression set in during and after the war of 1807-14 with Great Britain, this stimulus was naturally reduced. Nearly the whole of the mercantile marine was captured, and the war expenditure resulted in the bankruptcy of the State in 1813. After the Napoleonic wars there was an increase in European agricultural production, with falling prices and consequent protectionist measures. Danish agriculture was particularly hard hit by the severance from Norway during and after the war because Danish grain had a monopolistic position in that country. It should be added, however, that already about 1800 the reform movement had begun to meet with opposition, both in the Kingdom and in the Duchies. There was a reaction against the French Revolution and its radical domestic henchmen, and this attitude increasingly marked the line taken by the Government and by large sections of the public in the following decades.

The Age of Patriotism differs from the period of the later national movements. It had been a cosmopolitan movement characterised by a predominantly practical reformism and general humanitarian approach. Its appreciation of national values was all along simple and vague, and its fundamental patriotic sentiment attached itself to the Monarchy as a whole, only vaguely to the local spheres of activity. However, this responsibility for society not only could change to zealous patriotic feelings under war conditions, but could also be focused on one or more of the constituent 'states' of the Monarchy. The latter kind of patriotism was destined to become of the greatest importance in the Danish-Norwegian-German state. Patriotism could be Danish, Schleswig-Holstein or Norwegian. The last-mentioned can, however, be disregarded here because of the break in the political connection; the other two must be examined as the direct precursors of the later national movements.

The origin of Danish patriotism was a reaction against the strong German element in leading positions. Aversion grew especially between 1770 and 1772 when a German Court Physician, J.F. Struensee by name, reigned supreme at Court and *ipso facto* in the state. He was overthrown by Danish circles led by Ove Guldberg, a Dane of middle-class extraction, whose influence was dominant till 1784. This meant a purely Danish policy, which at once manifested itself in ordinances decreeing Danish as the language of command in the army and the use of Danish in official letters not concerning the Duchies. To this was added in 1775 the introduction of Danish as a special school subject in the grammar schools (except in the Duchies). In 1776 a Danish-Norwegian-Holstein citizenship became a requirement for employment in the civil service. The insistence on this regulation was directed against foreigners and was everywhere hailed with enthusiasm as an expression of general patriotism embracing the triune Monarchy. Most foreigners in Danish service were Germans, and Guldberg held that Danish was to be principal language of the Monarchy, a policy which would strengthen fellow-feeling so that both Norwegians and Schleswig-Holsteiners should consider themselves Danes.

This policy was resumed by Frederik VI (1808-39), who had been Prince Regent during his father's illness from 1784 to 1808. He particularly wished to increase Danish influence in the Duchies as the basis of a uniform, centralised administration. In 1804 he appointed a Danish lawyer as head of the German Chancellery, and after 1806 when the First Reich was dissolved he issued a series of 'Danising' ordinances on the close connection of Holstein with the Danish Monarchy, the use of both Danish and German in official letters in the Duchies, preferential treatment of applicants proficient in Danish, and the extension of the area in Schleswig in which Danish was the language of church and school, etc.

These political moves paralleled a Danish patriotic current which, since the era of Struensee, had manifested itself in literary criticism of German influence, and had burst into enthusiasm at Nelson's attack on Copenhagen in 1801 and during the war of 1807-14. More important was a long period of increasing literary concentration on Danish-Scandinavian culture. It began in the eighteenth century with the writing of history, the publication of historical sources, studies in Old Norse literature and poetical treatment of subjects from Danish history. During the first decades of the nineteenth century this tendency gave a new impetus to Danish literature and other branches of intellectual life — in spite of the economic recession. Most influential were A. Oehlenschläger and N.F.S. Grundtvig, who created a fundamentally Danish patriotic poetry inspired by Danish history and by Old Norse literature and mythology, as well as B.S. Ingemann, whose widely read novels, three of which were translated into English, used themes from the Danish mediaeval past and offered a Danish analogy to Walter Scott. Ideologically, these authors were representative of a new attitude. They were influenced by German idealism and romanticism and by the censure of eighteenth century rationalism, which to their minds was very superficial. With them began a new Danish national consciousness, spreading after 1830, but still a purely literary movement with no definite national and political goals. These authors wholeheartedly accepted the existing United Monarchy without direct hostility to its German element.

The analogous Schleswig-Holstein patriotism developed later, but assumed a more definite shape. It had as background the administrative, cultural and economic association of the Duchies, with common church organisation since 1542, joint diets to 1712, a common civil service mostly educated at the University of Kiel, and a shared body of landowners, the landed aristocracy, with extensive privileges. The long association with the Kingdom had, however, left profound traces, and at the end of the eighteenth century the general attitude was chiefly in favour of continued loyal association with Denmark.

During the following period the general attitude began to change, and this was largely due to economic factors. Dissatisfaction began among the landed aristocracy when in 1802 the Government imposed taxes on real property overriding its exemption. The aristocracy pleaded its old privileges, among them the right of granting supplies, but without success. On the contrary, armaments and war brought heavy taxes in their train, and in 1812 the finances of the Duchies, till then independent, were involved in the general inflation. After the national bankruptcy in 1813 the Government introduced a monetary union with a standard based on a state mortgage on the value of all real property, and withdrew the special Schleswig-Holstein currency. The latter measure aroused such strong opposition that it had to be abandoned, and as the currency and economy of the

Kingdom were still in a bad way, it was generally thought in the Duchies that the burden of association was disproportionate.

To this must be added an independent cultural development receiving fresh impetus from German literature in its idealistic-romantic heyday. This development centred on the University of Kiel, where a number of young professors, notably F.C. Dahlmann and N. Falck, were influenced by the strong national, liberal and religious currents in Germany aroused by the War of National Liberation against Napoleon. Under the settlement of Vienna (1815) Holstein had become a member state of the German confederation with the promise of a constitution based on the Estates of the Realm. The endeavours of the Kiel professors especially concentrated on having this constitution realised and extended to Schleswig. They based their argument on the historical unity of the Duchies, acknowledged by the Danish Kings, and initiated petitions from the Schleswig-Holstein towns and requests from the landed aristocracy, who wanted the old joint diets re-established.

All these proposals were turned down both by the Danish Government and the German Federal Diet, which pursued a very conservative policy. The agitation apparently died down after 1823. In spite of the element of German nationalism, the movement was still in its core homely Schleswig-Holstein patriotism. To be sure, it had rejected Danish centralism and desired greater independence, but it did not want to break with the United Monarchy and the Danish Royal House.

1830-64. The Breakthrough of the National Movements

The Danish-Schleswig-Holstein War of 1848-50 divides this period into two spans of years of which the former is of particular interest since it witnessed the breakthrough proper of nationalism. But it must be noted that from an economic point of view the period forms a whole characterised by almost unbroken progress both in the Kingdom and in the Duchies. The recession after the Napoleonic wars had reached its nadir in the 1820s when agriculture, the main resource, had been hard hit by adverse market conditions and falling prices. But then trading conditions changed as the European demand for agricultural products grew and the English market was progressively opened (1828, 1842 and 1846). From the 1820s to the 1850s the Kingdom's average export of animals was doubled. The price of grain doubled between the late 1820s and the late 1850s, and the rise in price of animal products was almost as big.

For a long time the Duchies were clearly in the van of the market. Their currency was stable and they had bigger exports of butter and a bigger industrial sector, especially in Holstein. The foreign trade of the Kingdom till 1848 was dominated by Hamburg and Altona (the largest town in Holstein, with 28,000 inhabitants in 1840), whereas Copenhagen was stagnant. But during the 1830s the finances of the Kingdom were stabilised, and in the 1840s its export of grain to England was nearly doubled. Its provincial towns began to grow more rapidly about 1840 and the capital about 1845. In spite of everything Copenhagen was still by far the biggest city in the Monarchy and now grew with increasing speed, in ten years (1845-55) by 26,000 to 155,000. The total increase in population in the Kingdom, about 33 per cent between 1834 to 1860, was greater than in the Duchies.

Economically, the time after 1830 was reminiscent of the palmy days of Danish overseas trade before the war in 1807. It was also marked by the resumption of the public debate and the civil reforming efforts which characterised the Age of Patriotism, but with the difference that the activities were now of a political nature leading to ever stronger claims being laid to political power secured through a free constitution. First and foremost, the time from 1830 to 1848 witnessed the breakthrough of political liberalism, both in the Kingdom and in the Duchies.

The revival of the public debate was originally due to the July revolution of 1830 in Paris and to a radical Schleswig-Holstein claim to a constitution prompted by that event. This claim was met by the Government with the introduction of a constitution comprising the entire Monarchy and based on the Estates of the Realm with four consultative assemblies sitting every two years, one for Holstein, one for Schleswig, one for North Jutland and one for Zealand (with the surrounding islands). The first elections and the assemblies themselves, which began sitting in 1835-36, gave a further stimulus to the debate. The debate called forth numerous pamphlets, and many newspapers and periodicals dabbled in politics. The right of voting depended on the possession of real estate, favouring landowners but also allowing some well-to-do villagers to get to the assemblies, but the debates were dominated by a disproportionate number of officials, people with a university education and prominent industrialists and tradesmen.

Patriotism's fund of ideas supplied the main body of opinion both for the Government and for the opposition. Both sides aimed at arousing the 'public spirit' and of working for the common good. The debates also turned to a high degree on general questions of reform in attempts to combine liberal desiderata with the interests of the taxpayers. Delegates demanded publication of their debates and of the budgets, retrenchment, local government developments, liberalisation of trade, reduction of the privileges of the nobility such as freedom from duties and the right of coursing, and minor judicial, agricultural and school reforms. But the debates also called forth national sentiments and claims, and in the 1840s these came increasingly to the fore.

Bound up with all this was the representative principle legitimised by the assemblies. Patriotism embraced the state as such, and was in principle 'State patriotism', loyal at least to the existing United Monarchy and to the Crown as its symbol. But the dynastic policy lost its dominance as 'the people' came to be considered the highest authority, for 'the people' was conceived as a national, i.e. a linguistic, cultural and historical unity, either Danish or Schleswig-Holstein. The usage therefore changed gradually from 'patriotic' to 'national'. The 'fatherland' became 'the land of the people', its historically given homeland, 'public spirit' became 'the national Genius' (*Volksgeist*), and the common good assumed the character of tasks of national reform.

The assemblies played an important part in this development because they were inclined to identify themselves with either the Danish or the Schleswig-Holstein people and to demand greater powers by an amalgamation of the two Danish assemblies on the one hand and the two Schleswig-Holstein assemblies on the other. This reflected political liberalism. Because Schleswig was bilingual, a crucial national question would at once come to the fore: where was the boundary between the Danish and the German peoples? The policy of the Kings (Frederik VI and Christian VIII, 1839-48) was a cautious unitary one, aiming at political integration of the Kingdom and the Duchies with due deference to all parties. But it proved to be more and more difficult to walk the tightrope between conflicting national interests. These crystallised three national movements, which will be discussed below: a Schleswig-Holstein, a Danish and a North Schleswig movement.

The Schleswig-Holstein movement could build upon the endeavours of Dahlmann and Falck, but in 1830 it received a firmer basis in a pamphlet by Uwe Jens Lornsen, a young official in the German Chancellery. This was for a consistently liberal constitutional programme, the unification of Schleswig and Holstein as an independent national unity within a personal union similar to that of Norway and Sweden. But the centre of gravity in the constitution thus put forward was a jointly elected body vested with the right of both making laws and voting taxes. At first leading Schleswig-Holsteiners felt this to be too radical. Lornsen himself was put in prison and incapacitated by illness. His programme had, however, became the yardstick of the young university men dabbling in politics and was supplemented with the ideas of Schleswig-Holstein's historical claim to a joint diet. In 1838 both the Schleswig assembly and a committee appointed by the Holstein assembly voted for the amalgamation of the assemblies of these two Duchies.

The turn of the tide set in when in 1840 a Royal ordinance was promulgated decreeing Danish as the language in the Courts and of local authorities in North Schleswig. This was supported in that province and in the Kingdom, but was resisted fiercely in the assemblies of the Duchies. These now not only demanded amalgamation, but their parties were united in pursuing an anti-Danish policy, decidedly separate from that of the Government. In 1844 they even associated themselves with a duke of the House of Augustenborg, who laid a claim to the succession in both Duchies, and when in 1846 the King rejected this separatism, feeling ran high. The Holstein assembly lodged a complaint with the German Confederation, the Schleswig assembly demanded admission to the Confederation, and, the members resigning their seats, both assemblies were dissolved.

The separatist movement was also backed by economic arguments. The financial policy of the United Monarchy, which had brought about a growing national debt, had already been criticised by Lornsen in the Schleswig-Holstein assemblies. The same disapproval was also voiced in the Kingdom, but it carried weight particularly in the Duchies, because it was felt that the Kingdom, economically the weaker party, was being favoured at the expense of the Duchies.

D

In the 1840s this view resulted in strong demands in the assemblies for a separation of the finances of the Kingdom and the Duchies. This was the result of a single-minded propaganda campaign from about 1842, criticising economic conditions since the state bankruptcy in 1813 and the connection between the currencies of the Kingdom and of the Duchies, warning the Schleswigers of financial loss resulting from closer connection with the Kingdom and emphasising the advantages accruing from accession to the Prussian customs union.

The merit of this case is questionable. As mentioned, there had been economic progress in the Kingdom, and trade between the Kingdom and the Duchies was flourishing. When in 1838, in spite of protests from Copenhagen, the Government repealed the greater part of the protective duty at the Konge River, the Kingdom was opened up to Holstein industry, and trade between the Kingdom and the Duchies was doubled in ten years. The centres of this trade were Kiel and Flensborg, and the latter also took over a great deal of the trade with the Danish West Indies.

Of greater importance as a background to Schleswig-Holsteinism was a flourishing cultural and public life. In the '30s and '40s, the Schleswig-Holstein church carried the impress of a strong neo-orthodox Lutheran movement among the clergy, who tried to make the work in church and school effective and to rally the national church and make it independent through a representative church synod. After 1815 there was a great intake of students at the University of Kiel, and these were very closely held together through their associations and clubs, which were very much alive with debates on topical themes. In this way, there emerged a conscious Schleswig-Holstein class of university men and officials whose attitude manifested itself *inter alia* through vigorous protests against the employment of Danish clergymen and the introduction of Danish as the language of the Courts in North Schleswig. The University also became the centre of exhaustive studies of the history of the Duchies, stressing their historic rights to form an independent unity. About 1840, this view permeated the books for use in the schools.

To this came the intensified public discussion resulting from the debates in the assemblies and the topical political issues. A broad national movement emerged with mass meetings, national choral societies and numerous petitions, the use of the Schleswig-Holstein national anthem, national flag and other national symbols, and interminable debates in pamphlets and newspapers. All this received strong stimulus from the contemporary movement towards German unity in Germany itself. The independence of Schleswig-Holstein and the unification of Germany were not conceived of as conflicting goals but became, to many, two sides to the same question.

The corresponding national movement in the Kingdom developed comparatively late. From the outset the Schleswig-Holsteiners' constitutional questions were looked upon with apathy, and the German element in Copenhagen was no longer a problem. The liberal forces were stronger than in the Duchies, but until the beginning of the '40s they chiefly rallied round reform and constitutional issues of the Kingdom. On the whole, the contemporary public saw no national problems in the financial and constitutional questions at issue in the Kingdom.

It became of great importance that the cultural efflorescence continued in many fields, especially in poetry and art. Of contemporary or later European fame were Hans Andersen, S. Kierkegaard, B. Thorvaldsen, and in science, H.C. Oersted, and A. Oehlenschläger, N.F.S. Grundtvig and B.S. Ingemann were still important influences. All this gave rise to national self-esteem and deepened the sense of the specific values of Danish culture. Inevitably it had an effect on the relation between Danish and German in the Duchy of Schleswig, a problem which was to become the national bone of contention in the '40s.

Originally, the national issue was raised as a predominantly cultural problem, curiously enough by a Kiel professor, Christian Paulsen by name, a native of Flensborg of German-speaking upper middle-class parentage. During his time of study in Germany he was seized with the same liberal and national ideas as aroused the enthusiasm of his fellow-students; but in his case these led to a study of Danish literature and a conscious Danish-Schleswig national feeling. In 1832 he was induced to write a refutation of Lornsen's Schleswig-Holstein programme in German, arguing in favour of the constitutional unity of Schleswig and Denmark and also of the introduction of Danish as the language of the Courts in North Schleswig and the medium of instruction in the towns and in Middle Schleswig. His chief point was that the people of Schleswig were predominantly Danish by virtue of language, mentality and traditions, but that they were spiritually impoverished by exclusion from the corresponding higher culture. Therefore standard Danish should be furthered and the national consciousness developed by means of Danish literature and Danish educational establishments, teachers and officials.

During the following years Paulsen worked for these ideas and saw to it that not only was the language question raised in the Schleswig assembly in 1836 and 1838, but also that it aroused interest in liberal circles in Copenhagen. These were closely connected with literary circles and between them they organised a society for the promotion of the freedom of the press and for the dissemination of good literature. In 1835 it had 5,000 members, most of them in Copenhagen.

It was only natural that in 1836 this society should extend its activities into North Schleswig, where it worked particularly by issuing Danish fiction, and other literature.

Its engagement had become national, and this held good to a still higher degree of an analogous effort of wider scope, the organisation in 1843 of a national subscription for the promotion of a Danish educational service in Schleswig, with a special view to calling a Danish-Schleswig official class into being. The purpose was still a cultural one, rooted in the university education, and the originators were still the liberal Copenhagen intelligentsia headed by professors and big businessmen, chiefly supported by officials, students, authors, etc. But the subscription reflected a conscious Danish national movement and was a clear challenge to the Schleswig-Holsteiners. At the same time links with the other Scandinavian countries were suggested. Danish nationality and culture were regarded as part of Scandinavian culture, and the idea of Scandinavian fellowship found enthusiastic supporters in the Scandinavian university towns, where a number of inter-Scandinavian student meetings were held in the '40s.

In the early '40s the Liberals also developed a national programme. The question of Schleswig's connection with Denmark had already been raised when in 1838 the two Danish consultative assemblies had petitioned for their amalgamation. When they met again in 1840, they received many petitions for an amalgamation of the two Danish assemblies with that of Schleswig into one representative body with the right of voting taxes. In spite of sympathy for this, the deputies found it wiser to show restraint, and turned to supporting the Government's unitary policy in order to preserve the existing Confederacy. But the Schleswig-Holstein protests against the introduction of Danish as the language of the courts of North Schleswig and against the equal status of the languages in the North Schleswig assembly called forth strong reactions in the Kingdom, especially between 1842 and 1844. This was the case both for the assemblies and in the general public discussion which, in popular petitions (for instance one had 10,000 names, 4,000 of them from Copenhagen), demanded protection of 'the Danish nationality' in Schleswig. This discussion led to the welding together of the liberal and the national forces in the National Liberal Party. Its goal was a union of Denmark and Schleswig as far as the River Eider with a joint free constitution.

Separate mention must be made of the national development in North Schleswig, because it differed from trends in both Denmark and Schleswig-Holstein. The difference was based on a social difference. The movements already mentioned were built on the bourgeois intelligentsia, but the national development peculiar to North Schleswig was built on the peasantry, generally looked down on as a lower social class. Behind this peasant movement was the early breaking up of most landed estates and the ensuing independence of the peasants, who often owned large farms. Also peasant prosperity there was more marked than in the analogous class in the Kingdom. Peasant affluence became the basis of social self-esteem, which might turn against German-educated officialdom, but which might also bring affinity with the German culture of the upper classes in its train. Knowledge of German was not only a must, but also the high road to success for the social climber.

Politically, the North Schleswig peasants were above all conservative. They were hesitant at initiating political activity which was dominated by the higher classes, and from the outset they stood aloof from the liberal and national ideas of the middle classes. The peasantry stuck to the established order and were satisfied with the intermediate status of Schleswig which secured commercial relations with the South and brought to them advantages over the peasantry of the Kingdom, among other things greater local influence. But they held the Danish King in great esteem. The peasants felt themselves to be loyal subjects in duty bound to the existing institutions and laws, all emanations of the Royal power. This attitude was particularly encouraged by the Lutheran National Church. The clergy were in close contact with the population and were responsible for the educational system and the moral and religious instruction of the people. The church was particularly influential among the rural people of North Schleswig especially in the south, in the neighbourhood of Aabenraa and Tonder, where in the '30s and '40s the clergy, inspired by the Schleswig-Holstein clerical movement, did a considerable amount of work in the service of the church. In this area the population took little interest in the contemporary political and national commotion.

Political concern was greater in the north, particularly around Haderslev, and Danish national propaganda focused especially on this neighbourhood. This was first and foremost because of Chr. Flor, who, like Paulsen, was a professor in the University of Kiel but, unlike him, of Danish descent. He was inspired by N.F.S. Grundtvig's peculiar cultural vision. Grundtvig's poetical, historical and mythological work was prodigious, but he had always opposed the Danish cultural élite: the only author with whom he was closely connected was his fellow-poet Ingemann. However, he had gained influence with the peasantry and with young clerics through his theological reaction against rationalism, and in the 1830s he tried to call forth an analogous cultural opposition against the prevailing university education. His ideas were founded on Old Norse literature and on the traditions of the simple Danish folk, who were to have the opportunity for a higher non-academic education through the foundation of Folk High Schools.

Flor's attachment to Grundtvig put up a barrier between him and the highbrows of Danish National Liberalism. His goal was not primarily liberal or politico-national, but to make the peasantry stand on their own feet independently of the intelligentsia. The means to this goal was to be a new Danish 'folk culture', first in Schleswig, then in Denmark. So far he could collaborate with Paulsen in strengthening the position of the Danish language, but it was particularly his own work that brought the Danish-Schleswig agrarian movement into being.

The demand for Danish in the courts was supported mostly by petitions inspired by Flor and coming from the rural districts, and it was introduced into the Schleswig assembly by representatives of the peasantry in 1836 and 1838. In 1838-40 Flor started three Danish newspapers in North Schleswig, most important among them the *Dannevirke*, published in Haderslev. Its editor, P.C. Koch, was as enthusiastic over Grundtvig as Flor himself, and it had a relatively wide circulation among the peasantry. On the initiative of Koch, sixty or seventy Danish lending libraries were established, all but a few in the villages. The promulgation of the Royal ordinance of 1840 was received with a large address of thanks, composed by Flor, which met with widespread approval among the peasantry in North Schleswig. In 1844 Flor reached his primary goal: the establishment of a Danish 'folk high school' in North Schleswig, the first realisation of Grundtvig's idea of a 'school for life'.

Politically, Flor was very moderate. During its first years the *Dannevirke* was conservative, royalist and pro-government, critical of liberalism and of Schleswig-Holsteinism. It was radical only in its deprecation of the suppression of the people and the vernacular by German officialdom. This attitude was no doubt consonant with that of the peasantry. Originally, the Danish-Schleswig movement was not so much based on a Danish-national consciousness as on the conservatism of the peasantry and their practical problems in point of language, and to this were added a number of circumstances, socio-economic, administrative and religious. For instance, the well-to-do and proud peasantry in the vicinity of Haderslev had for long been quarrelling with the officials, particularly on financial matters, and were now backed by the *Dannevirke*. In the island of Als and the adjacent peninsula of Sundeved the Duke of Augustenborg was very influential as a landowner, but not as a spokesman of the Schleswig-Holstein cause because he caused bad blood by his behaviour to the tenants and the clergy, who were partly attached to the church of the Kingdom. Also the north-western part of Schleswig was attached to the Kingdom in ecclesiastical matters, and the great majority of the clergy and the teachers were Danes or had been educated in Denmark.

From about 1842 Flor was partly eclipsed by a former Schleswig-Holstein politician of extreme liberal views. This brought in its train a more uncompromising Danish policy, provocative behaviour in the assembly, liberal opinions in the *Dannevirke*, large meetings and attempts at founding a party organisation. The reaction against this was strong also. In the rural populace large groups dissociated themselves from this policy, which, it was feared, would result in the incorporation of North Schleswig into the Kingdom. But still less did people want to be incorporated into Germany, and therefore the radical Schleswig-Holstein separatism of the mid-40s again called forth a pro-Danish feeling now shared more widely. It was clearly expressed at the last election to the consultative assemblies in 1847, in which the majority voted for Danish-Schleswig candidates in nearly all the rural districts of North Schleswig.

The war between Denmark, Schleswig-Holstein and Prussia of 1848-50 is of interest only as the culmination of the national movements.

The outbreak was an after-effect of the Paris revolution of 1848, which spread revolutionary ferment far and wide, and into Denmark and Schleswig-Holstein. The spokesmen for the revolutionary ideas came from mutually hostile yet kindred circles, which in the Kingdom rallied round Copenhagen and in Schleswig-Holstein round Kiel. In both cities National Liberal partisans placed themselves at the head of large popular demonstrations, demanding liberal constitutions and union with the Duchy of Schleswig, in Copenhagen concomitant with a separation from Holstein, in Kiel concomitant with the incorporation of Schleswig into the German Confederacy and a separation of the united Duchies from the Kingdom. In Copenhagen Frederik VII (1848-64), who had recently succeeded to the throne, yielded and appointed a National Liberal government. In Kiel a provisional government was set up, which at once prepared for an armed rising. In spite of the resulting war the political development still ran along parallel lines. Both in the Kingdom and in Schleswig-Holstein constituent assemblies were elected, which prepared closely related constitutions with democratically elected parliaments.

South Schleswig and most towns in Schleswig rallied round the government in Kiel, but among the rural populace of North Schleswig a strong pro-Danish excitement arose with popular assemblies and councils. There was widespread arming of local defence volunteers, who harassed the Schleswig-Holstein officials and resisted taxation. The great majority now supported the Danish-Schleswig leaders, who wanted closer links with Denmark and yet the preservation of Schleswig's exceptional position. However, the movement was soon checked by the military occupation of nearly the whole of Schleswig by Prussia and Schleswig-Holstein.

In a way, the war also put an end to the earlier trend of national development. Its mainspring had been the public debate, the consultative assemblies and popular propaganda, and till this point it had made a constant appeal to the will of the people as the supreme authority. Consequently, proposals suggesting the partition of Schleswig in accordance with national sympathies had influential supporters in both Copenhagen and Kiel in 1848. But the national movements had also argued in favour of historical and dynastic rights which covered the whole of Schleswig irrespective of the wishes of the populace. The passions of war in combination with military requirements for the suppression of national sedition resulted in the predominance of the dynastic views in Denmark, whereas the Schleswig-Holsteiners still adhered to their historic rights.

The Schleswig-Holstein occupation of North Schleswig was tantamount to the suppression of the Danish movement and the removal of pro-Danish officials. The subsequent Danish influence in North Schleswig from 1849-50 meant a reversal of this procedure, which was completed on a large scale after the final Danish victory in 1850. Altogether at least 250 Schleswig officials and employees were dismissed or fled the country, among them about 100 clergymen, who had played a prominent part as spokesmen for the Schleswig-Holstein cause. The peace terms prevented a change of the constitutional status, but not an absolutist Danish administration of Schleswig, which sought to extend Danish nationality through numerous Danish officials and through the introduction of Danish as the language of church and school in Middle Schleswig and the towns of North Schleswig.

However, the national boundary lines and views did not change materially between 1850 and 1864. In Denmark a complicated pattern of conflict arose between the National Liberal Party, a conservative unitary party, and a peasant movement with some leaning towards Grundtvig. The Schleswig-Holsteiners forgot the revolutionary spirit of 1848 and were now arguing from a purely legitimist platform. More important was their indignation at Danish power politics. This feeling evoked stronger and stronger response in Germany and thereby laid the psychological foundation of the Prussian war of revenge in 1864.

The Development of Nationalism in Denmark, 1864-1914

Lorenz Rerup

THE development of nationalism in Denmark in the half century after 1864 was strongly influenced by the great transition Danish society passed through in the period up to World War I. This transition began many years before the disastrous war of 1864, accelerating gradually and advancing and broadening especially in the decades about the turn of the century. Among its important antecedents were the rural reforms between 1769 and 1788, Denmark's successful adjustment to international trade (from 1845 on she was related so closely to Britain that the price-indexes ran in parallel), and the introduction of the constitutional monarchy in 1848/49 with its forerunners in the 1830s. The transformation of Danish society went very deep:

Politically from a society ruled from above by the bureaucracy of the absolute king to a constitutional monarchy, at first governed by relatively small, well-established groups (conservative civil servants of high position, National Liberals usually of middle-class composition, estate owners), then, after a long constitutional struggle resulting in the *de facto* recognition of parliamentary democracy, changing over in 1901 from the 'Right' to the 'Left' —

Economically from a traditional and poor, only partially integrated, grain-producing country, to a modernised, highly integrated agricultural, industrial and commercial society, the most important export 'industry' being Danish agriculture, a processing industry importing grains and other feeding stuffs and subsequently exporting meat and dairy products. In 1830 the population numbered about 1.2 millions, of which 21 per cent lived in towns; in 1914 the population amounted to 2.9 millions, 45 per cent of them town dwellers. Despite this growth, the gross domestic product (at factor cost, per capita, in 1968 US dollars) was 275 in 1830, increasing to 414 in 1870, 624 in 1900 and 851 in 1914 —[1]

Culturally from a society with a small elite, based mainly on the towns, particularly on Copenhagen, which had experienced higher education, and with a large peasantry which had, since 1814, enjoyed a compulsory but primitive elementary education to one comprising various elites, a diminished but not yet closed gap between town and country, and alternative ways of education, especially the Folk High Schools, of greatest importance to the peasantry. The breakthrough of the press from the 1870s onward created, at the end of our period, a network of newspapers all over the country (the so-called four-paper system corresponding to the four main political parties) working up a public opinion now emancipated from the domination of the previous elite and based on a far broader foundation. The Labour Movement was also well consolidated at the end of the century, having been an important ally in the Liberal Left's political triumph in 1901. Instead of one leading elite with a one-way communication with a roughly spoken, quiescent people, we now find a system with several centres competing with each other for the attention of public opinion and an electorate highly mobilised by the constitutional struggle. The leading circles of the towns, at the beginning of the struggle completely dominated by National Liberal and Conservative points of view, were divided, and a lively Liberal and Radical Liberal intelligentsia had grown up. These centres are connected with, but not identical to, different social groups and political parties. They show a tendency toward a consensus nationalism, the final merger of which lies outside our period. Obviously such complex changes in society are the mainspring of the development of Danish nationalism during these years. The picture, however, is incomplete unless the defeat of 1864 and the consequences of this are considered as well.

Above all, the defeat of the war with Prussia and Austria meant that the Danish United Monarchy, with its connected, complicated problems producing national tensions, ceased to exist. In effect the Denmark that was left became a nation-state, although it still included Iceland, the Faroe Islands, Greenland and the Virgin Islands, all of these unable to exert any serious influence on the development of nationalism on the mainland, because too little integrated with it. But, of great importance, the post-war border, which apart from some minor adjustments followed the old borderline between the Duchy of Schleswig and the Kingdom of Denmark, divided one part of the Danish people from the other. Particular significance lay in the fact that the separated part had been the turning-point for national feelings and national efforts since the outset of the national movements. The consequences of this painful separation were support, on as large a scale as possible, for the patriots under the 'Prussian yoke' and waves of national sympathy and correspondingly bitter feelings towards Germany, especially from the 1870s when the Prussian policy of Germanisation or sheer oppression was strengthened. The defeat produced also the need for an ideology sustaining endurance, thus giving the suffering parts both a working programme and the vision of a better future.

Furthermore, the defeat stressed the fact, which was further strengthened both in 1866 and in 1871 when the last hopes of revenge with the aid of France were extinguished, of the enormous power of Prussia/Germany, Denmark's closest neighbour. Public feeling before 1864, in the light of the successful war of 1848-50, had indulged in dreams of security behind the Danevirke-position, of military aid from Sweden/Norway, or of intervention by Great Britain and/or Russia if, in spite of everything, the enemy should cross the borderline of the Kingdom proper. After the war there is evidence of a fear of catastrophe. It was feared that the country might be unequal to continuing as a nation. Perhaps Germany and Sweden would divide the remaining part at the Great Belt.

Conversely, an optimistic view was also discernible. Long before, agricultural progress, rising prices and population growth had made reclamation of the extensive moorlands of Jutland a profitable undertaking. In 1865 a large-scale reclamation, regarded as a national task of great importance, was initiated by the Danish Heath Society. An area larger than the whole of Danish-speaking North-Schleswig was actually reclaimed. In 1872 this movement acquired an appropriate motto, the idea for which curiously enough originated in Prussia after the defeat of Jena: 'What is lost outwardly must be gained inwardly'. The merger of a number of local companies into nationwide, semi-monopolistic organisations was also dressed up with national titles: The Danish Distilleries (1881), The Danish Sugar Factories (1872), The Danish Chicory Factories (1872), as also The United Steamship Company (1866), struck a national chord.

In spite of this there was no doubt — even in the minds of her own inhabitants — that Denmark was a small state. Danish foreign policy walked the tightrope of alliance-free neutrality. Although the Danish military forces were comparatively strong in proportion to the size of the country, after 1870 they were strictly intended for defence only. This situation did not exclude vigorous anti-German reactions. The Prussia of Bismarck was seen as the incarnation of brute militarism, the very word 'Prussian' became a piece of invective. The Radical Liberal Minister of Defence, Peter Munch (1870-1947), although cool-headed in regard to nationalism, noted with satisfaction in his diary in November 1918, on getting news of the armistice, that the bloody conflict was over, 'ending in the defeat of that Germany which through the ages had represented *the* great danger for Denmark and the strongest threat to those ideas on freedom and humanity' to which he had dedicated his life's work.[2] Surely he is symptomatic of more than his own generation.

Strong anti-German feelings were also important in the Defence Movement,[3] which, although started before 1864, burst into a blaze supported by public reaction when in 1879 it turned out that Prussia and Austria had abolished paragraph V of the 1866 Treaty of Prague. This paragraph stated, at the request of the French emperor, in a somewhat vague way, that the population of the 'northern districts' of Schleswig should have the opportunity to vote for cession of the territory to Denmark.[4] The Defence Cause became a very conspicuous bone of contention in the internal political struggle. For the party in power, the Right (the former National Liberals and the Conservatives, or the bourgeoisie and the estate owners), it was an effective plea that everybody assumed that the defence efforts were directed against Germany, although this argument was seldom mentioned in public and for good reasons never officially. When on occasion attempting a pro-German neutrality, the efforts of the government always took place in strict secrecy. German policy was unacceptable to the public at any time, although obviously there were slight differences in the degree of people's feelings, the Liberal Left as a rule being less nationalist in their opinions than other groups.

Above all, the existence of a tremendously powerful neighbour engendered a feeling of insecurity, necessitating an ideology capable of promoting a sense of security. One such was insistence on good behaviour. Some Right politicians would not risk the country's reputation in Europe by taking into the government politicians from the peasant opposition. Another was the redefining of the Danish view of Germany in such a way as to connect the threatening aspects with certain German circles. This might make possible the reversal of the injustice inflicted on Denmark in 1864 by other social groups in Germany coming into power. Social Democratic newspapers wrote at the turn of the century that a Social Democratic Germany would give the population of North-Schleswig 'the entire freedom'.[5]

The powerful economic, scientific and cultural progress of the new German Reich from the early 1870s generated similar views especially in the Liberal Left. It must generally be emphasised that neither Prussian brutality nor the general anti-German feeling seemed to hinder the study-tours of the young, the spa-journeys of well-to-do elders, the wanderings of the artisans, the contacts between the Social Democratic Parties, the undisguised attempts of the Right to imitate Bismarck's system of Social Insurance or, last but not least, trade between the two countries. Certainly Denmark's export statistics showed the share of exports to Germany to be declining and that to Great Britain to be increasing, but the share of imports from Germany was very considerable. After the war, Hamburg's previous importance in the export of grain and live cattle from Jutland dwindled. This was not unconnected with the railway policy of the National Liberals prior to 1864, a policy influenced by national and military views, leading to the construction of the port of Esbjerg, opened to traffic in 1874. Already in 1857, however, Hamburg's position in Danish trade had been weakened by the crisis of the same year, and the city's position changed even more when she was integrated in the new Reich. No matter what influence the new border exercised, it could not possibly be profitable to transport the increasing quantities of Danish food exports to Great Britain through Hamburg.

The defeat also had political consequences. It debilitated the National Liberals, ideologically the most distinguished elite, in power before and during the war. They were already worried about the peasants' tendency to elect people from their own ranks instead of 'the wiser, the more expert and the more opulent', i.e. the notables of National Liberalism. In the latter years of the Danish United Monarchy the complicated constitutional conditions had held the peasant opposition in check but, in the simplified position after the war, it became necessary to revise the constitution. This was done in 1866. In the constitution of 1849 the *Folketing* (Lower House) had an almost general suffrage which was not altered in the constitution of 1866. The *Landsting* (the Upper House), however, though originally constructed with a moderate income qualification, was now devised as a Conservative stronghold providing the great landowners with a dominant position. The constitution did not specify how solutions should be found in case of conflict between the houses. This formed the basis of a constitutional struggle, the point at issue being that the Left claimed supremacy of the *Folketing*, whereas the Right maintained a position favourable to the Establishment. The struggle reached a climax in 1875-94 during the premiership of Estrup (1825-1913). It had started in 1870 when the United Liberal Left attained a majority in the *Folketing* and continued until the 'change of system' of the installation of a government of the Left and the *de facto* introduction of parliamentarianism. This long struggle produced a very widespread opposition movement against the party in power, which at first was supported by the urban voters from their aversion to a régime of peasants and schoolteachers. In the 1880s and 1890s the Conservatives gradually lost their supporters, first in Copenhagen, later in the provincial towns. The vote in general elections reached 70 per cent in 1887. In the 1880s the structure of the parties shifted quickly from parliamentary groups to electoral-mass parties with nationwide organisations.[6] The cultural counterpart to this struggle against the political establishment was the development of non-elitist mass ideologies promoted by the explosively expanding press as well as by institutions like the Folk High Schools. The opposing mass ideologies emphasised the people's right to self-government, allotting a very modest place to the state and its institutions. In fact the state played only a humble part in the enormous changes undergone by society, a fact which corresponded to the liberal view of its rôle.

Finally the defeat resulted in the loss of the Duchy of Schleswig, inhabited in its northern part by 170,000-200,000 Danish-speaking people. In this population the idea of dividing the Duchy now began to gain ground. The ancient regional solidarity — with national preferences from the 1830s on — gave way to concepts of national integration with mainland Denmark even at the expense of division of the region. For example, in 1864 we find in Aabenraa a Danish-minded craftsman disgustedly observing the joy of his neighbours at the German bombardment of Dybböl which fills his heart with horror.[7] Paragraph V in the Treaty of Prague could induce only similar considerations. Sustained by this paragraph, the Danes in North-Schleswig entered into the so-called 'policy of protest' by addresses and deputations, making the most of every occasion to re-assert the need for quick fulfilment of this promise. Organisations to support this view were still lacking.

The Danes in Schleswig participated in the elections to the Prussian Diet but those elected refused to take the obligatory oath to the constitution and so were prevented from taking their seats. The young opted for Denmark. Taking Danish citizenship they avoided the detested Prussian conscription, at the price of their political rights in Schleswig. In later years the young left the country altogether. This policy caused heavy national losses. Measured by votes in the area north of the present-day border, there had been 23,072 Danish votes in 1867. Twenty years later the votes reached their lowest point, 11,752, and then rose to 16,447 in 1912.[8] For a movement based on farmers, the enforced emigration of its youth was ruinous, although it probably also minimised social tensions and contributed to the stagnation of the towns in North-Schleswig in Prussian times, thus emphasising the farmers' dominance of this region.[9] The formal abolition of paragraph V in 1878 (not proclaimed until 1879), which aimed at humiliating Denmark, did not deprive these confident farmers of their hope of reunion. In the 1880s the concept gained ground that long-term tactics would have to be changed. This view spread only slowly in the western parts of the country where agriculture was backward. The elected candidates took up their seats in the Diet to fight against German encroachment within the system. Indeed, in 1906 in the German Reichstag the leader of the Danes supported the German government in a dubious case to ensure the continuation of negotiations. In order to keep full political rights and their right to stay in the homeland, young men submitted to Prussian conscription.

Vigorous emigration climaxed in the quinquennium 1880-85 and later.fell off, decreasing drastically in the new century. Simultaneously, however, agriculture prospered. Emigration removed about 60,000 people from North-Schleswig and was far more intensive there than from Denmark. It was also more intensive than emigration from other parts of the Duchies. The intensity of emigration from North-Schleswig resembled, at any rate after 1871, that of some German states, annexed by Prussia in 1866.[10]

Most important, there was a considerable cultural and political effort at organisation, and the circulation of newspapers expanded. In 1880 a Voters' Association (*Vaelgerforening*) was set up and in 1892 a School Association (*Skoleforening*), was established to be responsible for sending youngsters on to schools in Denmark, frequently to Folk High Schools, after completing the Prussian elementary school. These organisations, which had many members, reached into every village of North-Schleswig. They tried to combat the official policy of Germanisation. This had been initiated in the schools in 1871 with six lessons a week in German, was accentuated in 1878 when both languages were made of the same standing, and completed in 1888 when only four lessons in religion were left to be taught in Danish. Also, from the end of the 1870s the state schools inclined to German propaganda, while the few existing Danish private schools were closed. The authorities in Denmark were unable to intervene, but private circles gave cautious support to Danish by supplying money, books, scholarships, etc. The real burden of the national struggle, however, was carried by the Danes in North-Schleswig. Their core, the farmers, in these decades built a sub-culture of democratic agricultural organisations, dairies etc, corresponding to those of their social equals in Denmark, who now became their models.

Worried about the Danish perseverance, the Prussian authorities no longer restricted the struggle to cultural and political aims. Periods of oppression — culminating under the notorious Chief Civil Servant of Schleswig-Holstein, v. Köller (1898-1901) — followed upon periods of conditional benevolence, e.g. the agreement of 1907, which solved some citizenship problems resulting from the previous options. Both policies were dictated by considerations of foreign policy. Realising, however, that it was ownership of land that constituted the strength of the Danes, the Germans tried to buy up farms in order to hand them over to German farmers.

After some initial success the struggle about land quickly became national and a counter-attack was organised in which, among others, an Association was formed on October 5th 1898 to collect money to keep threatened holdings in Danish hands. In 1909, when the Germans intensified the contest, a Credit Association of North-Schleswig (*Nordslesvigsk Kreditforening*) was founded which actually did buy up farms and deliver them over to skilful young Danes on favourable terms. Finally in 1913, *vis-á-vis* the prospect of huge German funds, a Land Protection Union (*Landevaern*) was established, the locally organised members of which were bound by pledge not to sell land to Germans.

The amazing endurance of the Danish inhabitants in North-Schleswig from 1864 till the reunion with Denmark in 1920 had a complicated background with interacting political, economic and cultural elements. The dominance of a confident, prosperous, rural population was essential to this, since it could make money by selling food to the growing industrial towns in Germany, while in return the Germans were unable to break the farmers' solidarity in the network of their organisations. Least of all was it possible for the Germans to get hold of their basic support, the land.

Nationalism to these people did not mean only the holding of some peculiar attitude, or the conservation of a common language. To a great extent it was a way of life, on which emancipation was based, language also being a symbol of democracy. Its strength gave to the Schleswig Danes the feeling of fair wind. After nearly fifty years of Prussian rule, their leader, H.P. Hanssen (1862-1936), said in 1913, 'We are in harmony with the bright spirits of life, we have ideals which we embrace with fervour and enthusiasm. For this reason we are also able to gain more people to the Danish cause.'[11]

Historians do not like the word 'if', but if North-Schleswig had been exposed to industrialisation as the island of Als was after World War II, or if its agriculture had suffered from a constant decline, possibly there would have been a very different picture. A possible indication of this is that of the national development in Flensborg. Without a sound socio-economic basis and despite immigration from North-Schleswig, the original Danish circles there nearly disappeared.

Hand in hand with the great transformation of society and influenced by the consequences of the defeat in 1864, especially by the fate of the Danes in North-Schleswig, a Danish nationalism matured to include steadily increasing parts of the population. In spite of political, social and cultural differences which still divided the population, the tendency was toward a consensus nationalism foreshadowing the result of the transformation, a new society with a common framework of values. This has not yet been explored systematically but, presumably, it could be studied by investigating the sources: newspapers, meetings, organisations, book-sales statistics, ephemeral literature, reviews, advertisements, features of the educational system, especially school books and the teachers' professional training, also material on the Folk High Schools including the practice inspired by these schools of starting meetings and lessons with a song. As hymns are used at service to remind congregations of christian thoughts and religious experiences, so these songs expressed national conceptions and historical experiences. Furthermore, this consensus nationalism should be studied in relation to the development of the political system, because this is obviously connected with the participation in public life of new and broader social groups. Consensus nationalism fitted their need for identification, legitimised their ambitions and aims, and answered their need for the understanding of the surrounding world. There is an enormous leap from the horizon familiar to a peasant in 1850, as a rule limited to his ordinary daily work, the nearest district and very little public matter, except in areas early stirred up by social or religious problems — to the outlook of the co-operative farmer at the turn of the century, embedded as he was in a web of organisations and political and economic activities, perhaps including membership of the committee of a Folk High School and having in his farming the opportunity to choose between different forms of production.

For many people among the lower-class town-dwellers the leap was hardly less. Their level of information and experience widened in a similar way. It would be a mistake to believe that all of these made the leap or made it in full, but presumably many did so. Clearly the elements of this consensus nationalism were more amorphous and to a lesser degree logically connected than the ideologies of the elites, but it appears to me that these elements can be listed as follows — although I wish to emphasise that my survey is only a personal impression based upon the rather sparse literature and on knowledge of the period in question:

(1) The consensus contained a fear of Germany in the sense of a state or a military power but not as a cultural entity or an economic power. Generally speaking any concept of a dominant state was disliked.

(2) It built on the concept of a people characterised by language, culture and habits, and by common history. Race and religion were considered unimportant. The key word was '*sindelag*', a state of mind, at any rate partly including a sense of loyalty.

(3) It contained ideas of a right in a 'people' to organise itself as it wished in a nation-state of its own. As democracy spread, for example in Germany, this idea also spread. Thus the existence of Denmark would be ensured in the long term and the injustice of 1864 could not last for ever. Free people could be assumed to be of goodwill.

(4) It contained the idea that Denmark bordered on kindred nordic people who were friends. This was especially emphasised in respect of the Norwegians, followed by the Germans and the British, in that order. The French and the Russians were felt to be more distant. To some extent these concepts reflected the ease of communication but the tendency of the political development of the countries had its significance.

(5) While being passive spectators to the world theatre, Danes felt they must develop a national culture. This idea was very comprehensive. It included both high and low culture, some national products (e.g. the Lur Brand on Danish Butter), and political and social relations. The poor and old needing help were to be supported, but only if found worthy of it. There were certain norms for this development. As many participants as possible would be included, for there was no exclusiveness. According to an interpretation of Danish history and traditions the development had to be smooth and without any drastic breaks. Some attitudes were looked upon as un-Danish — an emphasis on military virtues and qualities, pathos in speeches or the solemn celebration of national symbols — but there seem to have been almost no limits to irony and laughter. Privilege was evil, authority questionable, a certain informality decent. Above all, the development had to be '*folkelig*' (of the people), i.e. in harmony with a somewhat idealised concept of the Danish people.

(6) Naturally the consensus also contained elements of the usual national self-confidence and conceit.

This consensus nationalism combined elements from the ideology of the National Liberals, visions of Grundtvig and experiences of the new classes now participating in public life. At the turn of the century it became the dominant but by no means the only national ideology in Denmark.[12] In 1920 an agitated national opinion on the reunion of North-Schleswig with Denmark, stirred up by the Conservatives and by parts of the Liberal Party, and based on widespread public feeling, did not wish to surrender Flensborg and other districts of Schleswig although these showed a large German majority in the plebiscite of that year. Eventually the border was determined by the wishes of the people as indicated by the plebiscite. A comparison of public attitudes at the outbreak of war in 1870 and at 1914 showed the existence of other national ideologies too. In 1870 a vigorous opinion wished Denmark to declare war on Prussia in support of France. But the decision-makers kept their heads cool. In 1914 such a feeling was absent but in 1915 the government assumed that a critical situation would produce a strong popular opinion for entering into the war on the side of the allies.[13]

Obviously there existed considerable remnants of the rather aggressive nationalism especially connected with the Right and with the Defence Movement and exploited by these in attempts at winning mass support in opposition to the movement for parliamentarianism. The defence propaganda's aim was to inflame patriotism. The flag could intensify the sense of national honour. The cautious foreign policy was sometimes looked on as servile. The Germans ought constantly to be reminded of Denmark's unresolved border problem. It was held that strong military forces were a necessity, whatever the cost. Especially important was the fortification of Copenhagen. Then the capital could be held until one or more of the Great Powers of Europe could come to the rescue, encouraged by the need to preserve their own strategic and commercial interests in unimpeded access to the Baltic. This nationalism did not lack an heroic variant which considered an honourable fight to be necessary for the healthy existence of the nation, and which urged national unity. Any split in the nation would weaken it outwardly. In 1894 a Right politician considered it to be obvious that a small nation like Denmark in an exposed position must have a strong government.[14]

In another dimension also a tendency to uniformity could be seen. A harmless but characteristic manifestation was the attempt to denounce German flags as 'indecent'. In 1906 they were used side by side with other European flags to decorate shops in Copenhagen in the tourist season. But, considering the Prussian suppression of Danish flags in North-Schleswig, a Conservative wrote, 'when such a thing is possible, the mercenary spirit must be well on its way to being given pride of place'.[15] In 1911 an ostensibly unpatriotic article aroused a storm in the Conservative newspapers. It had been written by a leading civil servant — quite incidentally of Jewish origin — by request of the Ministry of Foreign Affairs and others, but even so, there was no lack of anti-Semitism in the press attacks.[16] In connection with the negotiations about the sale of the Virgin Islands at the beginning of the century a veritable Danish imperialism arose, although of limited strength. In this movement the aims of big business were neatly combined with views on the necessity of giving Danish youth something to strive for.

Another peculiar kind of nationalism which can be found both in Liberal and Conservative circles was characterised by a very high regard for the folk-concept, probably a development of Grundtvigian ideas untouched by liberal thoughts. This assumed the development of the people within a framework to be marked out by the loyalty of the people to itself. Outside influences were rejected as injurious unless integrated by means of a fruitful interplay with the cultural tradition of the people. An outstanding Danish historian, born in North-Schleswig and certainly no narrow-minded nationalist, was A.D. Jørgensen (1840-97) who was sincerely interested in a revival of the old cultural relations between Germany and Denmark once the injustice inflicted on his people had been redressed. He not only had objections to the Danish Social Democrats on account of their 'de-nationalising tendencies' but also to the famous literary critic Georg Brandes (1842-1927), who had 'thrown into our midst a foreign school of thought, of a most un-national shape, to a youth likewise suffering from a weak digestion on this point' — the last being a rap at the academic youth.[17] Surprisingly he also disliked the National Liberals, because the policy they applied to the problem of Schleswig was 'doctrinaire' and without sufficient regard for the life and the traditions of the United Monarchy. A.D. Jørgensen is a very fascinating person in his relationship to the development of Danish nationalism. I do not here refer to his personal, elaborated national ideology, on which he founded a momentous historical production, although it had a broad effect, especially outside university circles. One of his books, *Forty Tales of the Fatherland's History*, was distributed in 1882 in 10,000 copies among the Danes in North-Schleswig, becoming very popular and effectively counteracting the schools' attempts at indoctrinating pupils with German history. In our context, however, his importance lay both in his ability to co-ordinate widely differing groups from the Left and the Right in a common purpose to support the Danish population in North-Schleswig, and on his influence on the youth of North-Schleswig and their helpers in the Kingdom when the long-term view had to be taken. In a controversy in 1879-80 he repulsed the idea that, if once revised, the border of Denmark should be moved 'back to that place to which history bears witness of its having been from time immemorial' or that Denmark should embrace 'that part of Earth which Our Lord, ere the dawning of history, gave to the Danes, in which — neither in more nor in less — to develop their innate talents' as his right-wing Grundtvigian opponent had stated.

The vision of A.D. Jørgensen was quite different; 'we want the border of the kingdom placed where the people's frontier lies. Like every individual, every people retains the inalienable right of free self-determination; every other right or title can be lost.' More remarkably he declared that the historical border had to be given up, 'because it would invade the rights of another people and necessarily would bring us new struggles which we would have to meet without any confidence in the justice of our cause'.[18] This view triumphed in 1920, when North-Schleswig was reunited with Denmark, in opposition to those ideologies which were ready to take advantage of Germany's defeat and wished to recover more than the area legitimated by plebiscite. It was this view also that became connected with consensus nationalism and gained the status of a dogma when the succeeding events seemed to verify it. A.D. Jørgensen's concept of the exclusiveness of a people, directed against Socialists and Jews, was also shared by the prominent Liberal Left-politician and Folk High School leader Frede Bojsen (1841-1926) and by others. It remained solely their property despite its clear relation to the concept of the people as a specially qualified community. In 1884, however, it was still possible, when the Left opposition divided into two groups, to distinguish one as the 'European' Left, exposed to foreign ideals originating in the great French Revolution, whereas the other labelled itself the 'Danish' Left, and accused the former group of using 'clammy hands' to take away the 'warmth of the heart'.[19] Ten, fifteen years later, individuals might still be hounded in this way but not a group, still less a political party.

In connection with the political exploitation of nationalism clearly involved in the defence question, we also find a pronounced anti-nationalism, partly as a political reaction. This strove to ridicule nationalist phraseology — with considerable success — and questioned the defence policy, preferring a cautious foreign policy at any cost to a strong defence. The latter might even tempt an aggressor, the fortifications of Copenhagen being thought too large a sword in the hand of a weakling, as had been the case of the Danish navy in 1807. This tendency was also bound up with anti-militarist trends existing from early times in parts of the peasant movement, because the burdens of conscription had been solely borne by the peasantry until 1848. It did not make sense for the early Social Democrats to fight for a 'country which belongs to others'.

In Denmark the peculiar political struggle gave momentum to these anti-nationalistic ideas, although the greater part of the population was hardly opposed to the defence of the country, only to the fortification of Copenhagen and to expensive military forces. No doubt this trend moderated the utterances of consensus nationalism, and favoured a relaxed attitude to national symbols. Both in the Radical Left and in the Social Democratic Party an anti-nationalism persisted beyond our period. Another kind of anti-nationalism was to be found in the Home Mission (the Evangelical Movement) which was, from first to last, absorbed totally in religious problems. This was important in North-Schleswig where the Grundtvigian inhabitants devoted themselves eagerly to national endeavours, while the Evangelicals often became indifferent. In time the Evangelicals also received a touch of nationalism. It should also be mentioned that a number of leading Folk High Schoolmen were influenced by the 'European' Left and later on by the Radical Left and this paved a way for consensus nationalism too.[20]

In 1889, analysing the situation in North-Schleswig, A.D. Jørgensen emphasised that a conquest was by then far more terrible than in earlier times. 'Then the conqueror was content with a tribute and an outward obedience to his law. Now he demands the very personality in full.' In this connection he described what has here been called consensus nationalism. He was in advance of his time. Consensus nationalism was by then hardly developed in Denmark. A bitter political struggle divided the country. There was antagonism between rural and town dweller, and unsolved social problems persisted: 'Never before have state and municipality on a scale as now continuously undertaken new and comprehensive endeavours, never have they so penetrated private life, everywhere uniting, settling, and giving human efforts the indispensable momentum. Thus the public burdens increase daily, while simultaneously the needs of the citizen are increasingly met. It lies in the nature of things, however, that this state and this municipality should act in the interests of the citizen, being an expression of that very society's spirit and will. Thus it matters not that different political parties struggle and exercise government in turn. On the whole they will all promote the same interests and will agree on the most important national questions.'[21]

The spirit and will of which he talks, common interests and the agreement on the most important national questions, were all results of historical processes as intimated above. In the case of Denmark it must also be remembered that the great transformation of society was connected with considerable economic progress, which smoothed over the changes, and that it was not possible to pursue a more active foreign policy or to think of violent resistance against the Prussians. Naturally this has given a special colour to Danish nationalism.

NOTES

1.   Svend Aage Hansen, *Økonomisk vaekst i Danmark*, Vol I, (København, 1972), p.16. For an outline of the cultural development see H.P. Clausen, 'Hvor laenge varede det 19. aarhundrede kulturelt?', *Kulturelle, politiske og religiose bevaegelser i det 19. århundrede* (Det laerde Selskabs publikationsserie, ny serie, ed Stig Jorgensen, Vol I, Aarhus, 1973).
2.   P. Munch, *Erindringer 1914-1918*, (København, 1961), p.356.
3.   For a short summary of the defence movement and other Danish national movements see Povl Bagge, 'Zur Organisations — und Sozialgeschichte dänischer nationaler Bewegungen im 19. Jahrhundert', in *Sozialstruktur und Organisation europäischer Nationalbewegungen*, Theodor Schieder (ed) (München/Wien, 1971), pp.143-152.
4.   Franz de Jessen (ed), *Manuel Historique de la Question du Slesvig*, (Copenhagen, 1906), pp.309-310. For a summary of conditions in North-Schleswig 1864-1920, see Troels Fink, *Ceschichte des schleswigschen Grenzlandes*, (København, 1958).
5.   Povl Bagge, 'Nationalisme, antinationalisme og nationalfølelse i Danmark omkring 1900' in Festkrift til Astrid Friis (København, 1963), pp. 13-14. This paper is henceforth cited as Bagge.
6.   General reference to Niels Thomsen, 'Urbaniseringen og den politiske adfaerd (i Danmark)' in *Urbaniswringsprocessen i Norden*, Vol III (Oslo, 1977), pp. 143-176.
7.   *Martin Bahnsens Dagbøger 1864-66* (København, 1964), pp.36 and 40.
8.   Aksel Lassen, *Valg mellem tysk og dansk* (Aabenraa, 1976), p.155.
9.   G. Japsen, 'Betragtninger over den danske bevaegelse i Nordslesvig' in *Sonderjyske årbøger*, 1973, pp.63-75.
10.   Mr Hvidt, *Flugten til Amerika* (Aarhus, 1971), pp.266-267.
11.   H.P. Hanssen, *Fra Kampaarene*, Vol II (København, 1929), p.245.

12.   Bagge, pp.9-11.

13.   P. Munch, *Erindringer 1914-1918* (København, 1961), p.40; see Bagge p. 27.

14.   J.F. Scavenius, *Danmark og det danske Folka Fremtid* (København, 1894), p.41.

15.   Vilh. la Cour, *Dansk Selvfølelse* (Odense, 1906), p.11.

16.   L. Rerup (ed), *Marcus Rubins brevveksling 1870-1922*, Vol I (København, 1963), pp.(73)-(85).

17.   H. Jørgensen (ed), *A D Jørgensens Breve* (København, 1939), pp.137 and 288-289.

18.   A. D. Jørgensen, *Historiske Afhandlinger*, Vol IV (København, 1899), pp.5-6 and 8-9. See also in general L. Rerup, *A D Jørgensen* (København, 1965, German edition Flensburg 1967).

19.   *Schultz Danmarkshistorie*, Vol V (København, 1942), pp.322-323.

20.   Bagge, pp.8 and 14-17.

21.   A.D. Jørgensen, *Om Kampen for den danske Nationalitets Bevarelse i Nordslesvig*, (København, 1889), pp.10-11.

The above paper has been revised as regards language by Birte E Lav. My participation in the seminar and the language revision of this paper are due to the economic support of the Danish Social Science Research Council. L.R.

The editor has decided, for reasons of consistency, to use the German rather than the Danish form of Schleswig.

Nationalism in Finland
— and the Effects of Economic Factors upon it

Yrjö Blomstedt

WHEN speaking about nationalism in Finland, there is a need for some clarification. There have been, and still are to some extent, three different categories of nationalism in Finland. First, the geopolitical nationalism common to the people living in Finland, its political objective being first enlarged autonomy and then the achievement and preservation of full independence. Then there are two different language-based nationalist movements, the Swedish (Swecomanians) and the Finnish (Fennomanians), both striving for political and linguistic predominance. During the period from 1809 to 1917 there were two areas of possible national friction, one between Imperial Russia and the autonomous Grand Duchy of Finland, another between the Finns and the Swedes living together in Finland.

The inheritance of Swedish rule from the eighteenth century was very important. After the kingdom of Sweden lost its position of a European Great Power in 1721, it was divided in two parts separated from each other by the Gulf of Bothnia. Sweden was the mother country, Finland the 'satellite', but formally both enjoyed the same political rights. There was, however, opportunity for a desire for geographical separatism in Finland. The inhabitants, especially the noblemen, were continually and deeply dissatisfied with the government's economic measures. These measures were often appropriate for Sweden proper but unfortunate for Finland. Expressions of bitterness and envy were often heard, and to these was added a distrust — founded on experience — of the ability or even of the will of Sweden to defend Finland against Russian expansion westward. All this nourished separatist thoughts, particularly during periods of crisis such as the Oriental Crisis of the 1780s.

Finland in 1809 was an underdeveloped country. Most of the people were engaged in subsistence farming, and the only things they had to buy were salt and iron. Practically no industrial works existed and foreign trade was very limited.

Before the Napoleonic Wars there had been a period of prosperous trade and export for Finland: from 1764 to 1803 the Finnish shipyards sold more than 1500 ships (containing about 200,000 lasts), and 4 million barrels of tar were exported. In 1803 Finland exported a great deal of timber. But the annual period of export was short (from May to October), and because the Swedish government was nervous about the destruction of natural resources such as the forests there were restrictions on the cutting of timber for sawmills and tar pits.

In the District of Viipuri (Viborg), already since 1721 belonging to Russia, there was a flourishing sawmill industry with markets in St. Petersburg as well as in Germany, Denmark and England. The owners of the mills were often members of the Russian aristocracy. Thus Russian capitalists had a foothold when the province was incorporated with Finland in 1812.

I

Decisions of the Diet in Porvoo (Borga) in 1809 and the peace treaty of Hamina (Fredrikshamn) in 1809 transferred Finland from the Kingdom of Sweden to the Empire of Russia, with the status of an autonomous Grand Duchy. The Emperor was Grand Duke of the Duchy. All Finnish subjects of the Czar were automatically subjects of the Empire, but the Russian subjects of the Czar could obtain citizenship in Finland only by naturalisation. In the early years of Russian rule there were some vague attempts to make the economy of the Grand Duchy serve Russia, but these were soon abandoned. Surplus revenue from the Grand Duchy was already directed towards the Russian State Treasury, but this had no real meaning because the Finnish State Treasury was permanently in deficit. Later Finland got its own State Bank, the Bank of Finland.

The Finnish producers were in touch with the new and large markets of Russia. But the peace treaty also confirmed the low or non-existent customs duties on trade between Finland and Sweden. The customs border erected between Russia and Finland in 1811 was more or less a formality; its main purpose was to hinder the illegal transit trade of foreign goods through Finland to Russia.

The commercial treaty of 1818 between Russia and Sweden was less favourable to Finland, but as Finnish export of grain to the now self-supporting Sweden ended, Finnish peasants and grain merchants found markets in Russia. In the 1830s, however, Russia attempted to gain advantages over customs at the expense of Finland. This resulted in an enlarged import from Russia, which caused a natural response in the increase of Finnish exports to Russia.

One of the problems for the Finnish economy in the first decades of Russian rule was the use of parallel currencies, Swedish and Russian. But by the monetary reform of 1840 Swedish money was, for most purposes, ruled out. Only peasants, trading in Stockholm with food, for instance meat and butter, or with firewood, had the right to exchange the Swedish money they received into rouble bills issued by the Bank of Finland.

Russian 'selfishness' in trade and customs policy evoked in 1830 a Finnish economic patriotism, a longing to develop the country economically. The aristocratic-bureaucratic members of the ruling class were either indifferent or even hostile to romantic or sentimental nationalism, but at the same time they were aware of the danger from Russia. In politics, their device was perhaps *bene vixit, qui bene latuit* — the man (or country) lives well, who lives well hidden — but in the field of economics they thought that the right course was rapid development. A strong economy would be the best guarantee of survival for a close neighbour of the Russian giant.

From the 1840s on there were improved opportunities for this economic policy. The principle of reciprocity became common in international customs policy, and even the Russians adopted it and adapted it to Finland. The mighty Finnish Chief of Finances Lars Gabriel von Haartman, nicknamed 'His Dreadfulness', was able to obtain the right of unobtrusively reducing customs duties. He was, because of a long stay in Central Europe, an ardent supporter of canals. The building of the Saimaa canal was begun in the 1840s to carry traffic between inland and coastal towns. But von Haartman did not appreciate the role of railways in expanding exports. Canals, industry for the home market, and freedom from craft regulations were his enthusiasms.

Von Haartman was in charge until 1858. By then there was no place for an old, self-confident authoritarian who believed in the duty of the state to control the detailed workings of the economy. But he was the man who had laid the ground for economic take-off in Finland.

In and after 1848 the newly awakened European liberalism had echoes in Finland. During the Crimean War, when British and French ships devastated the shores of Finland, the merchants and shipowners showed a tendency towards separatism. They wished for international recognition that Finland was not a 'real' part of the belligerent Russian Empire. The reason for this was clearly a simple concern for their own property. Again during the Polish rising of 1863 Finnish merchant vessels wished to raise their own colours, so as not to be threatened as Russians. These attitudes found disfavour in St. Petersburg, but all the same Finland was allowed her own consuls in important ports.

The most significant development was in 1863 when the Finnish Diet (*Lantdag*) began again to meet. From then a major part in the economic decisions was made by the Diet in conjunction with the Emperor-Grand Duke. In 1863 Finland got its own currency, the Mark (1 Rouble = 4 Marks), and this period was also marked by the founding of the first commercial bank in 1862. Gradually, as Treasury expertise developed, the Grand Duchy was found to be very wealthy. J.L. Runeberg's words in the national anthem, 'our land is poor, so shall it be', were not really true. Already in von Haartman's time there had been steps taken towards a more liberal economy: the abolition of guild power, the cancellation of the restriction of sawmills, to water power, etc. European demand for timber resulted in a rapid growth of the sawmill industry and after the Franco-German War Finland suddenly appeared as a country no longer predominantly agrarian. Agriculture responded by moving over to livestock and dairy farming. Dairies were founded in hundreds. Then, in the 1880s, in every year a new paper mill or cellulose mill was set up.

Throughout the nineteenth century there had been difficulties over relations with Russia. Most of these were political in essence, or juridical, and they increased and became more severe after the creation of the German Reich, which changed the geopolitical situation in the Baltic and also influenced the basis of

Russian strategy. But in economic matters there had been few quarrels. For Russian capitalists making investments in Finland, the fact that Finland was a separate state with its own rules and laws, which differed from those of Russia, was both amazing and provoking. The owners of the Pitkäranta copper mines and works treated both the workers and the local Finnish official very harshly. The Russian Artillery Department, owner of the Raivola Iron Works in the Karelian Isthmus, forced through an Imperial Decree that created a Russian township inside Finland. At the Huutokoski Iron Works, owned by the famous N.I. Putilov, counterfeit weights were used. On the other hand, most of the merchant families of Russian origin which had settled in Finnish towns became in a few generations totally assimilated into Finnish society, so that they regarded themselves more as Swedish-speaking Finns than as Russians. The Kiseleffs in the sugar industry, the Sinebrychoffs in brewing, the Tichanoffs in iron and general merchandise, the Wavulins, the Uschakoffs, all were His Majesty's Finnish subjects. In the last decades of the nineteenth century and in the beginning of the twentieth there was dispute about Russian Jews who wanted to settle in Finland as petty dealers when dismissed after twenty or thirty years of Russian military service in Finland. The attitudes of Finns to this issue were more racist than nationalist. Also, many Finns had settled down in Russia, especially in St. Petersburg, and they had done well as factory owners, craftsmen and merchants.

Not even the slightest traces of Russian exploitation of Finland can be found. Russian customs policy in the 1880s was very protective to Finland as well as to Russia, so that the Finnish wood-processing industry had considerable trouble when exports to Russia were reduced. The Finns were not happy, but there was no obvious complaint. There was, on the whole, a stable reciprocity in trade and industry between Finland and Russia.

In the field of state finances the peculiar Finnish system of two kinds of state money (that of the Diets and that of the Emperor) caused many troubles, but these must be seen in connection with politics (the millions spent on the Neva bridge or on the army). The main concern was with Russian constitutional, not economic, oppression. During the first world war, when 80-96 per cent of Finnish exports went to Russia, and 50-60 per cent of her imports were from Russia, many businessmen did not support the idea of Finnish independence. The Finnish shoe industry, which had equipped the Imperial Army with millions of boots, was in opposition to the independence movement until the Bolshevik October Revolution.

II

Historical developments had, already in the eighteenth century, led to a nation with two languages. Roughly speaking the majority of rural people spoke Finnish, and the majority of the inhabitants of towns and cities, Swedish. Swedish was the language of the educated classes, too. Before the language struggle there were few Finnish-speaking industrialists, merchants, or other entrepreneurs. The number of Finnish-speaking merchants began to increase when new inland towns were founded in regions with a wholly Finnish hinterland (for instance Jyväskylä and Joensuu). When the parliament began in 1863 there was only a handful of Finnish-speaking members in the Estate of Burgesses, but by 1880 a third of this Estate belonged to the Finnish party.

In the 1860s and 1870s most of the Estate of Burgesses had been Swedish-speaking Liberals, and for them the language problem was at first no problem at all: one nation, two languages. In the companies and bank companies, founded before the 1880s, the members of the boards were mostly Swedish-speaking people, but some prominent Finnish speakers were also elected to the boards.

In the 1880s the rise of the Finnish Party and its claims for hegemony for the Finnish language frightened the Liberals. Efforts to found a real Liberal party failed. In one sense the Liberals were also nationalist. Some parts of Finland's economic life lay in foreign hands. This was especially the case in the assurance business. Liberal Finnish-Swedish businessmen founded the life assurance company Kaleva as part of the struggle against Swedish, German, Russian and British assurance agencies: the name was taken from national mythology. But in 1888 the company refused to extend assurance for Professor E.G. Palmén: 'because he is so gruesome a Fennomanian' was the reason given. On Boards of Trustees the Finns were gradually omitted.

Of the greater industrialists, only a few, for instance A. Ahlström and G.A. Serlachius, would declare for the Finnish Party. Then ensued what could perhaps logically be expected to occur in Russo-Finnish economic relations, but on a small scale. In 1889, Kansallis-Osake-Pankki was founded, the first Finnish banking company. Its very name was national, and a demonstration of the national ideology of young and ardent founders. These founders were not businessmen, industrialists or merchants, but just young university people and professionals. After the *cause célèbre* over Professor Palmén, a national Finnish assurance company was founded, Pohjola. Thus the economic field in Finland was divided into a large Swedish-speaking section and a much smaller Finnish-speaking one. Most of the giants in Finnish industry were Swedish, and a typical demonstration of their Swedish nationalism was for instance the enormous donation made by Ernst and Magnus Dahlström, which made it possible in 1919 to open a University for the Swedish nation in Finland. The Finns retorted with a popular subscription list for a new purely Finnish Univeristy. (The State University was and remains bilingual). Most of the subscribers to the Finnish University were peasants.

So, the final answer to the question of possible grievances in the field of economic life must be more or less negative. This may surprise those who expect Great Powers to suck out and drain their satellites and colonies, and also those who hold to the primacy of economics in historical causation. The history of Finland is distinctive and perhaps unusual.

'Let Us Be Finns'
— the Birth of Finland's National Culture

Matti Klinge

THE rise of Finland's national culture in the nineteenth century provides an opportunity for analysing the factors that influence the shaping of a cultural form: the political structure and links, the manifestations of isolation and special efforts to create a separate national culture, and the circles of influence which participated in this active endeavour. The development of Finland in the nineteenth century is an example of the moulding of a culture from the starting point of a changed political status and subsequent withdrawal from the earlier cultural affinity. Even in broad terms, the role of such a change in status is important, if not decisive, and that for at least two reasons. One, to which I shall soon return with reference to Finland, is institutional separation from the cultural and administrative tie of the earlier political connection. The other event that occurs with a change in political status is independence or autonomy. This is essential, for the birth of a national culture is the distinct definition of the geopolitical development within which a national culture evolves. With the change in political status there comes a definition of the geographical basis in accordance with the natural prerequisites and especially of the ethnic and traditional conditions on which the new culture is created.

The term 'people' or 'nation' is never so strictly circumscribed a concept as to be incontrovertible if based on ethnic or linguistic boundaries. We require a special political step which decides that these tribes or those regional units shall be separate while others fuse together. Knowledge of the culture and people to which we must belong then spreads from above, from the centres and cultural institutions controlled by them. And this doctrine tends in quite a number of remote districts and frontier regions to oppose sharply the local belief that the ethnically and linguistically close dwellers across the frontier are strangers while those who live far away in the centres are kin. The Catalans of southern France must turn their backs on the Catalans of northern Spain and their faces towards distant Paris, while the institutions on the other side of the frontier stress the importance of Madrid. The boundary has fixed the sphere in which each national culture has its being.

In Finnish conditions, this important change of status occurred in 1809 when under the Peace Treaty of Hamina a number of provinces listed by name were incorporated in Russia, and the victor had decided before the treaty was signed on its own institutions for the administrative area that was formed in this way. This area had never before constituted an administrative entity, though the main parts had from time to time been placed under a temporary common administration. A distinct but not precisely defined concept of 'Finland' had already originated earlier. The traditional administrative, political and trading centre was Stockholm, capital of the centrally governed kingdom of Sweden. The frontier adjustment left, on the Finnish side, many Swedish-speaking ethnic groups and, on the Swedish side, a large Finnish settlement. Lapland with its Lapps was also divided. On the eastern frontier, again, in relations with Russia, the new administrative area was enlarged with territories, some of which had earlier belonged to the Swedish realm proper, but had been hived off in various phases, and some of which had never belonged to it or had been taken for a short time only as the spoils of victory and had not come under the traditional Swedish-Finnish administration or enjoyed the political rights of the realm. But the greater part of Russia's tribes that spoke Finnish or closely related languages was *not* incorporated into the Grand Duchy of Finland. Thus, the geographic formation of Finland left it with two ethnic minorities which are still distinguishable, the Swedish linguistic minority and the Orthodox religious minority in Karelia. Beyond the new frontier were groups which might in one way or another have qualified for consideration when the regional entity of Finland was formed. There is especial reason to refer to these features of regional determination when discussing Finland. In the ensuing debate later in the nineteenth century on the essence of national culture, a debate which retained importance until World War II, there was a significant polarisation. On the one side there were those who stressed the role of the Swedish-speaking part of the people and emphasised western ties. On the other side there were those who in a sense used the Karelian population as a fulcrum for levering the argument on the national culture towards eastern origins.

The new geopolitical unit was not the only outcome of the separation of Finland from the Swedish realm. Sweden, too, was at the same time made into the geographical entity which generations by now have known. Although Norway was under the sovereignty of the King of Sweden, it retained its own administrative organs, language and institutions. A contrary situation existed in the bilingual Kingdom of Sweden which historians often call Sweden-Finland. The name depicts for present generations the size and boundaries of the realm. But, in the search for false historical continuity, it can readily lead us to forget — and both sides have been guilty of this — that the conception of both Sweden and Finland dates back to the year 1809. On the institutional level this is not immediately apparent for Sweden, for the old administration continued. In reality, the difference was enormous even at the institutional level, for the Revolution, the new constitution and the new royal house which rested on French revolutionary traditions involved a sharp break with the old. But it is especially at the cultural level that an entirely new Sweden begins to emerge after 1809. The creation of an altogether new national spirit began there immediately under the lead of great and minor poets. Prior to 1809, Sweden with its Lapps, Finns, Swedes and Pomeranians was still in principle a small empire the inhabitants of which were joined neither by language nor national spirit, but by a common ruler. The mental image of Sweden now is of a national state, the birthplace of Vikings and peasant romanticism, propagation of the people and the language. Right from the 1810s Geijer began to write and teach the history of the Swedish people. The historians before 1809 had been writing about the history of the state or the kingdom of Sweden.

It must be remembered that the development of Sweden was of decisive importance for the birth of Finland's national culture. An essential initial feature of the Finnish national culture can be seen in retrospect in the fact that the culture of the late eighteenth century by and large continued in Finland although it was strongly renounced in Sweden. Thus, the national moulding of Finland starts largely and simply from isolation. It no longer follows the path signposted by its former centre. The Swedish language continued to be the cultural and administrative tongue in Finland, and Swedish law and the Swedish constitution were preserved in Finland, but Sweden itself adopted a new form of government. The Swedish hymn book was revised under the direction of romantic poet-bishops soon after the separation. But the old Swedish hymn book remained in official use in Finland for another half century. And so on.

It might be thought that this isolation — in a way without any pains on Finland's part — from the former cultural contact which had given Finnish culture a specific character was due solely to the poverty of Finnish cultural resources. The preservation of a cultural profile already regarded as obsolete in Sweden might be seen as a phenomenon indicative of the withering of culture, its total inability to keep up with the times. Perhaps this was so to some extent. But a more essential consideration is that while Sweden plunged directly into the maelstrom of Romanticism — not only in the domain of art, literature and even politics, but also very manifestly in the humanist, natural and medical sciences — Finland was incorporated in the Russian Empire where romantic idealism was not to have the same influence. The ideals of rationalism and neo-humanism of the Age of the Enlightenment were prevalent, especially in the western capital of the realm, St. Petersburg. It was to this city that came both the highest nobility of Finland set on a military career and the broad masses from eastern Finland in search of additional means of livelihood. The population of St. Petersburg and its surrounding provinces had a nationally disparate character. German, Finn and Lutheranism were as perceptible as Russian and Orthodoxy. The European languages and the cultural tradition of the Age of the Enlightenment set the trend in court circles and among the aristocracy. The new centre for Finland came to manifest expressly and at many levels the influences of St. Petersburg which suitably extended Finland's own traditions of the enlightened age. The old political, administrative and even cultural centre had been Stockholm. There, too, a great part of the burghers had spoken German in the seventeenth and eighteenth centuries, and a large proportion of the lower classes, fishermen, maidservants and providers of firewood had been Finnish. Both Stockholm and Leningrad (St. Petersburg) still have a Finnish church, located fairly centrally. Helsinki, the new centre of Finland's administrative organs and culture, was built to show imposingly and concretely both to foreigners and to the Finns themselves that a

separate political unit, Finland, had come into existence. It was henceforth to be
the centre to which the periphery of Finland was to look.

Romanticism in Sweden, Germany and England was already directed both in
literature and in historical conception to idealisation of the German Middle Ages.
But the monumental centre of Helsinki was created in conformity with the
Petersburgian-Baltic neo-humanist-ideals. This 'Empire' style, which spread
everywhere with official blessing, became an essential mark of Finland and, thus,
of Finnish culture. Romantic idealism was a weak current also in Finnish
intellectual life. While the old University of Finland was still in Turku, a wave of
German-Swedish romanticism was felt there in the 1810s, but even then it was
weakened by the vigour of the local neo-humanist-rationalist tradition. When the
University moved to Helsinki at the end of the 1820s, both it and its influential
intelligentsia began to express primarily neo-humanist thinking. This, I would
repeat, is particularly important when comparing Finland's development with
Sweden's as an indicator of the differentiation of their mutual national culture.

The Finnish Literary Society was founded in Helsinki in 1831. Its aim was to
spread knowledge of the motherland and its history, to further the use of its tongue
and to develop literature in the Finnish language for both 'educated compatriots'
and the 'lower classes'. In its early years the Society defined its main objectives as
follows:

1. The achievement of a Swedish or German translation of *Kalevala*;
2. A compilation of Finnish mythology;
3. A clarification of the Finnish reflexive verb;
4. The production of a memorial publication in Finnish on Porthan;
5. A Finnish translation of Runeberg's poem *The Elk Hunters*; and
6. The compilation of a Finnish theory of poetry to establish whether Finnish
poetry was based on the quantity or the stress of the syllable.

The academic intelligentsia — the only one in the country — sought to begin
building up Finland's national culture. The cornerstones were historical research,
study of the language and folklore, and dissemination of the *Kalevala* and *Elk
Hunters*.

The *Kalevala* (1835) was Finland's national epic compiled by Lönnrot on
classical lines from poems discovered in Russian Karelia. Its especial importance
was that it laid the groundwork on which to build the national continuity, or rather
an illusion of it, of Finnish culture. The active desire of the Finns to make the
Kalevala known in foreign languages is natural against the background of this
continuity of national culture. The *Kalevala* as it were legitimises the aspiration
for a new national culture. The new Finnish national culture would not be
artificial or constrained, for in addition to history and language it had a monument
indicative of an artistic ancient culture of high standard.

Runeberg's *Elk Hunters* portrayed the Finnish landscape and common men and
women in the setting of antique bucolic ideals. Runeberg depicted the Finns as
harmonious, balanced people, cheerful and content even in their poverty. This
Arcadian idyll was the first and most profoundly effective Finnish patriotic
portrait. It is of the essence that Runeberg's picture of Finland is decisively non-

historical, based on neo-humanist admiration for the people and scenery, in which the ancient ideals of balance, moderation and harmony dominate. This view of the mother country was central still in the song *Our Land*, adopted as a national symbol in 1848, a national anthem which emphasises the aesthetic. Pljetnov, Rector of the University of St. Petersburg, kept in touch with Runeberg and wrote: 'What could be more pleasant and useful than to travel in a country where the beauty of Nature is in harmony with the customs and civilisation of the people. Switzerland had something similar earlier. But now natural beauty has been spoilt by the horror stories of the Revolution. Yes, I am ready to believe that there is only one country in the world for you and me in which we can find our idea of happiness, and that is Finland. If I mastered the two languages spoken there, I would not hesitate to adopt that country as my motherland . . .'. This passage dates from 1848, the year when stories of the horrors of the Revolution were despoiling natural beauty, to use Pljetnov's words. The beauty of Nature also embraced man's Rousseau-esque freedom from corruption. And this brings us to the question of how imperial Russia viewed the idea of Finland's national culture.

The Russian attitude had been outlined before the Peace of Hamina. The preservation, unchanged but appropriately supplemented, of the religion, official language, legislation and administrative organs of Finland meant in itself abandonment of the idea of assimilation. It was never Russia's intention to russify Finland and make it a part of Russia. Finland was occupied as a marchland protecting St. Petersburg, a buffer against Sweden and its western allies. The approval of a special administrative system for the country and the emphasis on its political existence by building a separate capital make it clear that the creation of a national culture was also one of the government's aims. The birth of a national culture could not anyway be a negative phenomenon from the government's point of view, for it widened the separation from Sweden. A national culture would gain the people's loyalty and infuse it with a spirit of resistance to possible Swedish revanchism. Thus, in the government's view, the *Elk Hunters*, *Kalevala* and the Finnish Literary Society were all positive phenomena, and were to be supported. The government slowly but purposefully moved towards increasing the grasp of the Finnish language among civil servants. In fact, knowledge of Finnish was made a requirement for some civil service examinations as early as in the 1840s after a lectorate in Finnish was established at the University in Helsinki in 1828. Research on Finnish-Ugric philology was begun at the St. Petersburg Academy of Sciences. The first professor of the Finnish language was appointed in Helsinki in 1850 at a time when chairs in modern languages were still very rare. Indeed, Finland had no chair in any other modern language for over two decades. After certain vicissitudes, the position of Finnish alongside Swedish as an official language was confirmed by government initiative in 1863 even before the parliament that convened then requested it, and before there was any other pressure on the government. These examples show that the claim often made in earlier literature about the negative attitude of the Russian government towards a Finnish national culture is wrong. The government opposed all revolutionary trends and western political doctrines such as socialism and democracy, but it

F

opposed nationalism only when it occurred in association with them, as it often did in nineteenth century Europe.

National and social thinking were combined in Finland in the mid-1840s by Snellman. He was an opposition man during the reign of Nicholas I, but a government man and even a member of the domestic government under Alexander II. Snellman's great idea was the replacement of a bureaucratic society with a civic society, but in Finnish conditions broad participation demanded a change in the language situation. It is important in this connection to remember that Snellman's doctrine embraced not only education of the masses but also naturalisation of the educated class, i.e. gradual 'finnification'. Snellman did not want to create a new leading stratum or elite directly through educating the people. He wished primarily to preserve the old elite, but change its language. This endeavour was largely successful. The movement across class lines injected new blood into the leading element, but the old leadership comprising noble, bourgeois and particularly clerical families remained in charge until the country gained its independence and even long after that, until the end of World War II. This can be perceived from the lists of cabinet ministers or rolls of senior civil servants, for example. Even when an 'outsider's' name appears, he was frequently linked by marriage, often very closely, with the upper class network of kin and, thus, with the net of traditions. It may perhaps be said that only the entry of the Agrarian Party leaders into the political leadership in connection with the gaining of independence infused a sizeable new force and agrarian emphasis into the elite. Because of its defeat in the Civil War of 1918 the working class had to wait until the time of World War II for a share in power. (cf. the Social Democrats in Sweden.)

The upper or middle class nature of the stratum that was developing and moulding the national culture is clearly discernible in the pictorial arts and even in literature. The dominant character in Finnish-language literature was Aleksis Kivi. He was familiar with the life of the people at their own level. He wrote his main works in the 1860s and 1870s, but was not widely known and recognised until the twentieth century. It was only after the great political and intellectual transitional period embracing the General Strike of 1905 and the subsequent years that the upper and middle classes were ready to abandon the Runebergian popular portrait for the realistic image of Kivi. The Finnish pictorial arts of the 1880s and 1890s produced a picture of the country and the people that until then had been drawn almost exclusively in words. It is typical that this picture of the native country was drawn very largely in Paris and for the most part mirrored the Runebergian harmonious idealism in the new media of bright colours inspired by the exoticism of Brittany and the fashion of Japan. It is symptomatic that one of the painters of this great period of Finnish art, one who had been least instructed and was of humble social origin, participated hardly at all in portraying the landscape of his country. We can still see today, mostly through the lens of the camera, the Finnish landscape as the *fin de siècle* Finnish painters saw it. Runeberg in his landscape poems gave the painters of Finland's golden era the guidelines to which *Kalevala* elements were added later. The art of painting thus remained for a long time, indeed until the period of political transition already referred to, an extension of the national cultural tradition that was shaped in the first half of the nineteenth century.

There are also artists and works which are suggestive of another line or part of Finnish national culture, its aristocratic tradition. The thin ranks of the Finnish nobility went over to the victor readily in 1809 and immediately afterwards. They were prompted by the political development and new trend in Stockholm. There had been sympathy on the Finnish side earlier for the era of King Gustavus III and its leading personalities. Some leading Gustavians became central figures in Finland's new administrative agencies. To them, Alexander I was closer to Gustavus III whom they missed than was Gustavus' son, to say nothing of Bernadotte who was thrust in by the Revolution. But the considerable rewards given to the nobility also played a role in gaining their general acquiescence and later loyalty. Moreover, noble titles continued to be bestowed fairly generously until 1905, whereas the practice had decreased in Sweden and other countries several decades earlier.

Finland's very earliest nationalist movement originated with the Finnish aristocracy. Their attitude had hardly any literary or linguistic influence, but it created a firm national tradition in the administrative sphere, the civil service and loyalty to the monarchy and gained rewards when its members took service with the Russian army. Representatives of this aristocratic national tradition are Count Rehbinder and Count Armfelt, both Minister Secretaries of State, Senator Baron von Haartman, painter Albert Edelfelt, Marshal of Finland Baron Mannerheim, and many cabinet ministers and statesmen of even independent Finland.

A part of this aristocratic tradition fused with the liberal trend which spread to Finland in the 1850s and which flowered with the beginning of regular parliamentary meetings in 1863. The liberal group approved of the Runebergian idea of the native country and people, but wished to add historical elements to it. Runeberg himself had begun later to fix attention on them, especially in Part II of the *Tales of Ensign Stahl* which appeared in 1860. The liberal concept of history emphasised the continuity of Finland's institutions, law, culture and parliament, even the continuity of religion which bound Finland with Sweden and with the west in general. In the liberal optimistic view of history, the institutional and cultural germanisation of the Finns was progress, movement towards a higher form of culture. The Swedish regime was accorded a positive colouring, and contrasted especially with the bureaucratic censorship of the reign of Nicholas. Pursuing this view of history, the liberals revived memories of the war of 1808-1809 so strongly that the Russians were annoyed.

The liberal trend was connected with the restructuring of the economy. The forestry industry gained momentum in the 1860s and 1870s, foreign trade expanded considerably, the railways enlarged the opportunities for trade, and legislation opened the way to the establishment of limited liability companies, private banks and the industrial use of labour, together with freedom of trade. The liberal tradition eventually had a long-term influence on Finnish national culture in the sciences and arts, politics and the economy. We might even say that Finnish urban culture has continued this tradition both spiritually and materially. It has borne the traditions of the Finnish press. The liberal trend cannot be judged solely against the influence of the political party that represented it, the so-called Swedish Party. For the development of the national culture, nineteenth century liberalism was a power group which stressed the role of institutions and history and stood for the continuity of western influence. Working under its wing for a long time was a weak Sweden-oriented trend which did not really come into the open until the parliamentary reform of 1906. But then the Swedish People's Party, which is small, has never been a group of Swedish nationalists proper; aristocratic and liberal traditions have been more important in it. The nineteenth century liberals had no aspiration to build a unilingual national culture. What they wanted was a culture which both linguistic groups could share. It favoured, not opposed, the advancement of the Finnish language, but did not regard any language as the sole or even salient attribute of the national culture.

If liberalism was the cultural trend of the advancing bourgeoisie and towns, its counterweight from the 1860s on was the Fennomania which stressed agrarian values and found its political support in the traditional rural community, among the farmers and the clergy. This trend gave itself out to be nationalist and saw the moral and material values of the traditional rural society as the underpinning of the national culture. The ideal was the independent, landowning farmer, living witness to the ancient agrarian continuity and a Finnish independence free as it were of external political events. The leader of the movement, Yrjö-Koskinen, developed a new historical view, the history of the Finnish *people*, in which the past was explained in the light of the needs that had led to the growth and strengthening of Finnish nationalism. Yrjö-Koskinen wanted to create historical continuity for the Finnish language culture which the Fennomans were building up and which was understood as national. Thus, Fennomania turned against emphasising external influences and their manifestations, especially western influences which were stronger in the prevailing cultural climate than the rather negligible eastern currents. Indeed, Fennomania was ready to approach Russia and the Russians with a view to displacing the liberal Swedish-language elements. A part of the Fennoman youth saw their movement as socially binding and approached the line taken by the Russian Populists (*Narodnichestvo*).

However, the Fennoman vision of a rural society left a large part of the population on the sidelines. This sector was the rural proletariat, the surplus agricultural population, some of whom moved around the turn of the century to the cities or emigrated to Russia or America. Similarly, the urban proletariat was excluded from this shaping of the national culture. The importance of these groups was not revealed until the General Strike of 1905 and the first elections by universal suffrage in which the socialists unexpectedly gained almost half the votes. At this juncture, the national culture was split by internal suspicion which was darkened, too, by a stiffening of Russian policy. Finland's quiet but distinctly advancing economic and cultural independence had raised the question of whether, in the changed international situation of the 1890s, the country was any longer the loyal buffer state envisaged in 1809. Opposition to the more aggresive policy of the Russians led at the turn of the century to intensified education and propaganda aimed at gathering broad groups of the population into the fold of united opinion. Enormous quantities of legal and historical pamphlets and Runeberg's poetry were distributed. After the first parliamentary elections, it was felt that the intellectual grounds for this activity had ceased to exist, though there was no change in Russian policy. Only after the Civil War of 1918 and after the rural leaders assumed public prominence was it possible cautiously to recommend the revival of the Runebergian picture of the people, put aside in 1905. But there emerged at the same time other proposals for the groundwork of a national culture.

National culture is, of course, a concept that is under constant revision. But it does include the information and traditions commonly essential to the people or a great part of the people, common explanations of the national character, landscape and history, unanimity on certain values.

For Finland, the creation of these common values and traditions really began after 1809. The primary connecting link between citizens both in Finland and elsewhere was for long the suzerainty of the same ruler, the same semi-religious respect for the monarchy which was the cement that held the people together regardless of language, tribe, religion and even social class. On this foundation arose new structures of common identification which were then consolidated by the school system into a code of fundamental national knowledge. To a Finland without history came first the *Kalevala* and the peasant idyll, then Runeberg's lyrics of the folk and the land, and gradually other literature of its own. Then came a national anthem, Finland's monuments to Porthan, Runeberg and Alexander II, and the press and the railway system. Finland got her own capital and own administrative agencies, then her own monetary unit, parliament and, finally, universal suffrage. Her own great triad, Runeberg-Snellman-Lönnrot, was canonised. A history was written which linked that people which had been contained within a given regional frame since 1809 with the twilight of antiquity. Finland learned the lesson contained in the policy of Alexander I when he said in 1809 that she had been raised to the rank of a nation. Hence the demand for a national consciousness: 'Swedes we are no longer, Russian we cannot become; let us be Finns'. It is a theme that has been expressed with many variations, first in the letters and exhortations of the aristocracy, then in the writings of the intelligentsia. It was voiced by swelling numbers of Fennomans and liberals. Finally, it was uttered from the lips of thousands of elementary school children, heard in the patriotic songs of countless choirs and in many other connections, with different nuances and in different forms.

Icelandic Nationalism and the Inspiration of History

Gunnar Karlsson

A TINY nation in a rich and easily accessible locale would probably not be able to tell a story of a long national struggle. She would have been absorbed or extinguished by her neighbours early in history. An equally small nation in a very remote and unattractive area might have been able to survive through history without having to struggle against other peoples, and without any special need for national sentiments. But where the territory of a small nation is bleak and difficult of access, but has, nonetheless, something valuable to offer, recurrent national struggle is bound to characterise her history. Such is the situation of Iceland.

We can discern at least three periods in Icelandic history when questions of national rights, national freedom or national survival have been great, even dominant, political issues. The first period spans the late thirteenth and early fourteenth centuries, when the union with Norway was coming into existence and taking its form. The second lasted from the 1830s until 1918, when Iceland became a separate state in a Union with Denmark. The third period started at the end of World War II, when the Americans proved unwilling to withdraw their wartime base from the country. The struggle over the American base and American influence in Iceland is still going on, and in latter years has become intertwined with other difficult matters: attitudes towards the economic unions of Europe, the EFTA and the EEC; the protection of the fishing grounds; and the question of foreign investment in heavy industry.

In this paper I shall confine myself to the second of the three periods: the period of struggle for independence from Denmark in the nineteenth and early twentieth centuries. But before I turn to my main subject I must give a very brief political history of Iceland, and recount the main steps in her acquisition of political independence.[1]

I

Shortly after Iceland's settlement by Norsemen, in the early tenth century, a common code of oral law came into use in the country, and an assembly called *Althing* was founded in a place called *Thingvellir*. There was nothing novel in the establishment of institutions of this type; such was the general practice wherever Norsemen, and perhaps any Germanic people, settled. The unusual thing about the Icelandic community was that it lasted, independent of a king, for more than four centuries.

In the years 1262-64 the Norwegian King gained power over Iceland, and in the late fourteenth century union with Denmark was added to the pre-existing union with Norway. As time went on, Iceland's ties with Denmark grew stronger than her ties with Norway; *de facto* she became a Danish, not a Norwegian, dependency. When the Danish-Norwegian union was dissolved in 1814 and Sweden claimed Norway, the Swedish negotiators evidently overlooked Norway's rights to sovereignty over Iceland, the Faroes and Greenland, and dominion over these countries became, by default, the unilateral prerogative of the Danish throne.

From the beginning of her union with Norway, Iceland had kept her own code of laws. It is quite complicated, and not perfectly clear, how the legislative power was divided between the Icelandic Althing and the King prior to the mid-seventeenth century, but after the introduction of an absolute monarchy (in 1662 in Iceland) the King was unquestionably vested with all legislative power in his monarchy. The Althing continued to be convened annually in Thingvellir, but served almost exclusively as an appeals court. In 1800 it was finally abandoned and succeeded by a court in Reykjavík. Nevertheless, the general rule seems to have been that no law was valid in Iceland unless it had been promulgated there. Judges sometimes used Danish and Norwegian laws in the absence of appropriate Icelandic legislation, but, in the main, Iceland was a separate law-district. That was the most important indication of the special status of the country when the Icelanders began their struggle for independence.

That struggle followed almost inevitably from the liberal development in Denmark. In the 1830s the King decided to set up four elected consultative assemblies in his monarchy, one for Zealand and the other islands, one for Jutland, one for Schleswig and one for Holstein. Then the question was bound to arise: what should be done with Iceland? At first she got two representatives at the assembly of the Danish islands, but that solution was highly unsatisfactory to the group of Icelandic students and intellectuals in Copenhagen who wanted the Icelandic Althing re-established as a consultative assembly for the country. This idea soon gained support from many Icelandic officials; and when King Christian VIII came to the Danish throne in 1839, he decided to grant the Icelanders their wish. The new Althing was summoned for the first time in 1845, not in Thingvellir, as originally intended, but in Reykjavík. Iceland's next step towards independence followed from the revolutionary movement in Europe in 1848. In that year, the King of Denmark abandoned his absolute monarchy and promised to grant his subjects a constitution. Again the question of Iceland's status within the new order arose. No answer was found to that question until a quarter of a century later.

After a complicated process of claims and refusals, proposals and counter-proposals, the Danish authorities decided to cut the Gordian knot. In 1871 the King issued a law on the status of Iceland which the Danish parliament had passed. This law, the Status Law, defined Iceland as an inseparable part of the

Danish realm with special national rights. Certain affairs were designated as domestic Icelandic affairs, including civil law, court jurisdiction (excepting the Supreme Court of Denmark, to which Icelandic cases could be submitted), police, church, education, public finances and national properties.

What then remained was the enactment of a constitution for Iceland specifying how the King (Government) and the Althing should share the power over Iceland's domestic affairs. Once again negotiations became deadlocked; but in 1874, when the Icelanders celebrated the thousand-year anniversary of the settlement of their country, the King presented a constitution to the nation. The Althing was vested with legislative power in domestic affairs together with the King. A ministry for Iceland was established, but in fact the Danish Minister of Justice held the post as a sideline. The only evident increase in power brought to Iceland by the Constitution lay in the fact that the King and his Government could no longer enforce legislation in Iceland without the sanction of the Althing. Both Althing and King could initiate laws, and both could veto them.

This arrangement was never satisfactory to the Icelandic nationalists, and very soon a struggle began for revision of the Constitution. No agreement was, however, reached until government by parliamentary majority had been introduced in Denmark. The Liberal government that took power there in 1901 proved willing to yield to Iceland's demands, and in 1904 Home Rule was introduced. An Icelandic minister for domestic affairs, resident in Reykjavík, was appointed on the basis of the majority in the Althing.

The next round was fought over the replacement of the Status Law by a new Union Act. This time World War I paved the way for a very satisfactory settlement for Iceland. During the war Iceland had been largely cut off from Denmark because of the war at sea. Furthermore, after the defeat of Germany, the Danes made a claim for the return of the territory in Schleswig which was inhabited by Danish-speaking people, and therefore they could not very well refuse the nationalist arguments of Icelanders. So in 1918 a treaty was concluded by which Iceland became a separate state in a personal Union with Denmark. The treaty gave the citizens of each country equal rights, and the foreign affairs of both countries were to stay in the hands of the Danish authorities. After twenty-five years either country was entitled to terminate the treaty. This treaty of 1918 actually put an end to the struggle for independence in Iceland. No one was ever interested in amending the treaty, and people waited patiently for it to expire. Practically speaking, the Union was dissolved with Germany's occupation of Denmark in 1940, but Iceland waited until 1944 to dissolve it formally and to establish a republic.

Space does not allow me to go into the internal strife over nationalist issues. On the whole, however, it was the most radical demands which seem to have enjoyed the greatest support of the people at any time. I dare not say that a majority of the people supported the nationalist cause, because voting rights were severely restricted throughout the nineteenth century, and participation in general elections and other political activities was always limited. But those who showed any interest in politics were, most of them, usually on the side of the most radical nationalists. There was no political movement in the country except the liberal-nationalist movement, and it was due only to the intransigence of the Danes that the struggle for independence occupied nearly a century.

We have surveyed the political surface; now it is time to dig a bit deeper. Unlike the other contributors to this volume, it is my task to unearth both the economic and cultural roots of nationalism in my country. In a way this is fortunate, because in Iceland the two roots are very much intertwined. It is impracticable to treat the two aspects quite separately, but so far as possible I shall deal with the economic issues first.

II

The Icelanders were a poverty-ridden people in the first half of the nineteenth century. The population consisted almost entirely of poor farmers and rural labourers; around 90 per cent of the 50,000 people living in the country made their living from primitive animal husbandry and fishing. A primitive life is, of course, seen as a misfortune only if you know of something better. The Icelanders knew of two societies with which they would naturally compare their own. One was Denmark, the 'big brother' in the Union, evidently a much more highly developed society. The other was the Iceland of the past, known through the medieval texts preserved in Icelandic manuscripts.

The Icelandic medieval manuscripts include sagas, poetry, codes of law, translations of foreign literature and texts of various other kinds. To give some idea of their quantity, the preserved texts composed in Iceland in the twelfth, thirteenth and fourteenth centuries would fill perhaps 40-60 volumes of average size. The most remarkable of these texts, from our point of view, are the Icelandic sagas (or 'family sagas', as they are sometimes called in English), which tell stories of Icelandic farmers of the tenth and eleventh centuries. The sagas usually describe a prosperous life. Their heroes walk around in colourful clothes with good weapons, they hold sumptuous feasts, they sail to Norway in their own ships, stay with the King and receive presents from him. The veracity of this picture of the life of tenth and eleventh century farmers is strongly in doubt today. But in the nineteenth century people definitely believed in it, and it must have been a constant challenge to the humbly dressed Icelanders of that time.

Icelandic patriotism and glorification of the past antedate political nationalism. The eighteenth century Icelandic poet Eggert Ólafsson showed equal reverence for his King and his homeland. He seems to have been just as fond of the bureaucratic Danish monarchy as of old Icelandic wedding customs.[2] But by the eighteenth century the notion of Iceland's glorious past had already been introduced into economic discussions. At that time several attempts, mostly unsuccessful, were being made to improve the stagnant economy of Iceland, to introduce new industries, advanced technology, and so on. One of these undertakings, with which I happen to be especially well acquainted, was an attempt to grow grain in Iceland. Grain-growing had been abandoned in the late

Middle Ages; its eighteenth century advocates knew no better argument for its re-introduction than the evidence of the sagas that grain had been grown successfully in the country in earlier times.[3] In this way, the past could serve as a guide to new and better ways of living.

Icelandic students and intellectuals in Copenhagen in the first half of the nineteenth century were very familiar with such arguments from tradition. It must have been a revelation for them to become acquainted with a theory of nationalism which told them why life had been better in earlier times. This theory, whose main expositor was the German philosopher Johann Gottfried Herder, said, very simply, that every nation was endowed with its peculiar national soul or national spirit. Real progress, for any nation, was bound to be directed by the standards set by its national spirit. Accordingly, a nation which was free was likely to act in a natural way and make progress, while a nation under foreign rule, with foreign institutions pressed upon her, was bound to stagnate. Icelanders knew that their society had been prosperous in saga times, when it had been free. It was poor in their own time, when it was unfree. Obviously, then, the way to progress lay through national freedom. No wonder that one of the Icelandic intellectuals in Copenhagen in the 1830s, pastor Tómas Saemundsson, said that Herder's *Ideen zur Philosophie der Geschichte der Menschheit* was 'considered the most profound and sublime inquiry into World History which exists in German'.[4]

The influence of Herder's philosophy on nationalism in Iceland in these years is evident in the struggle which was fought over the location and organisation of the re-established Althing. Tómas Saemundsson and his co-editors of the nationalistic periodical *Fjölnir* insisted strongly that the Althing be convened in the old meeting-place Thingvellir and organised as far as possible in the same way as its medieval ancestor. They were opposed by the most influential leader of the liberal-nationalist movement, the philologist Jón Sigurdsson, who was more interested in developing a modern society in Iceland with a capital city as its centre. He joined forces with the more conservative top officials in Iceland to have the Althing summoned in Reykjavík.

It has been customary among Icelandic historians to sneer a little at the extreme nationalists who wanted to revive a medieval assembly in Thingvellir in the mid-nineteenth century.[5] It has been overlooked that from the point of view of nineteenth century nationalism, their wish was a perfectly sober one. There was every reason to believe that the old Althing had been organised in accordance with the Icelandic national spirit. An assembly in Reykjavik, on the other hand, would be nothing but an imitation of foreign parliaments, organised according to the rules of foreigners.

III

It was not enough, of course, to argue that the backwardness of Iceland was due to oppression of the national spirit. The nationalists also looked for concrete manifestations of oppression and exploitation which had resulted from the Union.

The most obvious — and perhaps the only obvious — thing appeared to be foreign trade. Since 1602 the Danish state had monopolised all foreign trade in Iceland (which, because of the uniformity of domestic industries, was virtually the only trade worthy of the name that was conducted in the country). Trading licences had usually been sold to Danish merchants or concerns, although occasionally, for short periods, trade had been run by the state itself. In 1787 the monopoly was lifted and trade was opened to all Danish citizens, including Icelanders. But only a few Icelandic merchants managed to compete with their Danish colleagues. When complete freedom of trade was introduced in 1854, things did not alter much in this respect, and until the last quarter of the century Danish merchants completely dominated the trade of Iceland.

Naturally, the Icelanders were continually dissatisfied with their merchants. Icelandic farmers had the usual desire to receive more than they were receiving for their products, and the disparity of nationalities magnified their feelings of discontent. The early advocates of nationalism made good use of this. For instance, both of the already mentioned pioneers of the movement, Tómas Saemundsson and Jón Sigurdsson, wrote about trade and considered how it could be improved and brought into the hands of the Icelanders themselves.[6] They maintained that trade would be more favourable for Icelandic farmers if run by their fellow countrymen, and pointed out that the foreign merchants had removed the profits of the trade from the country. It was for this reason, they said, that capital had not accumulated in Iceland, no bourgeois industries had originated, and no towns had been formed. There is little doubt that Jón Sigurdsson owed much of his sudden popularity among the people to the fact that he touched on the problems of trade, which were familiar to everyone.

Another sort of discrimination, not serious for the general public, but quite important to the smaller group of Icelandic officials, was the granting of public positions in Iceland to foreigners. Throughout the period of foreign rule in Iceland the bulk of the officials were of Icelandic nationality. The clergy were almost exclusively Icelandic, a majority of the district magistrates (*sýslumenn*) were Icelanders, and occasionally, after the mid-eighteenth century, Icelanders rose to the highest posts of governors (*amtmenn, stiftamtmenn*) and national treasurers (*landfógetar*). However, every now and then a good post went to a Dane or a Norwegian, and this was viewed with jealousy by the Icelandic officials. An elderly Icelandic clergyman wrote in a letter in 1837:[7] 'Improper it seems to me and hardly beneficial that foreign or Danish men get the district magistracies, one after the other, but natives run around like lambs in a fold and have nowhere to stay; perhaps Danish clergymen will follow.' This remark is probably not symptomatic of nationalism, but rather of a narrow-mindedness on the part of those Icelandic officials who feared that Danish people would steal the few official positions in Iceland from their sons. Although not nationalist in itself, this fear must have made the Icelandic officials more open to nationalist ideas than they would otherwise have been.

Public finance was another issue raised by Icelandic nationalists. The Icelanders paid taxes to the King's revenue, and a part of the fines and compensations for major offences also went there. Iceland had her own system of taxes, quite different from the Danish system. It is therefore impossible to say whether the Icelanders were taxed more heavily than other subjects of the King, but nothing indicates that they were. And in the first half of the nineteenth century the income which the Danish state collected from Iceland did not come close to paying what it expended on the country. Iceland constantly accepted financial support, and, with time, that support slowly increased, for various reasons. Therefore, when the Icelandic nationalists raised the demand for separate finances, they faced an awkward dilemma. How could Iceland at the same time ask for financial independence and financial support from Denmark? Jón Sigurdsson turned to history for a solution to this dilemma and calculated how much money had passed from Iceland to Denmark during the entire period of Union. He considered not only taxes and fines but also income from the trade monopoly, the property (mostly landed property) of the Church which the King had expropriated after the Reformation, and diverse other things. From the sum of these he subtracted the expenses paid by the King's revenue to Iceland, and came to the conclusion that Denmark owed Iceland a huge sum of money. He did not want this sum repaid, but he argued that Denmark should pay interest on it, an interest which would have more than covered the deficit of Iceland as it was at that time.

As was to be expected, Jón Sigurdsson's arguments were not accepted in Denmark. It was pointed out that the sources he used did not allow him to make very exact calculations of money transfers centuries earlier. And even had they done so, no part of the state was entitled to make such claims on the other parts. Nevertheless, these arguments had great effect. In Denmark those politicians who wanted to do well by Iceland used the exploitation of the country in earlier times as an argument for financial support, even though they did not agree with Jón Sigurdsson's calculations. And what was more important, these arguments allowed Iceland to receive Danish support without embarrassment, and to argue freely about the amount.

The financial dispute was settled unilaterally by the Danish authorities with the Status Law of 1871. At the same time that the Danish parliament renounced all interference with Iceland's finances, it promised an annual contribution from the Treasury. The amount was considerably lower than the interest suggested by Jón Sigurdsson, but it was sufficient for Iceland to start running her own affairs without having to increase taxation or cut public enterprises. The contribution was paid annually until 1918, when Iceland became a separate state.

In my discussion of the economic aspects of nationalism, I have thus far dwelt mainly upon the early stages of the struggle for independence. As time went on, self-rule seems to have become more and more an end in itself; and it probably came to be taken for granted that Iceland would do better economically if she were allowed to act freely. Only one really important new issue cropped up. Toward the end of the nineteenth century, foreign (mostly British) trawlers began to harry the fishing grounds around Iceland; and here the Danes failed seriously in their duty to guard the interests of their dependency.[8]

Foreigners had been fishing off the coast of Iceland for centuries, usually without causing serious trouble. In earlier times, there was no generally accepted international rule about fishing limits; but the concept of such limits was well-known. At the beginning of the nineteenth century, Iceland was supposed to have a fishing limit of sixteen nautical miles, but the Danish government did not make any serious effort to protect it. During the latter half of the century the limit was reduced to four, and later to three, nautical miles. This was done in accordance with rules which seem to have originated mainly in the British government. The Danish authorities, however, represented them to the Icelanders as international laws, and so people were, of course, reluctant to venture any opposition to them.

Then, in the 1890s, British trawler fishing set in, and soon became a serious threat to the livelihood of Icelandic fishermen in certain parts of the country. The problem was not so much the fish the trawlers caught as the damage they did to the fishing gear of the small Icelandic boats. A storm of protest and complaint arose, but nothing could be done. Fishing rights and the protection of the fishing limit were common Danish-Icelandic affairs, according to the Statٴ٭ Law, and thus entirely in the hands of Danish authorities, who were heavily pressed by the British. Repeated attempts to get the most important area outside the three-mile limit (an area which lay off the south-west coast) protected from the trawlers proved fruitless. Even the protection of the three-mile limit was lax, and several facts support the conjecture that British threats kept the Danes from protecting the limit as efficiently as they could have done. Finally, in 1901, the Danish government gave up all attempts to solve the problem and concluded a treaty with Britain whereby the three-mile limit was fixed for fifty years. Despite some discontent in the affected fishing districts, this treaty did not attract much attention in Iceland. Fishing rights never became a national cause like the struggle for political freedom. It is surprising to see how at the same time that the Icelanders were claiming the right to rule over their land, they calmly watched the Danes give away their fishing grounds. It became the task of the third period of Icelandic nationalism to reclaim them.

IV

It is difficult to say whether Iceland had genuine economic grievances during her Union with Denmark; indeed, the matter may be regarded in at least two different ways. On the one hand it can be pointed out that Iceland was comparatively poorer than Denmark in the early nineteenth century. She lagged behind in economic development; and no part of the Icelandic population enjoyed luxury like that of the wealthiest part of the Danish upper classes. There were no proper manufactures in Iceland; and no building in the country could compare with a reasonably stately manor house in Denmark. But two things must be observed. Firstly, these nineteenth century differences may be largely attributed to different developments in the two countries during the second half of the eighteenth century. While that had been a relatively prosperous time in Denmark,

Iceland had been troubled with a number of bad years and a volcanic eruption which had had serious effects all over the country. Secondly, the differences under discussion probably affected only a fraction of the population of each nation. If we compare the overall status of the two nations throughout the Union period, it is doubtful whether the Icelanders had much reason to envy the Danes. Each nation had had her ups and downs, and while Iceland had suffered from natural disasters, Denmark had suffered from foreign wars. It is noteworthy that both nations may have attained populations in the High Middle Ages that were not surpassed until the nineteenth century. The inhabitants of Denmark are estimated at about a million in the thirteenth century, a number that was not reached again until shortly after 1800. Although we do not have exact figures from the Middle Ages, we can say with relative certainty that there were, in Iceland, around the year 1100, about 4500 self-supporting farmers, which indicates that the population was not less than 40,000: many scholars set it as high as 70,000. By comparison, the number in 1800 only was 47,000, and only in the 1870s did the population pass the 70,000 mark. The only thing for which the Danish state might clearly be blamed is the failure to distribute its eighteenth century wealth equally between Denmark and Iceland; and while that is something we may demand of a modern welfare state, it would be unreasonable to expect it from an eighteenth century monarchy.

On the other hand, we can ask the question whether Iceland would have done better without the Union. In other words: was the backwardness of the society due to foreign rule or was it due to inherently poor conditions in the country? Rejecting the nationalist theory that a free nation will always do better than an unfree one, my answer is that an independent Iceland would not have done better. Foreign trade was already in foreign hands before the introduction of the monopoly — even before the Union with Norway — and it is quite unlikely that the Icelanders would have managed to get control of it before they did, even had it not been monopolised. A convinced liberal might argue that free trade would have been better than monopoly, even though it was run by foreigners, but in my opinion this is doubtful, partly because the limited amount of trade in large parts of the country did not allow for any genuine competition. Again, foreign officials in Iceland were only a minor problem for a small domestic elite. Taxation would hardly have been substantially milder in an independent Icelandic society. Such a society would very likely have had to maintain an upper class in one form or another. The problem of the fishing grounds arose so late that we need not discuss it here; but in that case, too, Iceland would have been even more helpless on her own against the British than she was under Danish rule.

So it is very doubtful whether Iceland was exploited by Denmark. The idea of foreign exploitation was probably fancied, but, because it was backed by convincing arguments, it played an important part in the development of Icelandic nationalism. These arguments were, for the most part, taken from history: from the cultural heritage of the country.

V

Turning to the more purely cultural aspect, we must first observe that Iceland was in important respects a cultural entity of its own. The people spoke a language very unlike Danish. Icelandic and Danish are, to be sure, close relatives, but they have developed in very different ways. They are not nearly as similar as Danish and Swedish; their difference is more nearly that between Danish and English, each language being completely unintelligible to speakers of the other without special training.

Notably, Iceland had her own gymnasia, although for university education Icelanders had to go to Copenhagen. No primary school system existed in the country until after 1900, and, apart from a few schools run on a private or local basis, the education of children was left in the hands of their parents, under the supervision of parish ministers. The Icelandic protestant Church used the Icelandic language exclusively. A printing-office was run in the country from the sixteenth century onwards, where essential religious books, and also other books were published in Icelandic. While literature enjoyed no heyday during the period of Union, prior to the nineteenth century, epic poetry was continually being written — in Icelandic — and the sagas were copied again and again. No attempt was ever made to prohibit the use of Icelandic, or to introduce the general use of Danish.

Thus, native culture stood relatively strong in Iceland when the nationalist movement started. Nevertheless, it was thought to face two serious threats. One was the use of Danish, or a mixture of Danish and Icelandic, in the villages, where the influence of Danish merchants was greatest. In 1813-15 the Danish linguist Rasmus Christian Rask stayed in Iceland in order to gather first-hand knowledge of the language. He was very pessimistic about its future after his stay, and forecast that in a hundred years' time no one would speak Icelandic in Reykjavik, and that the language would become extinct within two hundred years.[9] Rask's first forecast has certainly not come true, whatever the outcome of his second may prove to be. Rask's mistake was due to his overestimation of the villages as a cultural force, as against the countryside. After all, only a small minority of the nation lived in the villages, and the rural population spoke a relatively pure language. It therefore proved an easy task for the nineteenth century nationalists to purge the most conspicuous Danish influences from the language. This was done through a propaganda campaign; and I can add that this campaign has persisted in Icelandic schools up to the present day. Schoolteachers are still hunting for words of Danish origin in the essays of their pupils.

The second supposed threat to Icelandic culture was the use of Danish in the administration. When the nationalist movement started, Icelandic laws were issued in Danish, and only an unauthorised translation was published in Icelandic. Danish was also widely used in official correspondence in Iceland. Almost from the moment of its re-establishment in 1845 the Althing pestered the Government with petitions to have these practices changed, and gradually the petitions had some effect. In 1859 the King decided to issue Icelandic laws in both Icelandic and

Danish, but it was not until 1891 that the King began to sign only the Icelandic text (which he, of course, did not understand).

On the other hand the Government was never persuaded to prescribe the use of Icelandic in official correspondence, though it was ready to make provisions to insure that officials in Iceland had some knowledge of Icelandic. After 1844, applicants for official positions in Iceland were required to present a certificate of their knowledge of Icelandic. In 1857 a new regulation was issued whereby all non-Icelandic applicants were required to pass an examination given by the professor of Old Norse in Copenhagen or the teacher of Icelandic at the Grammar School in Reykjavík. It was sometimes said that the demands made in these exams were not very high; in any case, the examinations soon lost their significance, because men of Icelandic nationality came to occupy most of the official posts in Iceland. Hilmar Finsen, who became Governor in 1865 and resigned in 1883, was the last high official of Danish birth in Iceland, and even he was of partly Icelandic extraction. As regards lower posts, they were only exceptionally given to Danes after the 1860s.

At the same time, members of the Icelandic official class became so imbued with nationalist views that they gradually abandoned the use of Danish among themselves. Danish came to be used only in correspondence with the Icelandic Department in Copenhagen, which was manned by at least as many Danes as Icelanders. In 1904 this Department was replaced by a Ministry in Reykjavík, which of course used Icelandic, except in correspondence with Danish authorities.

VI

We must conclude that there was not much substance to the cultural grievances discussed above. But I have still to discuss another aspect of the cultural basis of nationalism: the importance of Iceland's historical heritage in her struggle for independence.

It is noteworthy that, right up until 1918, Icelandic demands for independence were based on a juridical-historical theory developed by Jón Sigurdsson. He referred to the treaty, still preserved, made between the King of Norway and the Icelanders in 1262, when Iceland first entered into Union. That treaty seemed to prove that Iceland was subject to the rule of the Norwegian King, not of the Norwegian people. Later the King's mandate was transferred to the Danish King, whom the Icelanders accepted, still later (in 1662) as their absolute ruler.

When the King, in 1848, returned his absolute power, he could only return it to the Icelandic nation, not to the Danish nation or to her representatives. This meant in fact that Iceland was a separate state in a personal union with Denmark. Of course, Jón Sigurdsson's theory had certain weaknesses that were soon pointed out by the Danes. It is doubtful whether a theory of this kind can correctly draw upon the authority of medieval arrangements, when subsequent constitutional ideas are so entirely different. Nevertheless, Jón Sigurdsson's theory served well the purpose for which it was mainly intended, namely that of convincing his fellow

G

countrymen that they had the right to demand self-government, and providing them with arguments in support of their demands.

For arguments were the only weapons of the Icelandic nationalists; they were completely unable, and unwilling, to resort to force of any kind. Iceland's battle for independence was fought with extraordinary peacefulness: no shot was fired, nobody was arrested or kept in prison. Why, then, did the Danish government make efforts to come to an agreement with the Icelandic nationalists, deprived, as they were, of ultimate political power? Here, I think, the cultural heritage comes in again. Danish politics were, during much of the nineteenth century, dominated by the National-Liberal party who had a predominantly friendly attitude towards Iceland. Iceland was the country where the language of ancient Scandinavia was considered to have been preserved — much more perfectly, indeed, than any linguist now believes it was. Stories of medieval Danish kings were to be found in Icelandic manuscripts, which were at that time more highly esteemed as historical sources then than they are nowadays.

These things were enough to make Danish nationalists fond of Iceland and anxious to be on friendly terms with her people. For the very same reason, of course, they were determined to keep Iceland within the Danish state. Because they were proud of Iceland they did not want to lose her. But it was impossible for them to close their ears to the dissatisfaction in Iceland, and so they were tempted to give in, step by step, and even to agree to financial support for the half-free Icelandic society.

VII

It is my main conclusion that the nationalist movement in Iceland in the nineteenth century was not grounded in genuine grievances against Denmark, either economic or cultural. Icelandic nationalism was, above all, inspired by history. Their historical heritage gave the Icelanders the idea that they had been discriminated against in the Union. It made them extremely sensitive to threats to their national culture. It gave them the necessary self-reliance to demand independence, and supplied them with arguments with which to fight. Finally, it made the Danes relatively receptive to their demands. Thus, the nationalist movement in Iceland owes both its origin and its success to the cultural heritage of the nation.

NOTES

1. The main works about Iceland's political status and her struggle for independence are the following: Einar Arnórsson, *Réttarsaga Albingis* (Reykjavík, 1945). — Einar Arnórsson, *Althingi og frelsisbaráttan 1845-1874* (Reykjavík, 1949). — Björn Thórdarson, *Althingi og frelsisbaráttan 1874-1944* (Reykjavík, 1951). — Páll E. Ólason, *Jón Sigurdsson* I-V (Reykjavík, 1929-33). — Short surveys in English are to be found in Gylfi Th. Gíslason,

The Problem of Being an Icelander. Past, Present and Future (Reykjavík, 1973), 9-40; and *Iceland 874-1974*. Handbook published by the Central Bank of Iceland (Reykjavík, 1975), 33-57.

2. Vilhjálmur T. Gíslason, *Eggert Ólafsson* (Reykjavík, 1926).

3. Gunnar Karlsson, Um kornyrkjutilraunir á Íslandi á 17. og 18, öld (Unpublished thesis at the University of Iceland 1964), 6-8, 32.

4. Tómas Saemundsson, *Ferdabók* (Reykjavík, 1947), 112: ... eru álitnar fyrir djúpsaerustu og haestu athugasemdir yfir veraldarsöguna sem til eru á thýzku.

5. See e.g. Sverrir Kristjánsson, Endurreisn althingis, *Saga* IX (1971), 117. — Bergsteinn Jónsson, Fjölnismenn og thjódarsagan. Andmaelaraeda vid doktorsyörn Adalgeirs Kristjánssonar 7. september 1974, *Skírnir* CIL (1975), 196.

6. Tómas Saemundsson, *Thrjár ritgjördir: 1. Um hina íslendsku kaupverslun* ... (Kaupmannahöfn 1841), 1-72. — Jón Sigurdsson, 'Um verzlun á Islandi', *Ný félagsrit* III (1843), 1-127.

7. Quoted in Gunnar Karlsson, *Frelsisbarátta sudur-thingeyinga og Jón á Gautlöndum* (Reykjavík 1977), 24: 'Otilhlýdilegt sýnist mér thad og mun varla verda affaragott ad útlendir eda danskir fá hér sýslum(anns)embaetti einn eftir annan en innlendir hlaupa um stekk og fá hvörgi ad drepa sér nidur; kannski danskir prestar fari líka ad koma hér á eftir.'

8. Björn Thorsteinsson, *Tíu thorskastríd 1415-1976* (Reykjavík, 1976), 155-202.

9. *Saga Íslendinga* VII. Timabilid 1770-1830. Upplýsingaröld. Samid hefir Thorkell Jóhannesson (Reykjavík, 1950), 430-31.

The Cultural Basis of Modern Irish Nationalism

L. M. Cullen

THE wellsprings of Irish nationalism, no less than of any other phenomenon, are complex. From the 1880s the tendency to find deep-rooted economic factors for Irish discontent was marked, and the economic factors stressed at that stage — a grossly defective land system and, over the centuries, a hostile English legislative policy — have been drawn in the twentieth century into more sophisticated, and sometimes Marxist, models. Ultimately, of course, nationalism has fed on both economic and non-economic sources for its survival and development. The problem is not one of identifying these sources, but of determining their relative weight. Essentially, the economic explanations imply a class causation which need not necessarily involve either Marxist models or phraseology: the relationship between oppressed and oppressor, sometimes set in an agrarian context on its own, sometimes in a wider colonial context. Even something as complex and bewildering as the 1798 rebellion in Leinster, with its ferocity, has to be accounted for in these approaches on a largely economic basis of rural oppression: essentially resentment of the burthen of rent and tithes.[1] Its markedly sectarian character is explained by the impact on Catholic public opinion of pogroms in the north by Orangemen, and by a rural fear of Orangemen spreading far afield in the intangible and mysterious fashion of the *grande peur* in rural France in 1789. Ironically, because of its assumed class origins something as potent and cataclysmic as the rebellion is ultimately under-estimated: its significant and powerful links with previous history or with later history have been scarcely examined even in summary fashion because its causes are assumed to have been similar to those held to have operated generally throughout modern Irish history. The difficulties the traditional explanation poses in economic — and class — terms are of course enormous, and may be looked at very briefly at this stage to illustrate the problems such general explanations raise. Why did County Kilkenny for instance remain quiet (or for that matter County Tipperary where military oppression before the rebellion was, as in Wexford, severe) whereas Wexford just across the waters of the Barrow burst into conflagration? The contrast is especially interesting because Kilkenny, and not Wexford, both before and after 1798, had been the centre of resistance to tithe payment. Moreover, class conflict in County Kilkenny had long been sharper, with a very marked conflict of interest between smallholder and large farmer and as in County Tipperary took place on Catholic estates as well as on others. Kilkenny, too, had long been the seat of violent rural disorders — abductions, arson, faction fights — so that it would have seemed the more likely region in which rural discontent, if its causes had been narrowly economic, should have assumed its most violent form.

It is difficult also to distinguish the continuing elements in Irish nationalism from those which operated over the preceding century, because Irish history as a detailed study dates only from the 1860s, and our understanding of its underlying forces is heavily influenced by the factors regarded at that stage as significant and which have assumed a disproportionate place in later history in accounting for all of Irish social development over the last three centuries. The picture of Irish discontent which came to be painted not simply in current terms but in what was claimed to be its historical background was also heavily influenced by the historicist approach both in England and Ireland in the 1860s to law, which encouraged the belief that Irish society had once been tribal with its land held communally and that Irish discontent was motivated by the urge to restore customary rights in land in place of English contractual practice.[2] Thus, in writings which were numerous in the 1870s, unrest relating to land no longer appeared simply as a current political and social problem but as one the roots of which lay deep in the past and which represented fundamental and long-standing aspirations motivated by a populist desire to restore the land to the people. Yet the formulation of this claim was quite recent. Fintan Lalor for instance in the 1840s had been prepared to allow a place to landlords in his new Ireland, provided they owned allegiance to the Irish nation,[3] and the Fenian leader Charles Kickham as late as the 1870s was prepared to accept landlords provided they met a rather general criterion of being decent and tolerant.[4] The overwhelming importance attached to landownership as the long-term factor which conditioned the very course of Irish history, as opposed to the simple but bitter fact of growing political embitteredness towards landlords which was beginning to challenge their right to a place in Ireland at all, first emerged in the writings of Isaac Butt in the 1860s.[5] The transformation of growing political hostility to landlords into a belief that the undoing of the land system answered long-standing historical need was unintentionally promoted by Prendergast's *The Cromwellian settlement of Ireland*, scholarly in its approach, which appeared in 1865 when the Irish political climate was at a rancorous political and sectarian pitch. When Predergast wrote of the 'transplantation of a nation',[6] he was making an aristocratic equation between the landowners of the seventeenth century and the nation. Within less than two years the very general strictures of the type Lalor had made were transformed by Isaac Butt, himself a conservative with a small 'c' as well as a Protestant, into a sweeping assertion that Ireland's agrarian problems of the nineteenth century could be traced back to the Cromwellian plantation. The impact of the book combined with the growing general resentment of landlords, who were held responsible for clearances in the Famine years and for the large emigration of subsequent years, and with the growing sectarian bitterness to which the often foolhardy landlord support for non-denominational education against the wishes of Catholic tenantry and priests contributed, produced a powerful myth which gave a historical backing to the growing hostility to the landlords. It preceded the appearance of Froude's *The English in Ireland* in 1872-4 which from a unionist stance seemed to support the historical theme of an oppressive land system. The celebrated land-agent, Steuart Trench, a shrewd and sympathetic observer of the Irish scene, already saw the shape of things to come in 1868:

> Some look upon the wealthy Saxon and prosperous Protestant as an invader who, notwithstanding the prescription of three hundred years, ought now to be deprived of his possessions, and expelled from the soil of Ireland.[7]

It is not necessary before an audience of economic and social historians to observe that there are economic elements in history. But the view which sees them as fundamental factors in influencing the course of Irish history is very doubtful. Revisionist views have increasingly challenged the inaccuracies of the crude interpretation of Irish landed relationships. It has already been argued that English policy was less devastating than suggested in the writings, British and Irish, of the nineteenth century, and the smuggling trade, which loomed large in the accounts by Froude and Lecky of Irish conditions and which seemed to offer a convincing though incalculable measure of the response to repressive policies, is largely a figment of the historical imagination. In fact revisionist history, sweeping and convincing though it may be, has the result of rehabilitating the traditional factors in history, and indeed of strengthening them because the allegedly oppressive social and economic framework which has often been given as much prominence as, or more than, political and religious factors, seems more benign than once believed. If the land system and the economic behaviour of landlords as a class were not reprehensible, the importance of religious and cultural factors in their own right becomes more obvious, because there can be no doubt that Ireland was a country with an increasingly poisoned and intolerant climate. Moreover, while Ireland was of course more backward than England in the nineteenth century and opinion was increasingly aware of this, this condition preceded the industrial revolution and even the great measures in English policy that in the seventeenth century or later affected Ireland. If Irish incomes in 1911 were only 62 per cent of British, the proportion was in fact if anything higher than it had been in the seventeenth century. *Per capita* Irish income seems in fact to have oscillated in a range of 44 to 70 per cent of British income between the 1680s and the present day, with low points in the 1680s, 1840s and 1930s, and high points in the 1770s, 1900s and 1970s.[8] Indeed, if one wishes to become increasingly speculative, one can put the contrast even further back into history. The description by the French nobleman, Creton, of his arrival in Waterford with Richard II's expedition in 1399[9] suggests that to the experienced traveller living conditions seemed poor and the organisation of work primitive in what was at that date one of the two main centres of the Anglo-Norman colony in Ireland.

The increasingly tense political situation in Ireland seems therefore to rest on a non-economic base, and certainly the dramatic deterioration in Anglo-Irish relationships and in class relations in Ireland in the 1860s is scarcely explicable except in the context of a wide and interrelated group of factors. Of course to the extent that public opinion believed that Ireland had been grievously wronged materially, the belief could be a potent force in causing, or gaining support for, resentments based on economic considerations. The Famine and post-Famine emigration, both of which were unique in nineteenth century western Europe, were certainly a catalyst in the deterioration of Irish attitudes and seemed to direct people towards economic or agrarian causes. In addition, the belief that Ireland had been overtaxed was increasingly held in the second half of the century — it was the subject of an influential though inconclusive report by a Royal Commission in the 1890s — and overtaxation was one of the most ubiquitous assertions of Irish nationalists in the decade before 1914. An all-pervasive belief in material injury coloured Irish thinking, boosted in nationalist tracts by extensive quotations from the rolling periods of Froude's prose and more sparingly, because the wording was more cautious, from the more sober pen of Lecky. The belief gained further currency on two counts. First, the late nineteenth century was an increasingly materialist age, and expectations not only of holding onto gains but of improving on them were general. Second, as a result of emigration and of education, Irishmen had a heightened perception of the gap between Irish and foreign living standards. What had long been evident to serious writers, was now evident to every Irishman. The consequent sense of loss was heightenend by the naive and almost medieval belief of Irishmen (as of the inhabitants of remote regions in time or space everywhere) that their environment was naturally fertile. Eamon de Valera's wife — a schoolteacher — for instance told her children that 'she believed that Ireland is much more beautiful, and much more fertile, than any other country on the face of the earth'.[10]

Ultimately the forces which have made Irish nationalism the distinctive product that it is are more social and cultural, moulded in a long and complex history of Anglo-Irish contacts, than economic forces related to any well-defined course of economic events, even if in the more interdependent world, culturally and economically, of the industrial revolution, some of its symbols and stated beliefs have become economic in expression. The main spring of Irish nationalism, and its outstanding single characteristic, is the chameleon one of race. The resentment of outsiders, already evident in medieval Ireland and by no means peculiar to Ireland, was not only carried forward into the seventeenth and eighteenth centuries, but took on an exasperated form in that period. Norman and Irish had partly amalgamated, but given the heightened racial sense that several centuries of inconclusive struggle had produced, resentment of new intruders, culturally very advanced and lending themselves to absorption to a much more limited extent than their Norman predecessors, was bound to be expressed in a racial form. The emphasis on race, pedigree, antiquity, medieval in origin and character, is repeated throughout the seventeenth and eighteenth centuries. It offers a continuity with earlier views, but seems increasingly archaic by contrast with the outlook and modes of expression of peoples in the more advanced areas of Europe at the time. The process was helped of course by the fact that Irish culture was partly oral; hence its transmission controlled by an intensely conservative and limited group of literate professional individuals. What is interesting in the nationalist literature of the late nineteenth and early twentieth centuries is the emerging cult of using terms with marked racial connotations: Saxon, Gall, Sasanach, West Briton. Some of these terms were taken from seventeenth and eighteenth century literature in Irish. But their ready imitation in English and their frequent and often vituperative employment betray a profound and deep racial antipathy. The fact that Bulfin's book, which to modern tastes is not only aggressively anti-English in this sense but sometimes puerile in its attitudes,[11] was much admired at the time, indicates how general and unqualified acceptance of this outlook was. Englishmen or people of English origin were thus seen not as individuals who were good or bad for their own personal qualities, but first and foremost as being characterised by belonging to a resented race. This is a racialist outlook — significantly, Bulfin for instance, the author of *Rambles in Eirinn*, had an anti-Jewish streak. While the tone does of course relate to racialist attitudes which were emerging in Europe and in imperialist Britain — and there were distinctly racialist views in many British attitudes to the Irish — the Irish outlook was essentially a homespun, non-intellectual product.

Deep-rooted resentments meant that Irishmen in the nineteenth century had a very poor ability to absorb or even to tolerate difference. In fact, tolerance declined sharply in the nineteenth century. In the eighteenth century there were still many instances of close personal and social contacts which warrant caution in translating broad national attitudes into corresponding intolerance at the personal or local level. But political conditions decayed steadily throughout the nineteenth century, and the worsening national climate was accompanied by increasing remoteness between classes and religions at local level. In the 1860s Lecky's interest in Grattan, 'the hero of unsullied purity', can be explained in part by his looking towards a form of leadership which would cross the sectarian divide. In extenuation of Irish attitudes it has of course to be recognised that they were closely related to a sharp reversal of political stances: Protestants were becoming Unionist, whereas Catholics who had supported the Union were now becoming repealers. When the general meeting of the Royal Bank boiled over in 1890 at the failure of the Bank to employ even a single Catholic, the terms in which the Bank's sole Catholic director was castigated suggest that it was the Bank's political complexion as much as its recruitment policy which gave offence.

Some degree of comprehension was easier of course to attain, even if very imperfectly, in the paternalistic society of the seventeenth and eighteenth centuries than in the democratic society of the nineteenth century. Moreover it was at all times easier to accept landlords of foreign origin than tenants from outside. This illustrates the fundamental fallacy in looking at changes in landownership in themselves as being responsible for bad rural relations in Ireland. It was changes in tenants which more effectively menaced good relations. And while colonial tenant and native tenant sometimes lived peaceably side by side, a growing body of tenants of one religion with its implications for a shift in the sectarian balance of land occupancy in a parish could be explosive, especially in the more densely populated countryside of the eighteenth century or where it menaced the interests of the larger farmers or of an extended family group of landholders. In other words, tension was not caused automatically by the presence of outsiders but by the extent of the threat they posed to local interest groups. The spread of colonists beyond the original regions of British settlement in Ulster into other regions produced long-lasting tensions on a shifting frontier. Armagh was the greatest single cockpit of change. First settled by English, and bearing more than any other county in Ireland the imprint of seventeenth century English settlement, it later attracted Presbyterians in large numbers, and finally in the late eighteenth century the submerged Catholics within the county had begun to re-assert themselves. The consequence was that the Anglicans of the region, strongly emphasising loyalty to established authority, founded the Orange Order in 1795. In Armagh, in contrast to south Antrim where Presbyterians, radical in their political outlook, supported the United Irishmen, the Order was also supported by Presbyterian tenants, usually more substantial than the Anglican. This was because Anglican and Presbyterian alike in the same county were at increasing loggerheads with the indigenous inhabitants of mid-Armagh.

Apart from abortive attempts at English settlements in the seventeenth century, it was only under the celebrated Johnstown of the Fews, remembered in hostile Gaelic tradition more than in history, in the first quarter of the eighteenth century that English law and order had been effectively established in south Armagh and outside settlers brought in on a permanent basis. At the beginning of the century an unsuccessful attempt was made to establish a town at Johnstown Fews, and a castle was erected for the protection of the settlers. The subsequent erection of a military barracks completed the military pacification of the region. Under the long administration of the landlord-rector Hugh Hill from 1728 to 1773, change was pushed further in the huge parish of Creggan which embraced much of the barony of the Fews. One of the first charter schools in Ireland was set up in 1737, leases were set at advantageous terms to outsiders, the success of the policy being reflected retrospectively in 1831 in the presence of substantial communities of members of the Church of Ireland in the parishes of Creggan, Newtownhamilton and Forkhill. The continued colonisation of the region is illustrated graphically in many features in the eighteenth century; it is reflected also in the creation of the town of Newtownhamilton in 1770 and of the parish of the same name three years later. Landlord-sponsored immigration was compounded by spontaneous Presbyterian infiltration into the region. By contrast the Presbyterians were widely scattered across the farm land of Newtownhamilton and Creggan, and in the former parish they outnumbered Anglicans by three to one in 1831. It was in these two parishes together with Forkhill, centres of sustained and determined Protestant immigration, rather than in the small parish of Jonesborough with a negligible Protestant community, that the most acute racial tensions existed. By the late 1780s the most tense situation in colonisation seemed to centre on Forkhill, so far the parish least subject to sustained settlement from the outside among the three major parishes. Under the will of a local landowner, Jackson, who died in 1787, provision was made for a school and for the founding of a Protestant colony on wasteland on the Jackson estate. In January 1789 hay, corn and turf at the glebe of the parish of Forkhill, the property of Rev. Edward Hudson who administered Jackson's will, was burned, and in July an attempt was made on his life. In 1791

Barkely, the Protestant schoolmaster at Mullaghbawn near Forkhill, and his family were murdered. It is no accident that south Armagh today is the region where rural opposition to British rule runs deepest. Crossmaglen, on which this opposition centres, is an urban creation of the eighteenth century, dominated by a great rectangular landlord-created square. The unrest spilled across into Louth and Meath, its characteristics being northern and the direction of tension and organisation both being identifiably from the north in the 1780s and 1790s. The same can be said of the rest of the fringe between Ulster and the rest of the island. At the far end of this frontier similar tensions can be identified, more particularly in Sligo, but also in Mayo. In fact, the Sligo-Mayo region had remarkably close ties with Armagh which was the focal point of the emerging sectarian unrest of the 1780s. There had been a steady drift of Presbyterians into this region especially into east Sligo in the eighteenth century. But the movement was accentuated by the growth of the linen industry in Mayo in the 1780s which encouraged the settlement of Armagh weavers. In turn when several thousand Catholic families were driven out of south Ulster in the Orange pogroms of 1795, they migrated to Mayo with which Armagh's ties were already multiple, counting on support from Mayo landowners intent on promoting the linen industry. These tensions are by no means irrelevant in the pattern of responses in north Connaught in 1798. They were particularly evident in the more eastern parts. Even a century later the sectarian hue of Sligo life comes across as a living force in the histories of the region written by Canon O'Rorke.[12]

Elsewhere such tensions could exist as well. The Palatines of County Limerick are an instance: their intrusion was resented at the time. The Defender unrest in the 1780s involved frontal assault on Palatine villages. An attack on Limerick city was proposed by the Defenders — or agrarian rebels — in 1800, and as late as the 1820s several Church of Ireland places of worship were attacked, a very rare manifestation of unrest in the Irish countryside where they generally enjoyed immunity. Evident though they are, the anti-Palatine tensions were relatively muted. In fact, the Palatines, praised universally in the eighteenth century because their standard of hygiene was superior to that of the natives — and cleanliness was next to godliness in the Anglo-Irish upper-class scale of values were a distinctly undynamic group. Few emigrated, they intermarried and subdivided their farms, remaining tightly encircled within their own original settlements, and despite landlord support showed remarkably little ability to move out to take over farms elsewhere. The result was that by the 1820s the average size of Palatine farms was very small, and Palatines were rarely among the largest farmers in the parishes which had Palatine settlements. Such an undynamic group, whatever their initial advantages, could hardly warrant opposition or resentment as deep as that stirred up by more determined settlers whether Presbyterians along the Ulster frontier or Church of Ireland members in some southern locations. Of the latter locations, the most remarkable was north Wexford, Wicklow and north Carlow, which is of special interest because this was the region where rebellion, when it broke out in 1798, assumed the character of a civil war with systematic house burning by both sides and carnage on a terrifying scale. What made the tensions before 1798 particularly serious in Counties Wexford and Wicklow was that not only did the Protestant community represent a substantial proportion of the rural population but that the Protestants were comparatively well-off. Many of them were substantial tenant farmers, among whom farm size was maintained by the mobility of the children of farm marriages. Thus in contrast to the Palatines or to the other sponsored Protestant settlements in the south of Ireland, Protestant farmers were usually the largest individual farmers within parishes and Protestant families the dominant group among the middle-sized and large farmers.

This pattern made the Wexford/Wicklow community almost unique in the southern three provinces: elsewhere, where the proportion of Protestants was high, many of them were industrial workers, and Protestants did not enjoy a comparable dominance of farm land. Even the Wicklow flannel industry was in the hands of sturdy Protestant hill farmers who disposed of the cloth at the Rathdrum flannel fairs, not in the hands of an industrial proletariat in the countryside. Wicklow had the highest proportion of Protestants of any county outside Ulster, and Wexford's Protestant population was heavily concentrated in the northern areas of the county, especially in the region around Gorey. North of a line from Kilmuckridge through Enniscorthy to Killann, most individual parishes even a generation after the rebellion had upwards of 15 to 20 per cent of Protestants. This fact and its importance have generally been overlooked. Pakenham has commented on the absurdity of Catholic fears in a region where Catholics outnumbered Protestants by thirty to one.[13] But in fact the reality was quite different, and was not lost on contemporaries. Arthur Young was surprised in 1776 in Courtown near Gorey to find a large congregation at service on Sunday: 'this is not often the case in Ireland out of a mass-house'.[14] In fact the proportion of Protestants was even higher, if we confine ourselves to tenant farmers. In 1831 in the small parish of Ardamine, just south of Courtown, 21 of the 40 tenants of 20 acres and upwards had Protestant surnames including seven of the eight largest.[15] Beyond the borders in Wicklow the proportion of Protestants generally was as high or even higher, amounting to 33 and 40 per cent in the Fitzwilliam parish unions of Carnew and Rathdrum, 40 per cent in the Powerscourt and Delgany parish unions in the north of the county with almost equally dense settlement along the east of the county from Delgany to the Wexford border. In such communities sectarian tensions further afield could readily meet a response of fear and hatred. Carnew and the neighbouring village of Tinahely were centres of two of the three Orange Lodges set up in County Wicklow. In both areas the yeomen even at their institution were predominantly Protestant. Their officious activity in the course of 1797 set a pattern followed in North Wexford in early 1798. The massacre of prisoners by the yeomanry at Carnew on 25th May 1798 was the spark which set off the powder keg in the entire region.

The most serious focal point of unrest was, however, around Gorey itself. Here were four compact parishes each, in 1831, with not less than a 30 per cent Protestant population. In Liskinfere or Clough parish, the proportion was 45 per cent, in Kilmichaelogue 35 per cent, and in Kiltennell and Killnahue 30 per cent.

The central point of tension lay in the parish of Killnahue which consisted of two clear-cut sections, a northern one where Protestants were only 20 per cent of the population, and a southern one where they were 56 per cent. There was a clear physical contrast between the two sections, the southern section covered with small gentry seats and numerous orchards, the northern section relatively barren of such features. In the parish at large Protestant economic dominance was very evident: in 1825 196 Protestant landholders compared with 144 Catholic, a dominance still more marked in the case of farms of 50 Irish acres and upwards: 37 Protestant compared with 10 Catholic.[16] The twelve largest tenancies were all Protestant. The parish was all the more remarkable because along the frontier between north and south stood the residences of two of the protagonists whose activity had contributed to the sharply deteriorating climate before the rebellion broke out: Hunter Gowan of Mount Nebo, who became a yeoman captain and magistrate in 1798, the only Wexford or Wicklow grand master present at the first meeting of the National Grand Orange Lodge in Dublin on 9th April 1798; and two miles away at Monaseed Myles Byrne, one of the leaders of the United Irishmen, who had already been actively spreading fears of an Orange pogrom. Both were social rivals ahead of the rebellion.

It is significant that the rebellion began in Wexford and not in Wicklow where the Protestant dominance at large was much more marked than in Wexford and where the absence of a Catholic rural middle class is reflected in the remarkable paucity of Catholic conversions to the established church in the eighteenth century. Given the presence of a Catholic middle class in the countryside, there was a social competitiveness that could not exist in County Wicklow. The most prominent Protestant families in the parish of Killnahue had several members among the landholders, illustrating a strongly entrenched position. The Byrnes were the sole Catholic family with a well-established interest, holding land in the staunchly Protestant south of the parish as well as in the more barren north of the parish. Tension in the parish before 1798 was therefore between dominant Protestant families and a single Catholic family with extensive interests in the parish. It was this competitiveness which was reflected in the conflicting political loyalties which sharpened in 1797 and 1798. The social competitiveness among the rural middle class was sharpened by their increasingly precarious economic position. From Oulart to Gorey, i.e. the region where the rebellion broke out and from which much of its Catholic leadership came, the land at the outset of the nineteenth century was largely in the hands of middlemen,[17] which in Wexford parlance meant farmers of around 300 Irish acres, part worked directly, part sublet. This system was now beginning to break down: middlemen could hope to retain the land they had worked directly, but had difficulty, as leases fell in, in holding on to the land which they had sublet. The changing structure of the countryside is reflected in the contrasts between the ambitious style of the larger residences and the insufficiency of farm acres to maintain them. In the Ordnance Survey of 1840, there are eleven gentry-type residences in the single parish of Killnahue; even fifteen years earlier, however, a sole farmer had held 217 Irish acres in the parish, and only four in all held 130 acres and upwards. In other words, farm size had fallen below the level which would generate an income large enough to maintain a gentry-type style of life. Change could not have worked itself out to this degree inside a generation: if their incomes and social prestige were already under pressure in 1798, as seems certain, the aggressiveness of the large tenant farmers in north Wexford, expressed in intense rivalry, born of desperation, between Catholic and Protestant middleman farmers becomes more comprehensible, as does the undoubted fact that the rebellion in Wexford seems to have been brought on by rivalries within a rural upper class rather than by seething unrest among smallholders and labourers.

All this should make it clear that while there are economic causes for social tensions, they must be seen in a framework of well-defined cultural patterns of relationships between communities. Unlike Kilkenny, where there were few Protestants before 1641 and where the Protestant community never became dynamic even in subsequent generations, Wexford had been a centre of sustained Protestant immigration largely of enterprising rural groups. The 1641 rebellion in Wexford had already been a bitter affair. Moreover, pre-1641 Protestant settlement in Wexford, the destruction of property and life in the 1641 rebellion and subsequent successful Protestant recolonisation took place broadly within the same region. Bitter memories and religious tensions which occasionally surfaced in the eighteenth century were already there before difficult economic circumstances and the intolerable pressures created by political developments brought things to a head in the 1790s. Bad religious relations were always close to the surface in Ireland; they were less evident only where one side was clearly dominant either numerically or in dynamism. Neither Armagh nor north Wexford on the evidence seems to have been economically stable at the end of the century, the instability due not to economic weakness — they were both among the most prosperous counties in Ireland in the 1790s — but to the impact of economic change. In consequence both regions became the centres of appalling sectarian strife in the 1790s, its bitterness reflecting the delicate balance between the different interest groups within the counties. Harmony is attainable in Irish circumstances only when one side is dominant; if it has increased on balance it has done so to a large extent because outside the north, the Protestant community, even more mobile than the Catholic, has suffered even more from emigration. In the north, by contrast, a conspicuously immobile Catholic population, less mobile in part for cultural and economic reasons than its southern Protestant counterpart, has threatened the fragile inter-community balance. Other factors are of course also relevant in the contrasting evolution of tolerance between north and south, but it seems necessary not to divorce tensions from close historical parallels which seem to offer little ground for easy optimism.

The difficulty of communities in combining is reflected in the character of Irish cultural interests, which have been very narrow and do not offer a bridge to comprehension. In fact, culture has tended to be an exclusive badge even when it is stripped of direct religious significance. Conflicts are reflected in the divisive interest in history. Irish interest in history has always been heavily commemorative but what is interesting is how almost instinctively an emphasis is placed on those facets which are calculated to produce a reaction of non-acceptance from the other side. Protestant opinion always emphasised heavily the memory of the 1641 massacres, interest in which had a new lease of life in the sectarian 1860s. This emphasis at that time was by no means isolated from a contrary lesson drawn by Catholics from the same span of years: obsession with the brutalities of Cromwell and the loss of land, with a new and almost hallucinatory emphasis being given to Cromwellian terror and confiscation. The 1798 rebellion in Leinster was widely celebrated in 1898 and with extraordinary fervour. What was a sectarian civil war was represented as a struggle for liberty. The organising support for commemoration seems to have come from the same sources as were promoting the Gaelic League and other nationalist activities at that time. Yet the 1798 rebellion with its painful memories was hardly calculated to provide a general rallying point for the population at large. Support for the commemorative activities and the source from which it was drawn reminds us how quickly the Gaelic League which was idealistic and broad-based to start with had become politically exclusive. In fact in the divided atmosphere of the late nineteenth century cultural interests became increasingly exclusive. Yet at the outset of the 1870s, with the Church of Ireland already disestablished and tenants thoroughly alienated from their landlords, thoughtful Protestants, anxious to make the case for a Protestant stake in a predominantly Catholic island, facing a crisis of identity, met the challenge by an interest in Irish culture and literature. In contrast to the first modern interest in Irish in the 1830s which came from individuals of Irish or, like Barron, Norman descent much of the interest in the 1880s came from the Anglo-Irish, notably from Russell, Maxwell Close and Hyde. The flowering of the literary revival is an even more dramatic illustration of this interest, which essentially sprang from a deep crisis of identity. But while the literary revival maintained a precarious independence and even fell foul of some nationalists as in the celebrated *Playboy* row in the Abbey Theatre, the language revival was from an early stage taken over by vocal nationalists, who first made it exclusive, nationalist and intolerant, and, secondly, politicised the movement. In other words the language, interest in the revival of which was in part due to the crisis in identity among the Anglo-Irish, quickly became an exclusive emblem the force of which in a divided community was inevitably divisive rather than healing. Nationalists never in fact faced up to the divisive force of the language movement in the form it actually took. This is illustrated very strikingly in the case of de Valera himself, for whom an end to partition and the revival of the language were the twin aims of the new state. He assumed, as did other nationalists, that northern Protestants would come to accept the language.[18] An awareness that they might not, or that they might have a right to dissent from goals which were chosen for them by nationalists, is nowhere evident.

The precise character which Irish nationalist aspirations acquired is closely tied up with the impact of school teaching. Teachers were in fact of immense importance in the growth of nationalism, and while nationalism is too powerful an emotion to be attributable to teachers, they profoundly influenced its character. It was in fact in the transmission of nationalism through teachers that it acquired its twofold character: its archaic, backward dimension, and its more modern facet, democratic and radical and in tune with the spirit of the new world of the French Revolution. The first teachers depended on patronage: they were usually employed as tutors to the children of well-off families. They were almost invariably poets or transcribers of the manuscript literature in Irish, and their employment as tutors was a natural progression from the patronage first extended to them as poets or scholars. In fact, in the medieval world which was just drawing to a close in Ireland, specialisation had not yet divorced teaching from poetry and scholarship as it had done in western Europe. As Irish culture was largely oral and teachers few before the 1780s, the division was necessarily slow to emerge. However, as the eighteenth century progressed the prestige of written culture meant that patronage for the largely oral culture of Gaelic literature declined, and poets necessarily relied heavily on teaching to make a living. But the close links between teaching and scholarship remained very evident in the active transcribing of manuscripts by teachers well into the nineteenth century. In the teachers two traditions fused: the aristocratic landed resentment at the revolution in land ownership and the downfall of the political power of the old Gaelic landed class in the seventeenth century, and the attractions of the democratic and radical ideas of the late eighteenth century which were imbibed by townsmen, often Protestant, but also, because they were literate, by the teachers. *Cox's Magazine*, which was very influential in the first decade of the nineteenth century, and which in the countryside was read out to the illiterate at crossroads by the literate,[19] presumably in many instances by the teacher, is an arresting illustration of the combination of resentments harking back to the seventeenth century and of the most radical ideas of the day. Set in a new mould, the resentments which had once been aristocratic in nature, necessarily acquired a more democratic edge. If allowance is made for the vague millenarianism that has lurked below the surface in all western European societies, the belief that the soil of Ireland was owned by all Irishmen was but one step forward. The greatly increased hatred of landlords that followed the Famine and the Famine-related emigration inevitably helped to transform vague millenarianism into a harder feeling in favour of the expropriation of the existing landowners. The number of teachers grew dramatically between 1780 and 1820 simply because of a growth in popular demand for literacy and because of the attractions of teaching as a profession for young men who were literate but had no other resources. The reasons for the establishment of a system of national education in 1831 forty years ahead of the rest of the British Isles have often been debated. In fact the National Board reflected the urge of the state to ensure that popular education was deprived of its independent impetus and put firmly under state control, and this explains also the very close attention of the National Board to the content of education and to the publishing of school books, in which it took the lead in these islands. The spread of literacy owed little to established institutions: its growth prompted landlords, whose interest in education had not been distinguished, and who were now alive to its subversive implications, to take a greater interest in schools, and established bodies such as the Church of Ireland, the Catholic Church and the State to get involved in a competitive struggle for the control of a subversive force, the control of which was coveted once each of them realised its significance. Teachers were described as dissolute, drunken and immoral, and their learning was mocked at as the pedantry of the half-educated. It was not simply that political subversion was assumed to connote immorality, but that it had to be established that men who were suspected of subversion were morally degenerate in order to make the case in favour of control more appealing.

The fears of subversive attitudes were on the whole well-founded. Even under the national system, the teachers were strongly nationalist (though prohibited by the Board's regulations from formal participation in political activities) and transmitted to their pupils in each generation the complex political outlook that had been developed by the teachers of the 1790s whose role incidentally in 1798 was more significant than has been generally realised. Teachers even under the national system saw themselves as successors to predecessors who had made a mark in the same parishes. Fr. Maurice Browne's account which may be assumed to reflect the outlook in his family in relation to his father's role as a national teacher is a good illustration of the sense of teaching traditions.[20] Dan Breen's *My fight for Irish Freedom* illustrates the impact of the teacher in the first decade of this century at Donohill, Co. Tipperary:

> He did not confine his history lesson to the official textbook. He gave us the naked facts about the English conquest of Ireland, and the manner in which our country was held in bondage. We learned about the Penal Laws, the systematic ruining of Irish trade, the elimination of our native language. He told us also of the ruthless manner in which Irish rebellions had been crushed. By the time that we had passed from his class, we were no longer content to grow up 'happy English children', as envisaged by the Board of Education. To the end of his days Charlie was in the habit of boasting of his rebel past-pupils.[21]

Teachers themselves of course imbibed the atmosphere of the times, so that they cannot be made independent factors in what was taking place. Charlie Walshe, Breen's teacher, had been engaged by the Gaelic League to teach Irish in the rural areas, so that in coming to national scholar teaching as a relief teacher, he represented these wider influences and not narrow professional ones. But national schoolteachers were, through their background, particularly open to these forces. Sinéad Flannagan, de Valera's future wife, was a primary schoolteacher, who 'for a number of years ... had devoted most of her spare time to studying and teaching Irish'.[22] Another teacher's approach, that of Daniel Corkery, has been immortalised not altogether flatteringly in the pages of one of his most famous pupils.[23] The crusading emphasis on the language, especially in the context of increasingly exclusive political views, was of course a novelty. There was a generation gap between the older teachers and the more subversive new ones, with their marked cultural and linguistic interests.[24] The generation gap was also clearly reflected in the Catholic clergy, the advanced nationalist and frequently linguistic views of many of the younger men contrasting with the more conservative views of older men. Rural priests like teachers were a potent force in the spread of the Gaelic League.

H

It must be said that the geographical distribution of support for nationalism is very complex. It does in fact seem to have some correlation with areas such as South Armagh, South Kilkenny, South Tipperary, West Cork and Kerry. It is worth noting that all these are areas where, at least in pockets, the sense of racial identity was strong, and where the old order and the language died late. A lingering support for modern republicanism is evident also in the region of the Slieve Bloom mountains, a refuge already for outlaws in the intense colonisation of the surrounding lowlands in the seventeenth century. It may thus be a product of a very strong sense of identity which survived in these areas, stronger than in neighbouring areas which were anglicised earlier and more completely. However, the more extreme republicans as opposed to nationalists have been usually individuals of modest social standing, and extreme views could reflect economic conditions and social stratification as much as or more than racial identity. The large number of recruits in the Munster counties in 1919 for the Irish republican army could be explained by the drying up of emigration during the war years in relatively stratified counties. Nationalism is thus something the strength of which is associated in a complex balance both with race and class. Religion was clearly a factor in 1798 although against a complex background. The long links embracing the 1641 rebellion, the 1798 outbreak and the 1898 commemoration may be reflected in the rapid rural spread of the Gaelic League in Co. Wexford. Wexford's nationalism seems thus at once strong in the sense of identification with the new Gaelic aspirations, and weak in the sense of still more militant activities. The 1798 rebellion, despite the prominence of a rural upper class in its causation, illustrates the importance of social divisions. It was uncommon in 1798 to find founding initiative for the Orange Order at the social level of Hunter Gowan; just as it was unusual for comfortable Catholic middlemen to risk their possessions by precipitating civil strife. The significance of social division emerges only when we realise that relations within this class were exacerbated by an economic rivalry which led them to believe that they had little to lose.[25] Militant republicanism in Wexford in the twentieth century had to be found a few steps down the social scale.

Irish nationalism is narrow and inward looking. It was thus extremely intolerant. It had difficulty in accommodating itself to other groups, and the unstable numerical relationship between religions was a prime factor in the Wexford rebellion. However, though the inability of mixed communities in Ireland to achieve a degree of comprehension is painfully evident, an unstable equilibrium is an exacerbating factor rather than a fundamental one. A sense of racial identity was pervasive, and it was only more evident where majority or minority was ill-defined because the tensions were more acute. Catholic views did not become more generous because of a more assured position. What was adduced as proof of tolerance was frequently superficial — the fact that any non-hostile contacts existed between groups at all. In the south of Ireland the Protestant population fell in the second half of the nineteenth century. Catholic dominance was not therefore at risk. Despite that, nationalism became more exclusive and intolerant.

The cultural renaissance was increasingly reduced to its linguistic content, and the wider cultural contacts imposed by Ireland's complex history were either denounced or ignored. There was a total and lasting lack of sympathy for the dimensions which could make Ireland's cultural appeal more general or comprehensive. In 1966 the fiftieth anniversary of the 1916 rebellion was commemorated in an orgy of celebrations; three years later the eight hundredth anniversary of the coming of the Normans passed in stony official silence. The Orangeman's long-standing addiction to the 12th of July is in no way out of character with this situation: it fits into it all too well. It need hardly be said that intolerance was not a monopoly of nationalists. Protestants, more generally in a minority, were frequently the more intolerant. The manifestations of exclusiveness and narrowness of view became more general all round. But it is necessary to single out the nationalist or majority view, if only because nationalists professed to lay claim to the whole island, and because instead of displaying the magnanimity and comprehension necessary to give effect to such views, nationalists became more assertive as the century wore on. The century seemed to end in a cacophony of assertiveness. Symbols and allegiances which had passed from the political to the cultural and linguistic were now being stressed on the nationalist side, and were increasingly foreign to unionists as growing cultural exclusiveness reduced the small band of Protestants who had toyed with linguistic and cultural nationalism, and on the unionist side the rights of a minority to secede was being formulated. Minorities are usually strident, as the northern unionists have certainly shown with a vengeance over the last century. But in one sense the nationalists were a minority as well. Till late in the century, nationalists and Catholics had the sense of being a minority in wealth or power. Hence their assertiveness was the strident one we associate with modern minorities. In this sense Irish nationalism was a product of colonialism: it did not predate it, but was in fact created by colonialism. Of the many contributions, cultural and material, of the British presence in Ireland, Irish nationalism, defined in terms of assertiveness springing from a sense of inferiority created by apparent impotence under the Union in the nineteenth century, is one. The more democratic political forms of the nineteenth century in fact exacerbated it, because they increased the sense of impotence by the contrast between the better-defined and rising demands of nationalism and the political immobilism imposed by the Union. Later still in the twentieth century, it is precisely the immobilism implied in partition that southern politicians have most resented. Only the intense sense of racial awareness in Irish nationalism seems to be of long standing, the thread linking the volatile moods of the nineteenth and twentieth centuries to the strong and somewhat exasperated sense of identity which runs through all of Irish history. This feeling predates colonialism, existing already in the ebb and flow of medieval conflict in which the Irish were the victors as often as they were the vanquished. It is the factor which holds together in a single panorama social groups as disparate as the chieftains, often mixed in race, of the march lands of the middle ages, the landowners who supported the Confederation in the 1640s and lost their lands, the large rural farmers of north Wexford risking all in 1798, the simple recruits in the countryside available for recruitment into the flying columns in 1919 only because emigration to the new world had dried up, and the inhabitants of Crossmaglen in the 1970s, not lovers of the IRA but not lovers of the British Army either.

NOTES

1.   T. Pakenham, *The year of liberty* (London, 1969), pp. 27, 35.

2.   C. Dewey, 'Celtic agrarian legislation and the Celtic revival: historicist implications of Gladstone's Irish and Scottish land acts', *Past and Present*, no. 64 (Aug. 1964), pp. 30-70.

3.   *Writings of James Fintan Lalor* (Dublin, 1895).

4.   Charles Kickham, *Knocknagow* (Dublin, 1879). See also B. O'Cathaoir, 'The Fenian best-seller', *Irish Times*, 13 Nov. 1973.

5.   Isaac Butt, *Land tenure in Ireland* (Dublin, 1866); *The Irish people and the Irish land* (Dublin, 1867).

6.   J. P. Prendergast, *The Cromwellian settlement of Ireland* (3rd. ed., Dublin, 1922), p. XXXV.

7.   W. Steuart Trench, *Realities of Irish life* (London, 1966 ed.), pp. 233-4.

8.   On some aspects of this question, see L. M. Cullen, 'Income, foreign trade and economic development: Ireland as a case study', unpublished paper read at New Orleans seminar on exports and economic growth, December 1975.

9.   Quoted in L. M. Cullen, *Life in Ireland* (London, 1968), p. 29.

10.   Recollections of one of her daughters, Máirín, quoted in Earl of Longford and T. P. O'Neill, *Eamon de Valera* (Dublin, 1970), p. 418.

11.   W. Bulfin, *Rambles in Eirinn* (Dublin, 1907).

12.   T. O'Rorke, *History of the parishes of Ballysodare and Kilvarnet* (Dublin, 1878); *History of Sligo: town and county* (Dublin, 1889).

13.   Pakenham, *op. cit.*, p. 143.

14.   A. Young, *Tour in Ireland* (1892 ed.), ii, 90.

15.   Public Record Office of Ireland, Dublin, TAB 31/30.

16.   Public Record Office of Ireland, Dublin, TAB 31/18.

17.   R. Fraser, *Statistical survey of the county of Wexford* (Dublin, 1807), p. 84.

18.   Pakenham and O'Neill, *op. cit.*, p. 460.

19.   W. Shaw Mason, *Parochial Survey of Ireland*, iii (Dublin, 1819), pp. 639-40.

20.   Joseph Brady, *The big sycamore* (Dublin, 1964), pp. 14, 27-8, 36-7, 368. Brady is a pseudonym for Fr. Maurice Browne.

21.   D. Breen, *My fight for Irish freedom* (Tralee, 1964), p. 13.

22.   Pakenham and O'Neill, *op. cit.*, p. 15.

23.   F. O'Connor, *An only Child* (London, 1970).

24.   E.g. see O'Connor, *op. cit.*, p. 114.

25.   This issue is to be discussed in a forthcoming book.

The Economic Background to the Historical Development of Welsh Nationalism

Colin Baber

AN admission I must make at the very start of this paper is that, try as I might, I have not succeeded in establishing an historical significance, in a direct, causal sense, of the economic foundations of a greater national consciousness, or of a formal political nationalist movement in Wales, and I therefore feel somewhat confused since my implicit economic determinism has largely deserted me in consideration of this topic. In many ways I feel that for Wales's experience a consideration of the economic, prior to the social and cultural bases of nationalism is in danger of seeing the cart before the horse, and to me at least, adds to the confusion. This might seem a negative and rather unconventional way of commencing an academic investigation, but as an economic historian, faced with exploring an area with such deep-rooted and emotive social and cultural ramifications, I have quickly been forced to discard the somewhat myopic form of analysis that economic historians are often charged with, and this in itself has profoundly affected my thinking in this connection. However it is certainly possible to perceive economic forces contributing to an environment which has eventually resulted, albeit spasmodically and often disappointingly for its proponents, in a positive and conscious nationalist movement in Wales. But as I hope to show, because much of this was done in retrospect, and was not really apparent to contemporary society as economic activity evolved, it is difficult to understand how economic influences entered into the real, causal matrix of Welsh national consciousness in a significant way. This does not, of course, intend to imply that in principle nationalism can only be a function of social, cultural or emotional forces, that economic causation is inevitably unimportant in the growth of national awareness, or in the sense of 'oneness' which emerges in a people which has long occupied a definite, geographical territory, with a consciousness of possessing a common history, whether it is preserved by oral tradition or by literature;[1] but that in Wales, economic forces have in historical terms served only as supportive or subordinate influences, rarely manifesting themselves in an overt manner as reasons for the growth of a Welsh national consciousness. In this vein, then, perhaps economic reasoning has occupied a more important role in underpinning the deliberate assertion of a Welsh national consciousness in modern times, which in itself 'is a very modern thing',[2] than it ever did in the past to contemporary Welsh society, though even then, the limited political achievements of Welsh national sentiment qualify its significance. In this way economic analysis is being put forward retrospectively, almost as a justification or rationalisation of the development, and also, more particularly, as a basis for the future growth of a greater national consciousness in political terms.

The assertion that 'economically speaking the history of Wales for nearly two centuries has been a history of exploitation'[3] fully explains this rationalisation. The theory of internal colonialism underpins this view of Welsh economic development, which Michael Hechter has explicitly asserted: 'Commerce and trade among members of the periphery tend to be monopolised by members of the core. Credit is similarly monopolised . . . The peripheral economy is forced into complementary development to the core, and thus becomes dependent on external markets . . . There is a relative lack of services, lower standard of living and higher level of frustration, measured by such indicators as alcoholism among members of the peripheral collectively. There is a national discrimination on the basis of language, religion or, in general, ethnicity. Thus the structural differences between groups are causally linked to cultural differences . . . That Wales as a region is disadvantaged in terms of income, employment, housing and education has decisive consequences for the individuals living there . . . the major financial institutions in the United Kingdom have always been English, and London has served as the primary repository of credit and investment capital. Thus when most individual investment decisions concerning the Celtic lands are made, they are largely decided in London by Englishmen who may be expected to have little knowledge, sympathy, or interest in these peripheral regions.'[4] This attitude then assumed that what was seen as being good for England was good for Wales. Wales as a separate entity seldom consciously entered into the making of economic decisions. Essentially the concept and idea of the 'British nation' was England writ large, and although this might have been more overtly apparent in social and cultural terms, it had significant economic undertones.

Perhaps the greatest difficulty faced in any attempt at an economic explanation of the growth of Welsh national consciousness, but something which needs clarification at the outset, is that Wales, far more than most other small countries, suffers from a geographical division which has distinct economic connotations. Although the comparative uniformity of the major part of the Principality, the upland interior, has emphasised its segregation and accentuated its peculiar culture, the polarisation of the two major economic regions, along the north-eastern and south coasts respectively, has given Wales anything but a concise economic background. The accentuation of this division, with the north-eastern coalfield aligning with the north-western region of England, and the South Wales coalfield also establishing strong commercial links in an easterly direction, quickly saw the two major Welsh industrial regions functioning completely independently of each other.[5] Thus the proximity and commercial significance of Bristol to South Wales, for example, saw a section of the city becoming known as the 'Welch Market' during the first half of the eighteenth century.[6]

Before the middle of the eighteenth century, apart from a few islands of small-scale commercial activity, Wales's economic progress was negligible and the country was dominated by subsistence agriculture. In particular there was little industrial tradition,[7] and so when the South Wales coalfield experienced its first real start in industrialisation during the second half of the eighteenth century it was as a result of an influx of English enterprise which brought with it capital, or the means and knowledge of attracting additional supplies, and in many cases the skilled labour, necessary to initiate production. Thus the four major iron works in South Wales which enabled the northern rim of the coalfield to become the foremost iron-producing region in Britain by 1820 all owed their existence and scale of activity to immigrant English entrepreneurs. The Guests at the Dowlais works and the Crawshays at Cyfartha achieved such an early dominance in the industrial life of the region largely because they were able to more fully exploit their English commercial links. From the very start, however, the nature of the industry which was fostered was not conducive to a broader and healthier spread of economic activity within South Wales itself. South Wales industrialised after the middle of the eighteenth century because ironstone and coal were found in juxtaposition along the northern rim of the coalfield, and it was also the convenient existence of mineral wealth that accounted for the accelerated furtherance of industrial activity with the growth of the sale-coal industry from the middle of the nineteenth century. This process of industrialisation did not foster diversification or the creation of an environment within which indigenous stimuli to further growth would be necessarily forthcoming. The finished products of Welsh industry were capital goods necessary for England's growing industrial power, or later for her hegemony in world trade. Thus by 1913, the South Wales coalfield attained an output of just over 56 million tons of coal, a third of which was exported, and much of the rest found its way to various English ports. In North Wales the picture was similar, if less extreme, with the coalfield of the north-east serving the industrial activities of Lancashire, Cheshire and Staffordshire and the slate-quarrying industry of the north-west depending significantly upon outside markets both in England and abroad. The failure of the substantial industrial activity at both ends of Wales to generate a greater diversification and a healthier economic environment created the arena for later charges of exploitation, and the fact that this occurred as a result of, and completely within the context of, the English economic machine further strengthened these views.

The nature and scale of the economic changes which had transformed Wales between 1750 and the end of the nineteenth century resulted in an environment which allowed few strongly held attitudes to prevail, other than those concerning the relationship between man, his employer and his place of work. The economic transformation of Wales was graphically reflected in immense demographic changes with a rapid growth in the size of the population, and its increasing concentration in the two coalfield areas, particularly in South Wales. Thus whereas in 1750, the population of Wales was less than half a million and fairly evenly dispersed, by 1911 there were 2,420,000 people living in Wales with over 65 per cent of them in the two coalfield counties of South Wales: Glamorgan and Monmouthshire. Apart from a high natural rate of growth, part of the general European demographic trend of the period, the massive growth of population in the southern coalmining districts owed much to the movement of people into the region for simple economic reasons. Before the 1870s the movement was predominantly from the surrounding Welsh counties, but as the period progressed, and communications improved, so the hinterland of the South Wales coalfield expanded geographically. This movement of people into the industrialising parts of South Wales from the rest of the country has been seen almost as the saviour of Welsh culture and national consciousness. In particular, it has been claimed that the Welsh language was saved by the redistribution of a growing population brought about by industrialisation.[8] Unlike some other countries — and the obvious example is Ireland — Wales's rural exodus did not lead to a massive out-migration of people taking with them their native tongue, culture and consciousness. But the fact that from the 1870s onwards the sources of immigrants to the South Wales coalfield extended, and particulary included the rural counties of southern and western England,[9] ensured that in the social melting pot of South Wales life at the end of the nineteenth century, although the language might very well have been strengthened by the concentration of people, there was little time, opportunity or desire for the flowering of a real sense of national consciousness.

The frantic industrialisation dominated socio-economic relationships in Wales and led not so much to greater national consciousness for the ordinary people, as to a variety of pressures and influences which touched them most often and immediately: there were manifested a growing concern for economic problems and the class conflict which became an indelible feature of life in the South Wales coalfield. The whole socio-economic system of Britain, of which Wales was a part, was conditioned to meet the needs of British capitalism. Until the last quarter of the nineteenth century, the controllers of the system, the British bourgeoisie, remained on the whole a progressive force in economic and political terms. They had secured for themselves, and for the community as a whole, almost a century of peace, bringing about a vast increase in the country's powers of economic production. These were fully exploited during the second half of the nineteenth century and the start of the present century by an almost blind adherence to the policy of free trade. Although there were serious social costs incurred, the level of real wages undoubtedly increased substantially over the whole period, and moderated considerably the social and economic grievances of the majority of the people. In addition, the political life of the country was democratised and the basis for universal literacy laid. These were historical achievements which along with other things had the effect of dampening down any real tendency towards nationalist sentiment.

But by the end of the nineteenth century the role of British industrial capitalism as a progressive force in economic and political affairs was well nigh spent. British energies became increasingly diverted from the constructive tasks of peace to the destructive and exhausting tasks of imperial warfare in all parts of the world, in part as a means of attempting to retain the economic status quo. After the first World War, chronic industrial unemployment and the persistent decline of agriculture became the dominant features of the economic life of the country, and universal literacy was turned into the social basis of a general culture dominated by the popular, and largely chauvinist, British press. These were disasters brought about by a ruling class which seemed to have outlived its social usefulness.

Wales experienced both the benefits and the costs brought about by this era of unbridled expansion of British capitalism. In economic terms the eighteenth and nineteenth centuries had brought Wales the benefits of modernisation, immense powers of production in iron, steel, coal and tinplate, greatly improved communications, bustling urban centres and a much increased population. But capitalism also brought with it more than its fair share of the costs universally associated with the system: the exploitation of working men; poor working and living conditions; straggling, unplanned towns and villages; cyclical variations in economic prosperity and unemployment. Undoubtedly the vicissitudes of the expansion of industrial capitalism were greatly aggravated in Wales by the fact that industry grew, not on a national and therefore more rational basis as in other countries, but to meet the requirements of British industrial and imperial supremacy, regardless of Wales as a national unit. Thus the main communications network was constructed to connect the Welsh industrial areas with neighbouring English regions, London or overseas ports, rather than with one another. While these logistic arrangements were entirely necessary, the result of the neglect of intra-regional communications was the creation of what could only be seen from a Welsh standpoint as an irrational economic structure consisting of separate industrial areas in North and South Wales, unconnected with each other, and poorly connected to their own surrounding rural areas. In addition, because the industrial development of Wales, especially in the south, was overwhelmingly based on the production of a limited number of capital goods, a situation which could be justified from the point of view of the system of British capitalism on the grounds of essential specialisation, it was from a specifically Welsh standpoint, of course, completely indefensible. The result was that whenever these industries underwent structural changes, as inevitably they did during the course of their development, there were no alternative viable economic activities within Wales itself to absorb the displaced labour, and to take the place of the older industries as generators of the principality's economic prosperity. In addition, not only did these developments symbolise the growing dependency which the Welsh economy was experiencing upon English capitalism, but they served as obstacles to the ability of Wales to practise effectively any real form of economic self-sufficiency.

The seeds of Anglophobia were also sown by the changing nature of agricultural productive relations. During the nineteenth century, as the coalfields of Wales were attracting intensive industrial activity, the pressure for agricultural production to become more efficient in response to an increase in the demand for food was, as in other parts of Britain, increased. Most of the landlords were thoroughly anglicised, both in language, sentiment and religion, while their tenants were Welsh and non-conformist. The gentry quickly lost touch with their tenantry, who were described even as late as 1796 as feudal[10] but who became increasingly democratic, a process which the industrialisation process ensured was maintained. The landowning class in Wales, like their English counterpart, recognised the economic gains to be made from more efficient agricultural production, and they sought expert assistance in fully exploiting their lands. There was thus a substantial and rapid increase in the number of estate agents or stewards in Wales, predominantly Englishmen, who often took a great delight in more effectively attuning an easy-going peasantry to the requirements of a commercial market. Such was the Welsh peasant's introduction to the Englishman at close quarters that the stewards as a class were despised and a widespread anti-English feeling in the rural areas arose.[11]

However, the manifestation of the various undercurrents of anglophobia during the period of the rapid economic transformation of Wales were few. Perhaps the most significant, certainly the most publicised, was the decision of Michael Jones, in order to save his compatriots from anglicisation, to establish in 1865 a Welsh settlement in Patagonia, a remote part of Argentina. He saw that Wales could not be freed in his own day because of English domination and Welsh servility, English landlordism in the rural areas, and English capitalism in the industrial parts.[12] But his work was a limited exception to the general experience, and under the influence of the tide of economic growth and industrial transformation the concerns of the vast majority of Welshmen during the eighteenth and nineteenth centuries did not extend very far beyond their own place of work and life. Although perhaps the *sais* steward, or coalowner, was despised, the translation of this into real, effective reaction and discontent was seen far more in the growth of a working class consciousness which attached a far greater significance to the adversary's economic and social standing than to his geographical and cultural origins. Generally up to the Great War, the British economic machine continued to function in a dominant manner, even though various weaknesses were increasingly experienced below the surface. Wales as a cog in it maintained its vital position.

During the 1920s and 1930s the Welsh economy was dominated by large-scale unemployment and this ensured that the basic sentiments and attitudes of the people which had been fashioned before 1914 were amplified. Any real semblance there had been of a national consciousness, illustrated most fully in the nationalism of the *Cymru Fydd* movement which lasted from 1886 to 1896, was quickly lost in the economically depressed years of the inter-war period, and served to corroborate the general lack of sympathy towards national consciousness as an economic end in itself. The level of unemployment in Wales was consistently and significantly higher than the British average, generally by as much as five times, though of course this varied both between different areas and over time. Thus whereas unemployment in Wales rarely fell below 20 per cent, the national figure for most of the inter-war years fluctuated around 6 per cent, while in 1934 the figure for Wales was 32.3 per cent and certain black spots such as Merthyr Tydfil — 61.9 per cent, Pontypridd — 53.2 per cent and Abertillery — 49.6 per cent made the figures for St. Albans — 3.9 per cent, Coventry — 5.1 per cent and Birmingham — 6.4 per cent look as if they referred to a different age and economic system. The causes of the collapse of the inter-war years were general, though technological change ensured that new industries cushioned its effects in some other economic regions of Britain, but they were intensified in Wales by the almost entire dependence of South Wales, where lived seventy per cent of the total Welsh population, on the basic industries of coal, steel, and tinplate. The moral and economic difficulties caused by the enforced idleness of large numbers of people for a prolonged period of time were intensely felt in Wales for most of the inter-war period. The most spectacular manifestation of this was the out-migration of people, largely to the Midland counties, the London area, and the south-east of England. Thus between 1921 and 1931 just over a quarter of a million people left Wales, the vast majority from the South Wales coalfield, and by the end of the 1930s the total outlfow was close to 430,000.

Within the depressed economic environment of the inter-war years, the development of a national consciousness in Wales was even more confused than it had been before 1914. The overwhelming effect of unemployment upon the political arena saw socialism rather than nationalism rapidly expand as the greatly hoped for saviour of the working man. However the period did see the formation, in 1925, of *Plaid Genedlaethol Cymru*[13] (the Welsh National Party) which quickly became the main political channel for national consciousness, but which had little real political effect before the coming of the Second World War. However, it was during this period that nationalist sentiments in Wales were strengthened by coherent economic thinking, and its historical development was, in a sense, retrospectively rationalised. This achievement owed its prominence largely to Dr. D.J. Davies, an economist, who had by 1939 effectively underpinned nationalist thinking with economic foundations.[14] Dr. Davies was profoundly influenced by the Danish experience which he saw as a perfect model on which Wales, also a small country, could develop economically along the lines advocated by Grundtvig, on the basis of agricultural and industrial cooperation.[15] He reacted against what he saw as the dominant way of perceiving the development of British civilisation, of which Wales was by now very much a part, as 'a materialist, universalist, internationalist analytic'[16] approach. He agreed that economic factors did play an important part in human history, but that they tend to control the progress and direction of man's achievement and evolution, rather than the reverse, and they had caused the spiritual decline of Welsh civilisation. He pointed to the Middle Ages when men were able to deliberately control economic life in the interest of what was conceived as spiritual ends (i.e. through guild regulations, the just price, etc.), asserting that 'men could do the same today if they were not hypnotised by materialism and the machine'.[17] He also championed the need for Wales to become economically self-sufficient, seeing the means by which England achieved her economic power during the nineteenth century as a strategic exploitation of other countries' resources, and that a 'Free Trade policy with its concentration on the export trade, leads to an utterly lop-sided and unhealthy development of the national life'.[18] This he saw as the primary reason for the uncontrolled industrialisation of South Wales and the neglect of Welsh agriculture, 'the destruction alike of natural beauty — a permanent thing of eternal value — and of the economic potentialities in the industrial areas'.[19] Essentially national consciousness was acquiring an economic foundation which could counter the abstract, analytic, objective approach which had dominated

British civilisation and expression. He and nationalist thinking generally recognised the organic nature of society, and saw that society could not be created, but that it is something to be discovered, that the society which then existed had been implanted in a Wales which had not been given the opportunity to develop the society which was latent in the nature and spirit of the historic Welsh people.

D.J. Davies was giving to Welsh national consciousness a form of retrospective economic rationalisation which was essentially founded on the idea of internal colonialism. The charge of exploitation, that the miracle of British industrial capitalism had been founded upon the economic development of Wales, which so skewed productive resources that Wales could not meet the needs of her own development, but which fully completed the wider needs of imperial Britain, was made explicitly, and has implicitly permeated nationalist thinking since. In the inter-war years, the manifestations of this economic rationalisation were increasingly made apparent. The contraction of the markets for coal, steel and tinplate dealt the economic buoyancy of South Wales a blow which still undermines the region's ability to share fully in Britain's economic progress, while the out-migration symbolised the malaise which was seen as the inevitable outcome of Britain's economic strategy over the preceding century or so. In looking at Wales's economic predicament, Dr. Davies then, and since then nationalist thinking, fashioned a model which is simplistically based upon the economic exploitation of Wales by England, the consequent creation of a narrow and badly balanced industrial structure, and the resultant economic and social decline of the country as the profitability of those forced industries eventually declined. This, it was seen, also wrought deep injury to Welsh culture, depriving Welshmen of a sense of their past and leaving them almost as barbarians with no history.

In one sense Davies was attempting to explain Wales's contemporary problems, and nationalist thinkers have continued up to the present in this philosophical vein to explain Wales's problems in terms of a basic historical approach which recognises that spiritual rather than material factors are of ultimate importance in the development of a true national consciousness. Thus it was seen as imperative that the traditions and cultural heritage of the Welsh people should be safeguarded to serve as a 'spiritual anchorage in facing the material problems'.[20] Certainly a causal interrelationship between the economic and the socio-cultural aspects of the fabric of Davies's analysis existed, with the result that the nationalist movement's view of things becomes somewhat blurred and confusing at times, but out of it there emerges a rationalisation of the economic bases of a national consciousness. The central point however is that these determinants of or justifications for a nationalist movement were not wholly apparent, and thus failed to function as real causal bases of the growth of Welsh national consciousness, at least before the Second World War. Thus, apart from the sporadic manifestations of nationalist expression seen in the Patagonia adventure, or the *Cymru Fydd* movement, it was not until the 1930s that nationalist sentiment, however strongly held it might have been, was articulated in economic terms. Generally the feelings of the ordinary people of Wales have been influenced far more by universal considerations of an economic nature than by the rights and wrongs of Wales's position within the British economic machine. The reactions have been not so much against imperial England, then, but against the iron master or coal owner, whether he came from Shropshire, Bristol, Falmouth, Llandinam, Cardiff or Timbuctoo.

However, the theme of economic exploitation by England as the basic cause of Wales's comparatively poor economic performance has been maintained both implicitly and explicitly as the primary basis for the Nationalist Party's progress in the period since the Second World War[21] and, since 1945, the nationalist movement in Wales has had greater, though still limited, political success. Certainly the democratisation of education has had a big part to play in this, but economic forces are still seen by the majority of the people in a British rather than in a Welsh light. Although the period has witnessed a move away from economic over-commitment in the production of a limited range of capital goods, the effects of an increasingly diversified economic structure have not been great. Indeed one should not exaggerate the changed nature of the Welsh economy. The memory of the difficulties encountered during the inter-war period still lives with a sizeable, though declining, proportion of the population. Although the demographic decline of the inter-war period has been stemmed, changes in the size, distribution and composition of the population have occurred which are still attributed to the exploitation thesis of internal colonialism. Now the majority of the Welsh people, some 80 per cent, live in what were the old counties of Glamorgan and Monmouthshire in the south, and Flint and Denbigh in the north.[22] The predominance of these counties over the more rural parts of Wales in demographic terms, while symbolising the dramatic effects that industrial development has had upon the character and distribution of population, is a constant reminder of the decline of the 'Welsh way of life' which has been the single most debilitating force in the comparatively limited growth of national consciousness in effective, political terms. Although one cannot but agree that Welsh society is far from being a special case in the wider British context,[23] the economic experiences of the past two hundred or so years have certainly not served to widen the gap between Welsh national consciousness, and the fact of belonging to bigger Britain.

The intermingling of Welsh with English has created a far more heterogeneous people in the most intensively populated districts which pays little regard to the nationalism of *Plaid Cymru*. In economic terms, the close interrelationship between activity in England and in Wales, the complementarity which has been strongly cemented between the two 'economies', and in particular the common experience which manual labour has experienced as part of the development of the British economic system, has forged a link which for many has proved far stronger than the theme of national consciousness and the cry of economic exploitation. The most vociferously patriotic Welshmen at Cardiff Arms Park, when Wales plays England in an international rugby union match, are at one and the same time the strongest supporters and advocates of the maintenance of the economic status quo. Generally speaking, then, it seems that although there might very well have been economic reasons why a greater national consciousness should have developed in Wales, these were recognised only in retrospect, largely by way of a rationalisation of what was being striven for politically. The whole era of British economic hegemony which had begun to experience difficulties in the early twentieth century resulted in a far greater demographic heterogeneity. This moved Wales further and further away from a social structure in any way conducive to the expression of national consciousness. Instead Wales and the rest of Britain's experiences ensured that when universal suffrage was achieved after 1886, it would be socialism rather than nationalism which dominated both formal political activities and the basic philosophy of the majority of Welshmen and women.

NOTES

1. J.F. Rees, *The Problem of Wales and other Essays*, (Cardiff, 1963) Chapter III, 'Of Welsh Nationality and Historians', pp. 27-8.
2. R.T. Jenkins, 'The Development of Nationalism in Wales', *Sociological Review*, XXVII 1935, p. 163.
3. Gwynfor Evans, *A National Future for Wales* (Swansea, 1975), p. 29.
4. Michael Hechter, *Internal Colonialism*, (London, 1975), pp. 108 and 109.
5. Emrys Jones, 'The Economic Division of Wales', in Davies Aberpennar, *A Collection of Writings in English* (Caernarvon, The Welsh Party, Swyddfa'r Blaid), p. 2.
6. A.H. John, *The Industrial Development of South Wales*, (Cardiff, 1950), p. 6.
7. Ibid., pp. 1-21.
8. Brinley Thomas (ed.), *The Welsh Economy: Studies in Expansion* (Cardiff, 1962) Chapter I, 'Wales and the Atlantic Economy', by Brinley Thomas, p. 26.
9. Brinley Thomas, 'The Migration of Labour into the Glamorganshire Coalfields 1861-1911', *Economica* 1930, pp. 294-6.
10. R.T. Jenkins, *loc.cit.*, p. 165.
11. *Ibid.*, p. 166.
12. D. Gwenallt Jones, 'National Movements in Wales in the Nineteenth Century', in *The Historical Basis of Welsh Nationalism: A Series of lectures*, (Cardiff, 1950), pp. 117-120.
13. This title was changed to *Plaid Cymru* (Welsh Party) in 1946.
14. I am greatly indebted to Dr. Ceinwen Thomas, Director of the Welsh Language Research Unit, at University College, Cardiff, for much of the information regarding the significance of Dr. Davies to the Welsh Nationalist movement.
15. Ceinwen Thomas (ed.), *Towards Welsh Freedom* (Cardiff, 1958). Dr. Thomas has in this volume brought together twenty-seven review articles which represent Dr. Davies's thinking on the subject of the economics of Welsh Nationalism, and in particular in her excellent introduction and biography of Dr. Davies, pp. 1-9, fully emphasises the formative influence which Denmark had upon his views.
16. *Ibid.*, p. 16.
17. *Ibid.*, p. 11.
18. *Ibid.*, p. 15.
19. *Idem.*
20. *Ibid.*, p. 16.
21. This has continued to be the predominant explanatory analysis, even though the

conclusions drawn from Professor Edward Nevin's work on the social accounts of Wales have tended to be the converse. See Edward Nevin, *The Social Accounts of the Welsh Economy 1948 to 1952* (Cardiff, 1956) and *The Social Accounts of the Welsh Economy 1948 to 1956* (Cardiff, 1957).

22.   As a result of the reorganisation of local government in 1974, the old county of Glamorgan was split into three new counties: West Glamorgan, Mid Glamorgan and South Glamorgan; the old county of Monmouthshire became Gwent, and Denbigh and Flint were combined into the new county of Clwyd.

23.   See A. Butt Phillip, *The Welsh Question: Nationalism in Welsh Politics 1945-1970* (Cardiff, 1975), Chapter 3 pp. 41-72.

Wales — the Cultural Bases of Nineteenth and Twentieth Century Nationalism

Glanmor Williams

AT the beginning of the nineteenth century the Welsh were one of the oldest nations in Europe in the sense that they had had for over a thousand years a strong awareness of their separate identity as a people.[1] The main ingredients of that consciousness had been a pride in their ethnic origins, their territory within its historic boundaries, their language and its literature, their religion, and that whole amalgam of shared experiences, vicissitudes and myths that made up their distinctive history. As far as their origins were concerned, although there was much confusion and uncertainty over details, on one cardinal point there was unity — the Welsh were descended from the oldest and most authentic inhabitants of the island of Britain. Their common territory was clearly defined, even if it had shrunk since the days when their earliest ancestors had ruled the whole island; at least the Welsh had for many centuries been in undisputed possession of the hills and valleys of Wales. Their language was unique to them within the British Isles and was unmistakably different from other languages spoken within those islands. Out of that language had emerged one of the oldest living literatures in Europe with an unbroken tradition stretching back over many centuries.[2] In religion they were almost without exception Protestants and, whether Anglican or Nonconformist by allegiance, the language of public worship for the great majority of them was Welsh. Unlike many of the smaller nations of Europe, the Welsh did not have to create for themselves *de novo* the cultural bases of nationalism.

This earlier consciousness of identity had come to its peak in the sixteenth and seventeenth centuries. Up until that time its chief protagonists had been the landowning gentry, the clergy, and the order of bards and littérateurs. However, for a period in the late seventeenth century and the eighteenth century it had seemed to be in grave danger. For a variety of reasons the landowners had become anglicised in speech and culture, and the poetic order, deprived of its customary patrons, had virtually disappeared. The seriousness of the threat had been offset — partially at least — by a remarkable renaissance of interest and enthusiasm which it provoked among men of middling status: clergymen especially, lawyers, professional men, and even craftsmen. Ideas associated with the Enlightenment and also with the rise of Romanticism penetrated into Wales and especially among patriotic Welsh exiles in London, who were among the most fervent advocates of them. Predictably, this led to a fresh emphasis on the history and antiquities of

J

Wales — real and mythical — for these men saw themselves as ardent descendants and upholders of their illustrious British forefathers. Alarmed by the neglect and decay of the literature, they set themselves 'the task of the cultivation of the British language' and a 'search into its antiquities'.[3] Many of their ideas concerning language, literature and history were dangerously uncritical, as indeed were those of romantics and patriots elsewhere in Europe. On the other hand, their beliefs in the supposed links between Welsh literature and the Druids, or between the Welsh language and that of God's chosen people, and the almost unbelievably ancient traditions associated with the Welsh and their culture, were delightfully exciting and flattering to national pride. Moreover, the remarkable extension of literacy in eighteenth century Wales, undertaken primarily for religious purposes, might well bring these intoxicating concepts to social groups hitherto largely immune from them.[4]

In spite of the age and venerability of these cultural bases, however, much of the nationalism of Wales, like that of many other parts of Europe, was largely a creation of the nineteenth century. The three most vigorous forces then at work in the country were: first, a marked growth of population with significantly increased upward social mobility; second, intensive industrialisation of parts of the country; and third, the rapid spread of religious nonconformity. The growth of population and the accompanying tendency towards upward social mobility among the more prosperous led to the emergence of more affluent and literate social groups of professional men, merchants, shopkeepers and skilled artisans in the rapidly growing little towns and of more comfortably off farmers in the countryside. Men of this kind were hungry for knowledge, diversion and, above all, for identity and reassurance through the medium of their own language and culture. Industrialisation, in the short run, was transforming the potentialities for the Welsh language.[5] Welsh speakers, unlike Irish or Gaelic speakers, were not obliged to abandon their language along with their old rural homes when they moved into industrial or urban areas in search of employment. They could take their language with them into their new environment. Furthermore, industry and trade were bringing wealth into Wales on a scale previously quite unprecedented. For the first time there existed a sufficiently large Welsh-speaking urban population and a wide enough margin of prosperity to support flourishing Welsh language societies and institutions; most importantly of all, to sustain a really vigorous publishing industry for Welsh books and journals. All this was being heavily reinforced by the phenomenal spread of Welsh nonconformity. The chapels were intensely Welsh in character and their commitment to achieving literacy among their members was total. Their ministers were an elite among the Welsh-speaking community, offering leadership not merely in religion but in all aspects of social and cultural life; they, above all others, were the great adepts in the manipulation of spoken and written Welsh as preachers and lecturers, poets and authors, and journalists and commentators.

How did this burgeoning sense of Welshness find expression in the nineteenth century? Much of it was canalised within the confines of religion, especially among Nonconformists. Religion offered not only emotional and spiritual consolations; it also brought intense intellectual excitement to many of its adherents who felt themselves to be emancipated from a world of ignorance and superstition into one of enlightenment which they could hope to master for themselves. Like all the more radical forms of Protestant belief, Welsh Nonconformity placed great emphasis on the responsibility of the individual believer to read and meditate on the Word. Nonconformist Sunday Schools, which adults as well as children attended, were the most significant medium of popular education for the greater part of the nineteenth century. The safeguarding of the Welsh language was widely regarded as being synonymous with upholding religion; to abandon Welsh was to run the risk of losing the faith. Furthermore, Welsh was thought to have the added advantage of inoculating those who spoke it against the insidious infections of the godlessness, vanities and political sedition that frequently found expression in English. Nonconformity at first tended to be narrow in its outlook and more than a little suspicious of the wider interests in social and cultural concerns, but by the middle of the century it had appreciably broadened its horizons.

This extension of perspectives could readily be seen in the extraordinary explosion of Welsh language publication in the Victorian era. As early as 1828 — and it became even more true in later decades — the editor of a Welsh language periodical put it very well:

> In comparison with earlier times the present age can be described as the *age of books* — *the age of readers* — the age when everyone is eagerly extending his hands to the tree of knowledge . . . It would have been unbelievable even at the beginning of this century that the printing-presses of Wales should have given birth to so many monthly journals as well as to a multitude of books on all aspects of knowledge.[6]

It has been estimated that some 8,500 Welsh books were published in the nineteenth century, as compared with 1,100 — 1,200 in the eighteenth century. Much of this output was religious in character — 370 editions of the Bible, for example, as compared with only 31 editions between the first Welsh Bible of 1588 and the end of the eighteenth century. There was also a great mass of books of more secular interest, histories of Wales, biographies and poetry being particularly popular. Perhaps the most convincing testimony to the liveliness and profitability of the Welsh book-market was that English and Scots publishers found it worth their while to commission Welsh authors and books and to maintain their own sales representatives in Wales. Even more impressive and more widely ranging in its influence was the growth of the Welsh language periodical and newspaper press. After a number of abortive ventures in the late eighteenth century, there were about thirty flourishing publications (most of them of a religious nature) by 1870. It is difficult not to be struck by the wide range and variety of their contents. Of their actual readership we know as yet far too little. But even if we make the cautious assumption that they were read by an elite of ministers and church elders, then they were reaching the groups and individuals strategically placed to mould, for the first time, an informed and self-conscious public opinion among the Welsh-speaking population over practically the whole of Wales. It must also have created an awareness of social and cultural distinctiveness among whole new social groups of industrial workers and tenant farmers for the first time. The experience of a Galician peasant, which was published as late as 1941, that neither he nor many of his fellows had fully realised that they were Poles until they started reading books and newspapers,[7] could well have been equally true of many of the Welsh in the nineteenth century.

Many of the people who bought and read these Welsh language publications would also have been the same people who supported the widely popular patriotic and literary societies of the age. Some of these were organised on the basis of the former principalities or provinces of Wales — Gwynedd or Gwent or Powys. Others were more local, and every Welsh town of any consequence boasted one or more of such societies. As might be expected, their aims were to foster and extend interest in the language, literature, history, antiquities, music and folk-culture of Wales. Two of their most typical activities were to celebrate the national day — Saint David's Day[8] (1 March) — and to organise *eisteddfodau*. The *eisteddfod* (an assembly for competitions in literature and music) was an exceptionally lively institution in nineteenth century Wales — not merely the national *Eisteddfod* held once a year but the hundreds of smaller ones held all over Wales.[9] The immense popularity of the *eisteddfodau* testified to the *kudos* which writers and above all poets enjoyed in Wales. The *Gorsedd* of the Bards, purporting to be of the direct descendants of the ancient poets and sages amongst the Druids — though, in reality, a late-eighteenth century invention of the arch-romantic Iolo Morganwg[10] — were held in enormous esteem; and it was the ambition of every Welshman with any pretensions to literary ability to acquire a bardic title. When so many individuals aspired to be poets, much of the verse was unavoidably pedestrian and banal. It was not the eisteddfodic poetry which gave birth to the best verse; on the contrary, it was the simpler and far more unpretentious lyrics which produced much the finest poems. What *was* impressive, though, was the extraordinarily widely diffused delight in literature, and not least in the highly complicated ancient alliterative measures of the *cynghanedd*, and the overwhelming channelling of Welsh aesthetic energies into language and into the written and spoken verbal arts. Their only rival was music, or rather singing, and this tended to be at its most popular when Welsh words were set to music. The visual arts came so far behind as to be almost out of sight.

Language also became inextricably tied up with political and social issues. Political developments are specifically excluded from our present brief; nevertheless, it may be important to make one or two general points. Political and social attitudes in Wales tended to become an extension of Nonconformity. To be Welsh and Nonconformist seemed to become increasingly synonymous with being opposed to an anglicised class of landowners and their associates and to the Anglican Church. Gradually this gave rise to a distinctively Welsh version of a concept originally associated with the French Revolution's emphasis on the rights and virtues of the will of the people. There emerged in Wales the idea of *y werin*: an idealised view of an extraordinary 'ordinary people' who were Welsh-speaking patriots dedicated to the virtues of religion, culture, freedom and international idealism; the products of the Nonconformist, democratic, vernacular society of the nineteenth century who had come into their own after centuries of oppression and neglect. This view of the unique merits of *y werin* has exercised a most potent influence in Welsh-speaking Wales for more than a century and is still far from extinct.

In view of what has been said already it will hardly come as a surprise to hear that it was round about the middle of the nineteenth century that the older Welsh patriotism turned into something recognisably like Welsh nationalism. No one has put the point better than the late R.T. Jenkins:

> Nationalism involves more . . . than an awareness of nationality, for it is a *deliberate assertion* thereof, and a *conscious direction of effort* towards some *external* manifestation which is conceived, rightly or wrongly, to be essential to the well-being of nationality. Granted these definitions it will be found that nationalism in Wales is . . . little older than the second half of the nineteenth century.[11]

Nor is it without significance that nearly all the Welsh words for 'nationalism', 'nationalist' and 'nationality' listed in the standard University of Wales *Dictionary of the Welsh Language* appear for the first time during the 1850s or the 1860s.[12] Most of the thrust of this emergent nationalism was directed towards cultural ends. It spurred on an energetic campaign for better education, though this was mounted on utilitarian as much as nationalist grounds. It led to the establishment of training colleges for teachers and to the foundation of three university colleges and eventually to the University of Wales in 1893. There was successful pressure for the teaching of Welsh as a school subject, the highly important Welsh Intermediate Education Act of 1889 set up secondary schools in Wales, and in 1896 the Central Welsh Board for the co-ordination of the educational system was instituted. In 1907 came the long-desired National Library of Wales and the National Museum. Side by side with all this, in the thirty or forty years before the First World War the foundations had been laid of a most remarkable renaissance in the history, learning and literature of Wales, which proved to be nothing short of a revolution. Some of the finest literature written in Welsh for centuries was written during these years. The critical study of the history, archaeology and language of Wales was firmly installed. The achievement was all the more remarkable because it necessitated the abandonment of many of the most cherished of earlier myths and shibboleths and because it was the work of a small nation pulling itself up by its own bootstraps with almost no help from a wealthy and cultivated aristocracy and upper middle class.

Cultural nationalism had gained so much momentum that it might have been expected to give rise also to the characteristic demand of so many comparable European nationalisms for the creation of a nation state. The ideas underlying such a demand are so widespread and familiar that they need not be expatiated upon in any detail. The nation was held to be a natural division of the human race endowed by God with its own unique character. It was founded primarily on language, which was the fundamental distinguishing feature of nationality. Its sacred patrimony of language, literature, custom and culture ought to be preserved pure and inviolable by those who shared in it. The only sure and effective way of doing so was by means of an independent sovereign state based on the culture-community of the nation, which was regarded as the only valid and justifiable form of political authority. While such aspirations elsewhere in Europe were well enough known in nineteenth century Wales, there was hardly any demand within the country for the creation of a nation state.

The absence of any serious demand seems to me to arise from the fact that there existed in Wales an unusual and highly interesting situation of two different kinds of nationalism which appeared to be compatible with one another at this stage. In addition to the kind of language-based 'new nation' nationalism already outlined, there was also an earlier, state-based, 'old nation' nationalism,[13] which had grown up over centuries of association with a monarchy which had incorporated two other nations in the island of Britain under its rule. (There are fascinating parallels to be traced in Spain, France, Sweden and Denmark.) Most of the Welsh in the nineteenth century — and for that matter in the twentieth century, too — regarded themselves as being British as well as Welsh and acknowledged themselves as being members of a wider political, cultural and linguistic community. They shared in that common and somewhat self-indulgent pride in the political, legal and social institutions of Great Britain and in the military, naval, colonial and commercial achievements of the British state. This was particularly true of the landowning class who thought of themselves, and were so regarded by others, as members of the ruling elite of the kingdom; but it was hardly less true of many other groups lower down the social scale. The minority who had had the advantages of formal education had received their instruction in English. Many more had a knowledge of English and greatly admired the writings of English authors of every kind — Milton, for example, was the most widely esteemed poet in Wales. The most influential of the patriots of the Romantic Revival in Wales, Iolo Morganwg, could refer with evident affection to Welsh and English as 'both my native languages'.[14] A number of regional and local newspapers in Wales were published in English, and the spread of communications of every kind made the language more widely diffused in Wales than ever it had been before. Moreover, even in the heyday of Welshness, some of the most influential of those who wrote and spoke in Welsh had their doubts about the viability of their native tongue. For instance, the foremost editor of a Welsh language journal in early and mid-Victorian Wales, David Rees of Llanelli, thought that Welsh was doomed to fairly near extinction and that the future lay with English. He believed that his fellow-Nonconformists must reconcile themselves to its fate and be prepared to cherish their politico-religious principles, which were more important than language, through the medium of English.[15] There were others who considered Welsh to be outmoded in the age of industry and commerce. Their attitude was expressed neatly enough in a cartoon in the *Welsh Punch*, where Welshness was depicted as an old lady dressed in traditional Welsh costume vainly waving an umbrella to hold back a railway engine, which represented the onward rush of business and technology.[16]

From the last quarter of the nineteenth century onwards, the increasing impact of new developments portended a pronounced extension of the future influence of English over the population of Wales and a correspondingly drastic reduction in that of Welsh. These trends were the product of two interlinked forces: the longer-term impact of industrialisation and the greater impact of the state on the lives of ordinary citizens. Whereas industrialisation in its earlier stages had powerfully stimulated the Welsh language and culture, in the longer run it had seriously detrimental effects upon them. In the later decades of the nineteenth century the pattern of industrial migration changed significantly. Following the creation of a railway network and the full opening-up of the coalfields, there poured into industrial Wales a mass migration of English speakers in numbers too large to be linguistically assimilated by Welsh-speaking communities. This is probably the most important single explanation for the decline in the number of those speaking the Welsh language. When enough English speakers came in not to have to learn Welsh to maintain normal social existence, a community became bi-lingual, and from there it was but a short step to becoming predominantly English in speech. In the heavily industrialised communities, moreover, the activities of local government, political parties and trade unions, the spread of daily newspapers, the greater ease of travel, and the advent of organised sport and commercial mass entertainment, all added to the use and diffusion of English. Just as important were the effects of the state's provision of free and compulsory schooling. Education was provided very largely in English, not only because this was government policy but also because what a majority of Welsh people wanted was that their children should leave school with a good knowledge of how to read and write English. Still more far-reaching, possibly, was the impact of the Welsh secondary schools set up under the Intermediate Education Act of 1889. They provided much greater educational opportunity and vastly increased social mobility; but they also creamed off many of the abler children, especially from the rural areas, and sent them out in shoals as teachers, ministers, doctors, and the like. Even those who remained had been largely educated in English.

Since 1918 the processes of change have become greatly intensified.[17] What has been most significant has been the breaking-down, on an unprecedented scale, of the relative isolation of the population. In an earlier period it had been this physical, linguistic and cultural seclusion which had insulated whole communities — some of them industrial, as well as the agricultural ones — against extraneous influences and ensured the transmission of an individual way of life, largely intact, from one generation to another. But in the 1920s and 1930s economic adversity cruelly dismantled much of the economic prosperity of industry and agriculture and destroyed the social optimism of the Victorian Age. Though the period since 1945 has not witnessed economic setbacks on anything like that scale, physical movement of people into and out of the country, and within its own borders, has been made easier and more frequent. Economic change and decline have led to large-scale migration out of the rural and older industrial communities alike — either to the more cosmopolitan coastal belts or out of Wales altogether. On the other hand, into many areas which were previously strongly Welsh has moved a sizeable influx of non-Welsh people for employment, retirement, second homes, tourism, or study. Furthermore, the media of mass entertainment and information, especially television, for the most part using the English language, have penetrated to the remotest hamlets and dwellings, where in previous centuries the language would almost never have been heard before.

During all this time some of the strongest bulwarks of earlier cultural nationalism have been breaking down. The romantic notions of language and history which had exercised so seductive a sway over Welsh emotions have been shattered by modern scholarship. Gone are the Celts of the Old Testament; banished are the language of Gomer son of Japhet and the Druidic sages and poets of the early British (except from the national *Eisteddfod*!); the better knowledge of history and language may have been more scientific but it has also been much less exciting and popular. Then again, the hold of organised religion, for centuries a lynchpin of the language, the linguistic community and the belief in a special relationship between the Welsh and the Deity has become much feebler. Not unrelated to the decline in religion has been the marked falling-away in the activity of local patriotic and literary societies. It is true that a surprisingly large number of Welsh books and other publications still appear in print, but they depend heavily on a considerable government subsidy, without which it would be virtually impossible to produce many of them. In so many spheres of contemporary life the Welsh language finds itself in competition with English. Such a competition is always bound to be unequal. Welsh is contending not with another small language like Irish or Gaelic but with a world language that has all the advantages that go with size, wealth and universality. On top of that, most people in Wales do not have to learn this immensely useful language the hard way but can pick it up without effort.

The resultant consequences for the numbers of those who speak Welsh have been extremely serious. In the Census of 1891, the first to record such information, the number of people in Wales who spoke Welsh was 898,914 or 54.4 per cent of the population. By the Census of 1921, although 928,183 spoke the language they represented only 37.2 per cent of the population. By 1931 those figures had fallen to 909,261 and 36.8 per cent respectively; by 1961 they were down to 656,000 and 26 per cent, and by 1971 had slumped to 547,000 and 20.8 per cent. Since language was the key to so much of the distinctive kind of nationalism to have grown up in nineteenth century Wales, it will readily be appreciated what damaging consequences this steep decline in the number of Welsh speakers has had on it.

There has been a widespread reaction of concern and regret at these developments — among the large majority who are not Welsh-speaking as well as among the minority who are. Many of these non-Welsh-speakers wish to see as much as possible of the Welshness of Wales preserved. They view with deep unease the dilution of national characteristics and the spread of bland and flavourless cosmopolitanism. They sympathise in general with attempts made to preserve and foster the language — as long as compulsion is not involved. There are many, of course, who are ardent supporters of national sporting teams and representatives. Considerable backing exists for national institutions such as the Welsh T.U.C., separate broadcasting services, bodies for the encouragement of the arts, and newspapers and journals specifically directed at Wales. 'Anglo-Welsh' literature, the efflorescence of musical composition and performance, and the achievements of the Welsh National Opera Company are widely admired.[18] Most Welsh people who do not speak Welsh nevertheless feel a well-marked sense of national identity. They usually resent any suggestion that they are not Welsh or that they are second-class Welshmen. They are conscious of an amalgam of many traits which shade them off from the English or the Irish or the Scots: a separate history, a prevalent radicalism in religion and politics, a deep dislike of class distinctions and snobbery, a warmth and ebullience of temperament, a deep attachment to their own kin and locality, a love of singing and rugby football, and the like. But, in general, they have not been and are not willing to think of their Welshness as the determining test of their political or cultural allegiance.

For many Welsh speakers, as might be imagined, the decline in the number of those speaking Welsh has been a catastrophe of the first order. They see language as the sheet-anchor of Welsh nationality and feel it to be incumbent on them to make the most desperate efforts to roll back the tide of language erosion. A large part of their energies has been directed to a variety of cultural institutions dedicated to the use of Welsh. A notable example is the national *Eisteddfod*, which for many years has been conducting all its proceedings in Welsh, in face of not inconsiderable criticism from some quarters. It is now a more indispensable focus than ever; itinerating from one locality to another each year, it becomes for the space of a week the Mecca of Welsh-speakers — even those who cannot physically be present turn their faces there in reverence, so to speak. The unpolitical and unmilitaristic youth movement, *Yr Urdd*, has, for fifty years or more, through its local branches, its summer camps, *eisteddfodau* and publications, encouraged the comprehensive use of Welsh and won a remarkable following among the young. From *Yr Urdd* came the initial impetus for the establishment of Welsh-language schools at the nursery, primary and secondary levels which have built up impressive momentum in recent decades. Interestingly enough, many parents who are not themselves Welsh-speaking have nevertheless chosen to send their children to these schools. Within the last few years there has been a significant extension of Welsh-language teaching in further education, teacher-training colleges and the university colleges. Though the departments of Welsh in the University of Wales have always been among the most powerful bastions of Welsh scholarship and literature, the use of Welsh for teaching other subjects has been very restricted. A demand regularly and vociferously urged in student circles at the present time is for the extension of such teaching. In view of the resounding emphasis always placed on education by linguistic nationalists in many European countries, the current agitation for Welsh-language teaching is not surprising; the puzzling feature, possibly, is that it did not emerge in strength much earlier.

Of all the contemporary organisations bent on upholding the Welsh language, the most active and clamant are *Mudiad yr Iaith Gymraeg* (Welsh Language Movement) and a similar but smaller rival group, *Adfer* (Restoration). The numbers in each group are small and the members youthful — in their 'teens and twenties — but they give expression in its most intense form to the tortured anxiety felt by them and by many others who are not members of their movement concerning the destiny of the Welsh language. Using non-violent methods of direct action as well as conventional propaganda, they have concentrated their protests and agitation exclusively on behalf of the language. While they exclude nothing from their programme which appears likely to strengthen the use of Welsh in public and private life, their primary targets have been increased recognition for the language in local government, education, broadcasting, road-signs, official forms and commercial advertising. The avowed object is to make it possible for Welsh speakers to live their lives wholly in Welsh. Recognising that such an objective could hardly be attainable outside *Y Fro Gymraeg* (The Welsh-speaking Heartland), i.e., those parts of North and West Wales where Welsh remains the language of the majority, the adherents of *Adfer* appear to have come to the point of view that a 'Quebec-style' autonomy, giving Welsh unquestioned supremacy in official and public usage in *Y Fro Gymraeg*, is the end at which to aim.

Many of the language campaigners inevitably have strong sympathy for the aims of political nationalism as espoused by *Plaid Cymru* (Welsh Nationalist Party), and vice versa.[19] But it is noticeable that adherents of the language movements insist that the central issue is the fate of the language, to which the attainment of political objectives must take second place. Nor is it a coincidence that among the linguistic and political nationalists alike, if indeed it is meaningful to draw a fine distinction between them, there has emerged a very strong inclination to see 'British' nationalism as the most insidious and sinister force in Wales. *Prydeindod* (Britishness) is condemned by them as the unscrupulous myth devised by English state-imperialism to hoodwink gullible Welsh — and Scots too! — so as to destroy the genuine indigenous nationalism. In other words, the two kinds of loyalty which for many centuries had been regarded as compatible, and even complementary to one another, are seen by contemporary linguistic nationalists as natural enemies. All the present signs, however, are that such a proposition makes little or no appeal to the majority and is, indeed, likely to awaken their suspicion and resentment.

For my own part I believe there is an urgent need for emphasising what the Welsh have in common rather than the differences between them. They are too small a people to indulge in the masochistic luxury of self-inflicted wounds.

NOTES

1.   For some general studies see D.M. Lloyd (ed.), *The Historical Basis of Welsh Nationalism* (Cardiff, 1950); Reginald Coupland, *Welsh and Scottish Nationalism* (London, 1954); Ll. Wyn Griffith, *The Welsh* (2nd. ed. Cardiff, 1954); Prys Morgan, *Background to Wales* (Llandybie, 1968); R. Brinley Jones (ed.), *Anatomy of Wales* (Cardiff, 1972); Gwynfor Evans, *Land of My Fathers* (Llandybie, 1973); David Williams, *A History of

Modern Wales (Revised ed., London, 1977); Glanmor Williams, *Religion, Language and Nationality in Wales* (Cardiff, 1979) and bibliography given therein.

2. Thomas Parry, *A History of Welsh Literature*. Transl. H.I. Bell (Oxford, 1955).

3. R.T. Jenkins and Helen Ramage, *A History of the Honourable Society of Cymmrodorion, 1751-1951* (London, 1951); Saunders Lewis, *A School of Welsh Augustans* (Wrexham, 1924).

4. C.E. Gittins (ed.), *Pioneers of Welsh Education* (Swansea, 1964); M.G. Jones, *The Charity School Movement* (Cambridge, 1938).

5. Brinley Thomas (ed.), *The Welsh Economy* (Cardiff, 1962), pp. 26-9.

6. *Y Gwyliedydd*, 1828, p. iv (my translation).

7. Elie Kedourie, *Nationalism* (Paperback ed., London, 1974), p. 120.

8. For Saint David's role in Welsh tradition, Williams, *Religion, Language, etc.*, chap. v.

9. Thomas Parry and Cynan (A.E. Jones), *The Story of the Eisteddfod* (Liverpool, undated).

10. Prys Morgan, *Iolo Morganwg* (Cardiff, 1975).

11. R.T. Jenkins, 'The development of nationalism in Wales', *The Sociological Review*, 1935, pp. 165-6.

12. *Geiriadur Prifysgol Cymru: A Dictionary of the Welsh Language* (Cardiff, 1950ff.), pp. 461-2.

13. H. Seton-Watson, *Nations and States* (London, 1977), chaps. 2-4, sums up useful distinctions between 'old' and 'new' nations.

14. Quoted in G.J. Williams, *Iolo Morganwg* (Cardiff, 1956), p. 102.

15. Glanmor Williams (ed.), *David Rees Llanelli* (Cardiff, 1950), pp. 49-51.

16. Lloyd (ed.), *Historical Basis*, p. 111.

17. Ieuan G. Jones, supplementary chapter to Williams, *Modern Wales*; A. Le Calvez, *Un Cas de bilinguisme: le Pays de Galles* (Lannion, 1970); Meic Stephens (ed.), *The Welsh Language Today* (Llandysul, 1973).

18. Meic Stephens (ed.), *The Arts in Wales, 1950-75* (Welsh Arts Council, 1979).

19. For recent Welsh politics, see Kenneth O. Morgan, *Wales in British Politics, 1868-1922* (Cardiff, 1970) and A. Butt Philip, *The Welsh Question* (Cardiff, 1975).

Nineteenth Century Scottish Nationalism: the Cultural Background

Rosalind Mitchison

IT is a commonplace that the Scots have a strong sense of national identity which, for the most part, has not been expressed in a demand for a separate political identity. In the nineteenth century they accepted a position of recognised cultural identity within Great Britain, asserted often by stress on points of pedantry, as in Sir Walter Scott's defence of the Scottish banknote in 1826.[1] Even the more explicit nationalism of the years after 1850 used a similar technique and concentrated on heraldry, Highland dress, the misuse of the word 'England' for 'Britain' and use of the word 'Scotch'.[2] Scottish nationalism has also to be seen in the context of a tacit English nationalism which has assumed that the various parts of the United Kingdom have delighted in becoming English. No strong demand spanning all classes for a clear political identity emerged in Scotland until the mid-twentieth century.

It is also a commonplace that the recognition of Scottish nationality spans a much greater gulf in Scotland than that between most Scots and the English, for it covers the society of the Highlands — different from lowland Scotland in language and literature, government (till the later eighteenth century) and religion — as well as the English speaking Lowlands. Scots in this century and the nineteenth have often stressed similarities between their society and countries in continental Europe, but the ease with which Scots have sought and found placement in England shows that this has been less significant than assimilation to that country. A correspondent to an Edinburgh newspaper stated ungrammatically in 1786 'we are not so different from the present English manners as they are from those of 1600'.[3] It would take more than a common use of Roman Law, Genevan Church discipline, a non-English pronunciation of classical languages and some odd words of French derivation to override the fact that the main influences on lowland culture since 1600 have either been derived directly from England or from experiences that Scotland and England had undergone together. This accentuates the surprising nature of the acceptance of a common national feeling in both Highlands and Lowlands. A reason for it may lie in the fine timing of eighteenth century cultural developments. Very soon after the Highlands ceased to be a political threat to the Lowlands, Gaelic culture caught the imagination of the world in two separate ways. The poetry of Ossian appealed to romantic ideas of barbaric simplicity, and the ardours with which the Highlands accepted extreme evangelicalism at the end of the eighteenth century gave them a 'holier than thou' aspect which reflected the pose of Scotland as a whole to England.

Scottish culture should be considered in those aspects of Scottish life and organisation which were either expressly left to the nation by the Act of Union with England of 1707, or which remained tacitly within Scottish control. Under the first heading came the Law of Scotland, family law, commercial law and land law, all completely separate from the English, though the use of the House of Lords as a common court of appeal gave opportunities for cross-fertilisation. The Church of Scotland, a presbyterian system accepting a Calvinist theology, was declared inviolate at the Union, though this did not prevent the Parliament of Great Britain forcing a patronage system on it a few years later, placing the parish minister into a relationship with the landowning class similar to that in England. Local government came in the eighteenth century to have a pattern of organised anarchy very similar to the English except that the Church in Scotland provided a tightly disciplined parish base. Finally the educational structure devised in seventeenth century Scotland of parish schools linked to the lower levels of University study was expanded and developed in the eighteenth century and formed the career base of many leading figures of the Scottish Enlightenment. It is through these institutions, Law, Church, local government and educational system, that we must look at the nineteenth century, and of course also through literature, science and the arts.

Scotland entered the nineteenth century on the top of a great wave of not entirely justified self-esteem, which made it inevitable that the country would soon experience the sense of decline. The Enlightenment had put her in the front of European academic culture, Scots had opened up whole new areas of study, formalised by later generations into separate disciplines of which the most innovative were geology and political economy. A separate, and even contradictory, current to this minority development had kept alive a popular evangelism. By 1800 this line of thought, austerely Calvinist, pedantically scrupulous in denying a role to the state in religion, often looking back through a haze of misrepresentation to what were seen as the 'good old days' of covenanting excess in the seventeenth century, had produced various dissenting sects, presbyterian in structure and sharing the confession of the established church.[4] Membership of these could include large proportions of the population in some areas, and common structure and dogma gave them a powerful pull on the established church. Even within the established church the evangelical party, badly organised, probably contained the majority of both parishioners and clergy. The new evangelicalism of the late eighteenth century, which penetrated the upper classes, added to this older current, and formed more separate communions. Calvinist groups of evangelical emphasis, whether old or new, confident personally in their grasp of salvation, were inclined to deny it to anyone who disagreed with them (an attitude which slipped easily into self-righteousness), and tended to be socially and politically conservative. It was not easy to suggest to such people that they might be wrong, or that the country to which they belonged could with profit borrow ideas or institutions from somewhere less obviously on the road to salvation. This form of national pride was expressed in 1834 by the temperance reformer John Dunlop:

I could not at first account for the circumstance that the external morality of the French appeared not particularly of a lower standard than that of Scotland ... I became satisfied that the superiority of our religious and civil institutions was evaded and neutralized by the intemperance of our inhabitants.

He went on to comment on 'the usages and etiquettes of the Scots, where liquor has become in great measure the authorized symbol of courtesy ... as necessary a point of etiquette as for an Arab to offer coffee'. But, though writing after the Napoleonic reforms in government, he was still convinced of the superiority of Scottish religious and civil institutions.[5]

A third source of confidence and esteem was the fact that the country had come through a period of rapid economic growth with the social hegemony of the upper class hardly disturbed. It is true that from the 1760s onwards this class had nervously watched the labouring population for signs of unwanted independence, that there had been radicalism, and trials of radicals, and that there was to be a sharp scare of a radical rising in 1820. But any comparison of radicalism between Scotland and England shows how much weaker it was in these early days in Scotland. Later radical opinion was captured by existing influences, so that it fuelled political whiggery in the 1830s, and chartism linked with the dissenting sects. By the late nineteenth century a conservative type of radicalism had become the normal form of Scottish political expression.[6] It was improbable that one small country should be an intellectual hothouse, a splendid example of social conformism and have a hot line to divine intentions, and if these conditions did appear to obtain for a short while it was most unlikely that they would persist. The Scots in 1800 were over-confident in their achievement and potential.

All the same the Scots managed to convince themselves, and quite often, their English neighbours, that they had the answers to the problems of the early nineteenth century. In *The Edinburgh Review*, the most influential journal of the day, they can at intervals be seen urging the English to borrow their system of education or to accept the basic plan of what, it was claimed, was their system of poor relief. They supplied the medical men who struggled with the early public health problems produced by rapid urbanisation, manned the medical services of the armed forces and produced the popular medical literature. The founding of *The Lancet* in 1823 was a belated English attempt to counteract the Scottish dominance.[7] The Scots told the English how to manage Savings Banks and to develop popular education. Finally from 1834 to 1843 they showed how to run a modern version of the mediaeval theme of the struggle between Church and State.

By the 1840s it should have become apparent to the Scots that, however much they were filled with secular or divine wisdom, their society was suffering from the social diseases of the day in a particularly acute form. The system of education was failing to cope with the problems produced by factory employment for children and with the large town. Scottish town government had collapsed in corruption and inefficiency. The first of a series of enquiries into the state of the Universities had shown, in 1831, that these institutions were not adapting to the needs of the professions. The response of skilled workers to the repression of Trade Unions had produced surreptitious organised violence which had continued after Unionism became legal.[8] The grisly Burke and Hare trial of 1828 had revealed a disgusting background to the achievements of medical education. The Chadwick report of 1842 showed up Scottish cities as more squalid and insanitary even than the great wen of London.[9] The series of pamphlets by W. P. Alison in the 1840s displayed a relationship between the excessive meanness and bad organisation of the Poor Law and the health problems of the cities.[10] Drunkenness was established as a peculiarly Scottish vice, and one which, at its then standard of living, the people really could not afford. And during this period of embarrassing disclosure the Scots ran their Church upon the rocks.

Quarrels between Church and State have always involved both parties usurping the rights and territory of the other, and that of nineteenth century Scotland was no exception. The evangelical party, by then dominant in the church, had attempted to override the law of patronage by giving parishioners an absolute veto on appointments. This would assimilate the powers of members of the establishment to those of dissenters within their churches. But the livings of the establishment were held by the law of the land, and the law recognised patronage. The result was a series of disputes, which widened the issues spread over nine years. The ecclesiastical courts rejected ministers for obedience to the civil courts and the civil courts prohibited ministers from preaching. The lawyer Henry Cockburn, who had a reverence for law, a sympathy with the church and enough historical sense to appreciate the damage being done to both institutions by the dispute, has left a series of contemporary comments. In 1839, 'if the law shall triumph, and unchecked patronage be restored we shall have ... a constant absorption of people into a new Voluntary Establishment, till the Church be a minority': in 1842, when a state victory appeared likely, 'This newly-discovered legal Church may be the best of all possible churches, but it is not the Church which any one Scotchman suspected he had adopted': after the crash, 'fanaticism has always been an essential part of Scotch Calvinism'. His retrospective criticism of the intemperance of the judges shows how much the authority of the law had weakened. 'Passion sometimes invades the Bench; and when it does it obstructs the discovery of truth as effectively as partiality can.'[11]

The church crisis convinced Scots that their attitude to religion was different from that of the English, and not understood by Parliament. It is difficult to go along fully with the latter view. Both sides, the General Assembly and the courts, had ignored the fact that in the inescapable area of the overlap of controls it behoved each to walk warily. But the quarrel was purely within Scotland. It was taken to Westminster before the final breach, but this was merely a despairing attempt to stave off the inevitable. No legislature could be expected to assent to changes in the law of property being made by some other body.

The final break or Disruption in 1843 meant that two fifths of the clergy marched out of the General Assembly to form a body which, though claiming to be the true Church of Scotland, used the name of the Free Church. To this adhered approximately half the membership of the old Church, in some areas very much more. Doctrinally there was nothing new, at least for a generation, for the new church's stance was that it was the continuation of the established church temporarily separated from the establishment. Psychologically, though the breach appeared a bold step, it was not intended to be so daring. The leaders expected such a complete departure from the establishment that the state would have to surrender. This miscalculation, both on politics and on the nature of modern civil government, was the source of much bitterness. The new church set out to form itself on the model of the old in everything from stone-built manses to knee breeches for the Moderator, and the ceaseless pursuit of funds for these aims distorted its social structure and accentuated the rancour. The splendid vision of half a modern country prepared to quarrel with its government degenerated into a degraded pattern of rancour, jealousy and moral pedantry. The issues that the country wasted time and ink over were to be whether God could be worshipped in temporary buildings, whether the trains that ran on Sunday to carry mail could also carry people,[12] and whether it was permissible to publish in the same volume both light and serious reading matter.[13] Neither theology nor church structure was at issue between these churches, though later on the Free Church could not avoid some swing to 'voluntaryism', that is to the abandonment of the ideal of an establishment. Mid-century, the main presbyterian groupings in Scotland, all adhering to the same confession, were the Church of Scotland, established but with patronage dead from the risk of the congregation's defection, the Free Church, disestablished but believing in establishment, and the United Presbyterians, formed out of old dissent, believing in voluntaryism. Each had its own local and social base. Logic led the established church to seek the legal abolition of patronage in 1874, and the two disestablished churches to unite eventually, but both these displays of reasonableness produced fresh bitterness and rivalry, and the latter created new schism. So did changes in theology and liturgy. The established church gradually abandoned literal adherence to the Westminster Confession, and all three churches, after heresy trials, belatedly decided against the idea of the literal truth of the Bible. The Free Church, to which adhered the bulk of the Highlands, was held by the fanaticism of this area rigorously to supralapsarianism, and for a long while to fundamentalism. It was also held to a low concept of the social nature of religion. In all these churches the congregation was more an audience for the message of the priesthood than a participating body (this can often be seen today in the architecture). In the Highlands an extreme sense of the rigours of the elect led ministers to pride themselves on selectivity and a short communion roll.[14] Even though the process of reunification of large parts of the fractured body of presbyterianism had begun by 1900, the position of the Scottish churches in the late nineteenth century was not one on which the confident sense of a country which had the answers to modern problems could be built. On the credit side, the Disruption blurred the inevitable nineteenth century process of secularisation, the taking over by the state of the social services of the church.

By 1900 extreme views of calvinist predestination were not only uncomfortable pastoral tools for many ministers, but were coming into prominence as a block to newer types of popular evangelism. The severe doctrine that the elect were a small

minority may have appealed to parish and small town communities in the
eighteenth century. In the late nineteenth century when new forms of mission
went down into the slums that the existing churches neglected, this was less easily
put across. There was, as a result, a growing split between traditional and popular
Calvinism.

Nineteenth century local government in Scotland suffered, as it did in England,
from the problem of creating coherence in a system of which the strength had been
total local autonomy, from the problems of using two contradictory principles in
doing so, the all-purpose authority and the *ad hoc*, and from a continuing belief in
the primacy of localism. The local unit, a concept never defined, was felt to have a
better appreciation of its true needs, as well as (more understandably) of its
willingness to pay for their satisfaction, than any central body. Untidiness was
increased by the duplication of burgh authorities which had resulted from the
unwillingness of the early nineteenth century Parliament to face the problems of
burgh collapse before it actually happened. There was further confusion as
overlapping structures for public health were created. Scotland's geography is one
very difficult to use as the basis for a coherent system of local government, so the
extreme localism of much of the nineteenth century was not a bad approach.
People in the north-east had little in common with those on Clydeside or in the
isles, either in relationships between the classes or in resources. But localism and a
confused pattern of rights and powers were no answer once the modern
concentration of population on Clydeside had become advanced. Social problems
came to the fore in the nineteenth century and in so far as they were tackled this
was done either at a Scottish national level or in Westminster. Acts of Parliament
had to be passed, inspectorates created, centralised boards or departments set up
to supervise. All this involved imposing concepts of social order derived from the
lowland middle class on the country as a whole. The most conspicuous example of
this was the imposition of an English speaking educational system on the Gaelic
speaking Highlands, largely at high cost to the localities. At the same time this
school structure offered an opportunity for the able and ambitious to leave the
area, and hastened the reduction of Gaelic society to a single class. The new
governing institutions of the period forced local culture into a stereotype.

Probably more important than these Scottish institutions was the legislation
forced on Britain as a whole as she grappled with the problems of a modern
economy. It was in this need for common solutions that the really subtle but
usually unacknowledged bonding of England and Scotland together took place.
'Anglicisation' is the wrong word for a process that forced controls and
adaptations on to both countries. In contrast to the conspicuous lack of legislation
of the eighteenth century, from the 1830s on there was a steady imposition of new
regulations on both countries. Sometimes, as in the matter of licensing laws, there
were minor differences between the two, but usually they were alike. Scotland as
well as England required regulations about working conditions in factories and
mines, noxious chemical emissions, the education of young children, the control of
crime, the adulteration of food, the protection of investors and travellers from the

dangers of railways, restrictions on the right of individuals to live without benefit of fresh air or sewage disposal. The list is endless, and in most cases a common Parliament devised identical or similar devices for control. All the new aspects of government had to be paid for by a system of taxation which deviated from the relatively privileged position Scotland had enjoyed in the eighteenth century. A further group of similarities came from spontaneous developments in daily life as the people of the two countries came to wear the same clothes, eat the same foods, and travel in the same trains.

The exemption of Scottish law and law courts from the effects of Union had not been particularly significant for most Scots most of the time. Landed property and inheritance were not concerns for most people, the law of marriage had considerable similarities between the two countries, the realities of feudal relationship, nominally surviving in Scots law, were whittled away by the lawyers, the relatively protected position of the suspected criminal in Scots law was a minority concern. But the new areas of law, usually common to the two countries, pressed on all and frequently.

Scotland's major social contribution to Britain over the last three centuries has been the creation of the professions. Starting with the clergy in the seventeenth century, a united group of people living by a formalised professional ethic, continuing with lawyers and schoolteachers, adding university professors, bankers and doctors in the eighteenth century, formalising the definitions of these groups and adding engineers in the nineteenth century, Scotland had made her mark in training and often exporting these middle-class men. Because of these professions the Universities of Scotland had been peculiarly important, both for the continuation of education at all levels within the country and for her international standing. The sudden efflorescence of the eighteenth century Enlightenment owed a great deal to the existence of functioning Universities, where professors, teaching levels which today would come under the heading of secondary education, were able, because of the pioneering nature of many of their studies, to embody in them transforming or creative thought. Of course this could not last. Classes which had to link up with the products of the parish schools, in some cases not yet taken much beyond basic literacy, and to the narrowly based curriculum of the burgh schools, could not indefinitely keep in the forefront of knowledge. The problem was partly met by a rise in the attendance age of many of the students, and by the new academies which fulfilled some of the functions of secondary education for a narrow social range, but it still was the case in the nineteenth century that if the Universities were to do only partly what patriotic Scots asserted in the Parliamentary debates on University education in 1858 that they did — offer a higher education to 'the youth of the nation' — they were bound to slip below the rising standards of the rest of western Europe. Changes in Scottish education were repeatedly thwarted by English dissenting Members of Parliament for English reasons. As was stated in the House in 1878, 'when there was a burning in Scotland there would be a vast amount of scorching in England'.[15] It was particularly galling that the older English Universities, which did not try to serve popular need, had woken from sloth and offered an education, highly specialised and, since offered to young men rather than to boys, more advanced than the Scottish. Scotland could not compete on numbers, since her rivals were drawing from the prosperous middle classes. Then the new University Colleges of the north of England, particularly Owen's College, Manchester, started to fill a social need similar to that in Scotland and did so with much greater adaptability. In Germany, as many who wished to reform the Scottish Universities pointed out, high scholarship and a wide range of subjects had become available in the Universities. Only with more money could Scotland offer variety and scholarship, and the existing lack of variety was not only an explanation of why the Scottish contribution was lacking in many fields but also why so many Arts students failed to complete a degree. Variety and specialisation would mean abandoning the traditional dominance of compulsory philosophy. Sydney Smith had engagingly described the effects of philosophy on the Scots in the early nineteenth century:

> They are so imbued with metaphysics that they even make love metaphysically. I overheard a young lady of my acquaintance at a dance in Edinburgh, exclaim, in a sudden pause in the music, 'What you say, my Lord, is very true in the aibstract, but' — here the fiddlers began fiddling furiously and the rest was lost.[16]

Putting philosophy into the young in their 'teens was done at the expense of equally desirable subjects, and when the new examinations for the Civil Service were instituted, it was on these other subjects that the examiners concentrated. The Scots, unless they had added further study at Oxford or on their own, were handicapped by youthfulness and by the wrong specialism. Pressure built up for the serious study of literature, classics and history.

So the Universities were under stress. They were kept in backwardness by the need to link with an inadequate school system and were out of touch with new thought. J. S. Blackie commented, 'the Professors of the Faculty of Arts . . . are supported in a great measure by poaching on the schools',[17] and, in a later broadside, asserted that Scottish education, 'except for medicine' was 'weighed in the balance and found wanting' by international standards. Arts faculties went in for 'local traditionalism, rigid routine, meagre furnishing, puerility and crudeness', and there was 'utter vacuity' on the historical side.[18] Blackie, as a specialist in classics, may have had a vested interest in departures from the old curriculum, and the same prejudice made him consider it a waste of time for professors of Greek to be engaged in teaching the alphabet. Another vested interest was that of the 'red Scots', as a recent writer has described the pushing young men who wished to exploit the English connection: 'cosmopolitan, self-avowedly enlightened and authoritarian, expanding into and exploiting bigger and more bountiful fields than their own country could provide. Back home lurked their black brothers, demotic, parochial and reactionary . . . resisting the encroachments of the English'.[19] National feeling ensured that Scots who went to work in England or the British Empire continued to regard themselves as Scots:

often they returned to Scotland for retirement. Their nationalism was no less valid than that of those who stayed behind, and it put pressure on the Universities to adjust to the need of people like themselves.

So here, it can be held, was a nationalist pressure acting against cultural national identity. Or was it? The concept is valid only if it is accepted that national identity involves simply the perpetuating of the past. This attitude was manifested by Sir Walter Scott to Francis Jeffrey in his anguished complaint against innovation: 'Little by little ... whatever your wishes may be you will destroy and undermine until nothing of what makes Scotland Scotland shall remain.'[20] It did not die with Scott. 'Red Scots', and most of those involved in higher education, suffered from an exaggerated veneration for the classics, perhaps because of an overready acceptance in the snobberies of English assimilation. This brought the particular weaknesses of the Scottish Universitities to the fore. Only in the most sophisticated schools was there a good preparation in the classics. The result was that on even the low level of latinity at the Universities most students still floundered. In 1876 in Glasgow 147 out of 261 first year students failed to pass in 'humanity' (as Latin was called) at the end of the first year in what was part of the compulsory foundation programme for all studies. These figures were submitted to the Royal Commission of 1878 by the professor who held that Scotland was 'the best educated country of Europe', and showed fully the problem of the link between schools and Universities.[21] The trouble was that even without the undue respect for the classics the problems could not be solved by insisting that what had served fourteen-year olds well in the 1770s was the only suitable curriculum for eighteen-year olds in the 1870s. The 'reformers' wished to introduce options into the Arts degree and even specialisation in science without an Arts foundation, partly to encourage more to complete degrees and partly to fill some notorious gaps. They suggested alternative specialised curricula.[22] But this Commission's report was ignored and alteration did not take place until the 1890s. Only then did it become possible for Scots to study history at a University level, and by then the history accepted as 'respectable' for study was an English-dominated British history, predominantly constitutional. This was, as a modern historian has pointed out, 'the classical age of Scottish historical scholarship', but the whole educational system of Scotland refused to give a serious place to Scottish history.[23] Scots were free to buttress their sense of nationality either from the sort of myths transmitted in the nursery uncorrected at a more critical age, or by private study of an intensive kind. (These variants can be seen expressed in the parliamentary debate over the abolition of patronage in the Church in 1874.)[24] Naturally the former was the more common method, and myths are powerful. Scottish nationality thus remained linked to a peculiarly childish and fictitious picture of the Scottish past.

So it was only belatedly, waiting on the expansion and financing of a pattern of secondary education, that Scots were able to regain a University training generally capable of sustaining scholarship and national prestige, and when regained it had this striking gap in national history. In some subjects, notably medicine, they had been in the lead all along. The intrusion of Scottish surgeons into English posts was a matter of outraged protest from the English in *The Lancet*.[25] Perhaps it was an achievement of the old predominance of philosophy that Scotland had been able in James Clerk Maxwell to produce the founder of modern physics. But in the Arts subjects there was a lot of leeway to be made up before scholarship could be a source of pride, and the supremacy of the early ninteenth century had been permanently lost.

Finally there is the area of literature and the arts. The visual arts were not a conspicuously successful area of Scottish creativity in the nineteenth century, either in the Lowlands or in the Highlands. The one significant innovator in the most important area of architecture, Charles Rennie Mackintosh, weakened his impact by poor business sense. His signature on a building is the image of the tower house, evocative of Scotland's rural and feudal past. This is doubtfully of relevance to the highly urbanised scene in which he worked. Literature also had become retrospective and small-town or rural in its emphasis. In Scott, early in the century, and Hogg, this did not derogate from its impact since these writers took the disputes of the past seriously, but in the later nineteenth century school, nicknamed 'the kailyard', the use of the nostalgia of rural settings was completely spurious. It was not a development encouraging to anyone with critical standards, and its finest memento is the savage counterblast it produced in George Douglas Brown's *The House with the Green Shutters*. But the fragmentation of Scottish society enabled some real literature to exist founded in rural life. The peasantry of the north-east produced its own classic novel, *Johnnie Gibb of Gushetneuk*, and the 'bothy' ballads. More striking was the revival of Gaelic literary enterprise in the Highlands. The Highlands were an area buffeted by economic disaster, forced into an unnatural social structure, compulsorily educated in a foreign language and in thrall to a puritan religion, which in attacking the genial manifestations of social life, such as the song, directly attacked the poetry which was also song. Yet poets continued to write, and the continuing vitality and use of Gaelic literature at last forced the outside world to start recording and collecting it. The only religiously encouraged form of poetry, the hymn, produced a native style of musical expression of great beauty.

A decline in Scottish culture, as it had been evaluated by educated Scots at the start of the nineteenth century, had been inevitable. At the end of the century Scottish achievement certainly stood lower than it had, in international terms, even though it was still conspicuous for a small country. In some respects, notably in the literature of the English-speaking part of the country, the decline was not merely relative but absolute. In academic achievement there had been a shift in some of the main areas of interest. Scots still provided much of the exploratory thought in geology and took a big part in some other sciences, but they had never been in a position to compete with the Germans in philological or literary studies, and their philosophers were no more sparkling than those of England. Nationality had not managed to make national history interesting to the nation. Even before the rise of modern motorised transport and media the country had become unified in culture, but except in the Gaelic areas this had been done at the cost of the break-up of the homogeneity of local cultures. The urban working class, cut off by the class structure of society from much of its heritage, had created its own sober and respectable way of life, but if the popular evangelism of the eighteenth century is to be regarded as an important social feature, then regret should be felt that the bulk of the working class were by 1900 dissociated from serious religion, while still suffering from the obstacles to the expression of their culture created by sabbatarianism.[26] The squabbles within the fragmented structure of the churches had often little to do with social or intellectual issues. The upper layers of the working class benefited from the fact that higher education was more generally available in Scotland than in many countries, but as, as individuals, they stepped up the ladder of education they tended to remove themselves and their abilities from the class that had bred them. The Catholic population of Scotland, by 1900 mostly of Irish extraction and to a notable degree even of Irish personal origin, was kept in thrall to Irish church issues by the prejudices and preferences of a clergy almost entirely drawn from Ireland.[27] The great bulk of Scotland's institutions had become, partly or wholly, assimilated to a common post-industrial type with the English under the pressures of the countries' shared experience. It is against these changes that the growth of organised nationalist sentiment in the Scotland of the 1890s should be seen. The demand for more national recognition appears closely related in Scotland to cultural decline and institutional failure.

NOTES

1.   N. T. Phillipson, 'Nationalism and Ideology', in J. N. Wolfe (ed.), *Government and Nationalism in Scotland* (1969), pp. 167-88.

2.   H. J. Hanham, *Scottish Nationalism*, ch 4. See particularly the activities of Theodore Napier.

3.   *Caledonian Mercury*, 8 April 1786.

4.   A. Drummond and J. Bulloch, *The Scottish Church, 1688-1843* (1973), chs 3 and 4.

5.   *Report of the Select Committee of the House of Commons into the prevailing vice of Intoxication among the Labouring Classes, PP* 1834 VIII, p. 394. I owe this reference to Dr. J. M. McCaffrey.

6.   See Gordon Donaldson, 'Scottish Devolution: the Historical Background', in Wolfe, *op. cit.*, p. 6. 'There was a Scottish political tradition distinct from that of England, but it lay in radicalism and not in nationalism.'

7.   I owe this point to Ms Rosalie Stott.

8.   See the report of the trial of the Glasgow Cotton Spinners, *The Scotsman*, 13 January 1838.

9.   M. W. Flinn (ed.), *The Sanitary Condition of the Labouring Population of Great Britain by Edwin Chadwick 1842* (1965).

10.   The best known is *Observations on the Management of the Poor in Scotland and its effects on the health of the great towns* (1840).

11.   *Journal* (1874), I, pp. 247, 315; II, pp. 38, 41.

12.   C. J. A. Robertson, 'Early Scottish Railways and the Observance of the Sabbath', *Scottish Historical Review* (hereafter *SHR*) LVII (1978), pp. 143-67.

13. D. Macleod, *Memoir of Norman Macleod DD* (1876), II, pp. 135-48.

14. A. Drummond and J. Bulloch, *The Church in Victorian Scotland 1843-74* (1975), p. 322.

15. *Hansard*, 3rd series, Vol. 240; 1738-99.

16. Quoted in Michael Joyce, *Edinburgh: the Golden Age* (1951), p. 66.

17. *On the Advancement of Learning in Scotland* (1855), p. 39.

18. *Letter to the People of Scotland on the Reform of their Academical Institutions* (1888), p. 5.

19. C. Harvie, *Scotland and Nationalism* (1977), p. 17.

20. J. G. Lockart, *Life of Sir Walter Scott* (1902), II, p. 284.

21. *Report of the Royal Commission on the Universities of Scotland*. Evidence *PP*, 1878, XXXIII, p. 558.

22. The Commission is discussed in G. Davie, *The Democratic Intellect* (1961), ch 4. I find some difficulty in relating his comments to the material in the Report. There is, for instance, considerable distance between Davie's statement that the Commission wished 'the old general degree to be virtually abolished' and the statement in the Report, 'the candidate for a degree in Arts should be allowed to proceed in the present course, if he please, and as, no doubt, many will still do'.

23. G. Donaldson in Wolfe, *op. cit.*, p. 6. Bruce P. Lenman, 'The Teaching of Scottish history in the Scottish Universities', *SHR*, LII (1973), pp. 165-90.

24. See in particular the remarks of the Earl of Selkirk, *Hansard*, 3rd. series, Vol. 219; 809-15.

25. A. J. Youngson, *The Scientific Revolution in Victorian Medicine* (1979), p. 85.

26. R. Q. Gray, *The Labour Aristocracy in Victorian Edinburgh* (1976). Hugh Wylie, 'Religion and the Working Class in Scotland, c. 1870-c. 1914', Edinburgh University MA thesis (1976), Economic History Department Library.

27. O. D. Edwards, 'The Catholic Press in Scotland since the Restoration of the Hierarchy', *Innes Review*, XXIX (1978), pp. 156-82.

The Economic Case for Nationalism: Scotland

R. H. Campbell

AN examination of the economic case for nationalism must show that in a historical situation contemporaries believed that their country or region faced an economic problem or opportunity, and that the problem or opportunity was more likely to be tackled effectively by alternative political arrangements. It must also assess the validity of the analysis of the economic problem by contemporaries, since a political remedy aimed at tackling an assumed but not the real problem would solve the latter only by chance. More probably it would fail and an unstable political situation emerge.

Symptoms of an economic problem in Scotland — both as judged by contemporaries and as judged by latter-day historians — are usually thought to be revealed by comparisons with Scotland's own earlier performance or with the achievements of other parts of the United Kingdom, so that nationalism may be seen 'in this context as a political response to the persistence of regional inequality'.[1] More recently comparisons have been made with conditions in countries overseas, but many, particularly those with the Scandinavian countries and with Ireland, are inept, because for long Scotland has been a highly industrialised and urbanised country, which they are not. The political remedies advanced usually imply therefore more active intervention by a devolved or independent administration to remove the possible regional discriminatory effects of legislation within the United Kingdom. Attitudes to these issues differed before 1914, between the wars, and after 1945.

I

Before 1914 contemporaries were aware of instances of relative decline in the Scottish economy compared with its earlier performance, especially through the emergence of intense competition in such earlier successes as the production and export of cotton goods and of pig iron. Against examples of decline can be set continuing successes, the most striking of which was the growth of the heavy industrial complex of coal, steel, shipbuilding and engineering, based on the natural resources of the central belt and on the engineering achievements of the west of Scotland. From a wider range of heavy engineering activities marine engineering achieved such distinction earlier in the nineteenth century that ships built elsewhere were sent to Scotland to have engines fitted. A steel industry geared to the needs of the shipyards grew from the 1870s and, as the use of steel became common in the 1880s, Scotland's existing comparative advantage in shipbuilding was reinforced. A record shipping tonnage was launched in 1913.[2]

Contemporaries may have been satisfied, but the historian can detect signs of impending danger even among the successes. Particularly in such older industries as textiles, in which comparative cost advantages were being steadily eroded through increasing competition, commercial acumen maintained profitable trading by the adoption of oligopolistic practices, notably after the amalgamation of J. and P. Coats and J. and J. Clark in 1896.[3] Other textile firms followed. In 1898 three Turkey Red dyeing concerns merged to form the United Turkey Red Company. In 1899 the calico-printers joined the Calico Printers' Association. The effects of the amalgamations varied. Thread production remained successful, especially in Paisley, but was increasingly overshadowed by Coats' activities elsewhere, but dyeing and calico-printing proved less so. Success in the heavy industries, though less defensively based, had its own seeds of future difficulty. The record export of almost 40 per cent of the output of coal in 1913 was partly to compensate for the loss of buoyant domestic consumption, especially in the ironworks — then consuming only about 6 per cent of the output — and helped towards the exhaustion of a vital natural asset. Equally ominous for the future, some of the more specialised branches of heavy industrial production depended on a few, and perhaps unreliable, sources of demand. Overseas customers were of overwhelming importance in some firms — especially in shipyards and among the manufacturers of steam locomotives — and in some shipyards the demand became even more concentrated as defence requirements before 1914 led to increased reliance on naval work. Both sources of demand had their own unpredictability. Before 1914 overseas customers were deserting traditional suppliers and defence demand rested on notoriously fickle public policy. Whether stability and success came from the adoption of defensive oligopolistic practices, as in textiles, or from the achievements of highly skilled but highly specialised production, as in shipbuilding, the historian is more aware of the relative absence in the industrial structure of even incipient growth of the newer light engineering, consumer-based industries. The origin and early growth of what there was lay in the specialist tradition, and so followed the bias of the existing engineering interests and did not move towards the standardised mass production of the future.

Whatever the evidence of relative decline from earlier years in the achievements of the Scottish economy, and even those symptoms of decay in the areas of success which the retrospective view of the historian may detect, contemporaries could and did regard the economic scene with satisfaction, especially in the centre of the industrial growth in the late nineteenth century in the west of Scotland. Few cities have probably been so aggressively proud of their industrial achievements as Glasgow before the First World War. It staged international exhibitions in 1888, and even more ostentatiously in 1901 to proclaim itself as the second city of the Empire and that Empire's workshop.[4] Though Glasgow was not Scotland, it could rightly regard itself as the centre, and its industrial experiences as typical of the whole, not only because 40 per cent of the total population lived in the counties of Dumbarton, Lanark and Renfrew in 1911. Its prevailing economic optimism could be applied generally to the central belt, and the outlying urban settlements of Dundee and Aberdeen had their own bases of prosperity. Dundee's volatile economy, heavily dependent as it was on jute, suffered increasingly from international competition, but chiefly in the cheaper goods. Aberdeen had a wider industrial basis and its diverse staples of fishing, shipbuilding, granite and supplying the needs of its agricultural hinterland gave it a more lasting stability even though its growth slackened in the later nineteenth century. In rural Scotland conditions were more varied. The drop in wheat prices in the late nineteenth century was not as detrimental to the prosperity of agriculture in much of Scotland because of its lesser dependence on wheat production among grain crops and the relatively greater dependence on livestock production,[5] but, though Scotland was no longer a rural society, the economic experience of some rural areas was admittedly a contrast. In their cases the remedy lay in emigration, both within Scotland and overseas. More than half the Scottish counties had reached their peak population by 1911. The problem was most recognised then and since in the Highlands, but it was a rural and not an exclusively Highland problem. By 1914 migration from both the rural north and south of Scotland was not offset by the natural increase. Partly the movement was to the industrialising areas, and that meant to Glasgow in particular. As early as the mid-nineteenth century it was the only area to receive a net inflow from all other parts of Scotland. Before 1914 conditions were changing. The net loss overall by migration was increasing: 10.4 per cent of the natural increase in 1891-1901, but 46.8 per cent in 1901-11 and 53.6 per cent in 1911-1921.[6] Yet there is another way of looking at the migration. It was a safety valve which operated in many areas even when the incentive to move was not the push of starvation but the push of a desire to better one's conditions. In the years before 1914 the Empire was the destination of most who felt the push, but even their experience does not nullify the conclusion that, though the historian may detect the beginnings of the relatively unfavourable comparisons on which any economic case for nationalism must be based, the economy was still regarded by contemporaries as generally prosperous. The instances where the generally optimistic interpretation did not apply were exceptional, generally in rural areas affecting only a small proportion of the population, who could always emigrate from these regions in any case.

If contemporaries were unaware of general problems in the Scottish economy before 1914, in practice there could be no economic case for nationalism in their eyes, but the rejection of an economic case before 1914 was based on even more fundamental considerations. Few accepted any role for government in the economy in any case. Even the attachment of the early labour movement to home rule can be interpreted only in a limited way as being based on the desirability of economic intervention by an independent Scottish administration. The Scottish Parliamentary Labour Party advocated home rule as the fifth of the eighteen points of its programme when it was formed in 1888, but as part of its advocacy of home rule all round — 'for each separate nationality or country in the British

Empire, with an Imperial Parliament for Imperial affairs'. The socialist advocacy of home rule as a specific solution of a recognised Scottish economic problem lay in the future. The increasingly interventionist role which government was following before 1914 was in social, not in economic, policy, and led to the advocacy of new political arrangements as practical means to more effective action. Sometimes the impetus came from resentment at the neglect of Scottish evidence of a social problem until confirmed, or even only grasped, when English evidence provided confirmation.[7] The lower standards of Scottish housing were less matters of public concern than those of England. Physical deterioration was officially identified in Scotland before the discovery in England gave rise to official concern.[8] Sometimes the impetus came from the delays which were part of local legislation and which led the Lord Provost of Glasgow to suggest in June 1914 'drastic devolution or Home-Rule-all-round' as a way of expediting the city's legislative moves towards municipal socialism.[9] Most strikingly of all, the impetus came in those limited areas, such as land tenure, in which government did have a responsibility and in which the law of Scotland was different. If there was discontent in such areas, it was easy to transform attempts to gain redress into nationalist political aspirations, as in the agitation for land reform in the Highlands, which could be linked to the Irish example,[10] but it also emerged in involved arguments that the mineral royalties of Scotland were already nationalised.[11]

Such isolated examples were only harbingers of the future. They do not affect the assertion that economic action was not considered a function of government before 1914. Economic issues appeared in nationalist political forms only incidentally. The strength of Liberal Unionism in the west of Scotland, breaking the old Liberal hegemony in Scotland, was indicative of the attitude of many of those living in Scotland — paradoxically often those of Irish descent — to the nationalist cause. The Scots were not inclined to favour home rule or nationalism, but whether they did so or not, their attitudes were determined not by economic, but by other issues. Whatever the reality of an economic case for nationalism in Scotland before 1914, none was imagined.

II

After 1918 both the state of the Scottish economy and the role of government in tackling its problems changed in ways which provided a much more fertile soil for the growth of the economic case for nationalism.

Economic difficulties were not unexpected in some areas at least after 1918, but in pre-war experience breaks in economic prosperity had usually ended fairly quickly and could be countered by such short-term expedients as cuts in wages, drawing on reserves, or accepting contracts at only prime costs, action all within the control of an individual firm and certainly not calling for any general change in the industrial structure or any need to seek external support.[12] Between the wars the depression was so extreme and so protracted that such short-term expedients were no longer adequate remedies and the possibility of a long-term solution through a change in the economic structure came to be accepted, often requiring co-operation or external encouragement. How that problem was understood and tackled is the key to any assessment of the economic case for nationalism in the last fifty years.

The ineffectiveness of the short-term remedies and so the existence of the long-term problem became evident only by the end of the 1920s. The industries on which much of Scotland's prosperity had been based before 1914 contracted and the reduction in their scale became permanent through amalgamations and schemes of industrial rationalisation. The concentration of the textile finishing trades continued. Calico-printing came to an end in Scotland; the once-famous chemical industry, which had grown to meet the needs of the textile industries, especially in the provision of bleaching powder, suffered similarly and alkali production ceased. The rationalisation of the heavy industries led to notable closures in steel and shipbuilding[13] and was a permanent recognition of the existing collapse of the heavy industries, which had reduced output drastically from the record levels achieved in coalmining and shipbuilding in 1913. Compensating expansion of new industrial growth was still lacking. An immediate post-war upsurge left little of permanence, and an absence of the production of aircraft, cars, motor-cycles and man-made fibres overshadowed such successful but more traditional light industries as paper-making and printing or food-processing, which tended to be concentrated in the east and not in the more acutely depressed west.[14]

The symptom of the collapse and of the lack of alternative expansion was the new and conspicuous social and economic problem of long-term unemployment in central Scotland, and — even more shatteringly — among some of its most skilled workers, giving an estimated permanent surplus of male labour of 100,000 in 1932[15] and a resigned acceptance of a lessened, but still permanent, surplus even in the relatively prosperous year of 1937.[16] Between the wars too the traditional option of migration for those affected by depression and unemployment assumed new forms. Internal migration offered fewer opportunities when the traditional reception area of Clydeside had high rates of unemployment. External migration continued the high level of the early twentieth century to reach a peak in the 1920s when it exceeded the natural increase of the decade and led to a decline in the population. The early 1930s recorded a net movement inwards, but one that declined as more Scots left to seek employment in England later in the decade. That was the only direction in which the safety valve operated in the 1930s, with obvious implications for political nationalism.[17] Unlike the years before 1914, the evidence of Scotland's economic decline compared with the country's earlier performance could not be ignored by contemporaries, but it was reinforced, and given a significant twist after 1918, by comparison with the superior economic performance of other parts of the United Kingdom, chiefly those which attracted Scottish migrants in the 1930s. When the need for amalgamations and rationalisation was accepted, the incidence of closures was thought to have fallen more heavily on Scotland, and even when amalgamations did not lead directly to closure, it was easy to believe that the passage of control from Scottish hands — as in such a critical area as banking — provided at least the potential for Scottish interests to be ignored. The apprehension left its mark. During the Second World War the then Secretary of State explained his desire to retain planning powers: 'It merely arises from the experience which Scotland has had of the transfer of Scottish interests to a U.K. basis, — calico printing and banking for example, — and Scotland is exceedingly restive with any further suggestion of that kind.'[18] Comparisons with other parts of the United Kingdom seldom recognised that the economic collapse of the industrial west of Scotland was not general and that in Edinburgh and the east lighter, though often traditional, industries ensured less unemployment, and that parts of England — Jarrow and Barrow from different sides — offered everything as grim as on Clydeside. But the transformation of the industrial fortunes of the west of Scotland, where the population was concentrated, was most dramatic and came to dominate political thought on the economic future of the country.

The acceptance by contemporaries of a long-term economic problem of structural adjustment by the late 1920s can be demonstrated, not so easily the acceptance of a remedy through political action and even less of one through nationalist political action. Though government intervention was on a scale unlike that before the war, it did not extend to the acceptance of responsibility for tackling economic problems even when evident and pressing. Government withdrew from much willing intervention, hardly surprisingly in the 1920s when the Treasury's main, indeed only, method of tackling the problem of unemployment was to cut wages, and, just as unwillingly, the agent in any strategy of industrial rescue or recovery became the Bank of England. As government came to assume a more active function its scope was still limited, to general schemes for rationalisation which were seen as being at least in part the source of Scottish industrial difficulties, or to specific policies or subventions, such as one to finish the Cunarder which was to become the *Queen Mary*. The limitations on the adoption of a more general approach to industrial recovery were evident in the earliest regional policy which started in 1934.[19] Conceived as a measure to improve the standard of social provision in areas suffering from social dereliction to that of other parts of the country, it soon became in addition a policy of trying to reduce unemployment where it was high, concentrated, and persistent. It was not seen as a policy of direct encouragement of industrial development until some minor legislative changes later in the 1930s and then only marginally. The policy was based on the belief that the increasing acceptance of government intervention in the life of its citizens should be a continuation and acceptance of government's responsibility to achieve social amelioration, which had been accepted before 1914, and not a strategy of regional industrial development. If the comparatively adverse condition of the Scottish economy was accepted, the relatively limited role in economic affairs still assigned to government did not lead easily or automatically to the advocacy of a remedy through political action. But in the inter-war years, especially in the 1930s, several factors were initiating a move in that direction, though not always consciously recognised.

Not all accepted a limited role in the economy for government, but an extract from a letter by Tom Johnston, the then Under-Secretary of State, on the closure of the shipyards following rationalisation shows the dilemma they faced: '... These decisions to close particular works in the hands of private ownership are, of course, the decisions of the owners and shareholders, and there is no power by which the Government can interfere ... You will, of course, appreciate the fact that so long as industry is in private hands and is run at the risk of and for the profit of shareholders appeals on the ground of public interest are not likely to have much effect.'[20] Johnston's view was, of course, more widely accepted among his political confederates, but, being in the position of a minority government, Labour was unable to carry that conception of the function of the government in the economy any further. Perhaps it would not have done so even with a majority, but, though Scottish members had ensured the leadership of the parliamentary Labour party for MacDonald in 1922,[21] the gulf between his thinking and theirs soon grew, and they at any rate would have opted for a more interventionist role for government. To that extent Johnston's views could be taken to represent those of a wider group. At the same time, they had witnessed the rise of Labour representation in Scotland until 1929 and so the prospect that socialism was likely to be achieved more quickly in Scotland than in the United Kingdom. Their advocacy of a nationalist solution, even though often couched in economic terms, should therefore be regarded primarily as a shortcut to socialism[22] and only secondarily, or consequently, as having an economic objective, except to those whose entire explanation of the political problem and solution was economic.

Even where only a relatively modest role attributed to government intervention in the economy was accepted, it was possible to consider it in a strictly Scottish context and, even more important, to consider that it was not operating to Scotland's advantage. The Scottish Office was aware of this issue in some of its submissions to inter-departmental discussion on the policies for the special areas.[23] A contentious issue from the earliest days was the geographical boundaries of the areas to be helped, which in Scotland excluded Glasgow and such contrasting, though equally depressed, areas as the Highlands and Islands or some of the fishing ports on the Moray Firth. The suggestion that the policy should therefore follow 'discretion without geographical limitation' was advanced but made little progress. Somewhat cynically the Scottish Office suggested that the Ministry of Labour was applying double standards in Scotland and England. Yet again in the last year of peace administrative pressure to limit the scheme was thought to take inadequate account of Scottish needs. While it was agreed that the provisions for social action might be repealed, as Scottish standards had been improved, the need for a continuation of the industrial provision remained pressing. Diversification of industry had made little progress, such improvement as had taken place being chiefly in the heavy industries and as a consequence of rearmament.

The same growing awareness of how even the limited nature of the government intervention of the time could be regarded as failing to meet the more specific needs of Scotland can also be illustrated both in popular economic literature of the

1930s and in the growth of non-political organisations to try to stimulate action. The literature was orthodox in its analysis, with much in common with all the comparative studies of depressed areas at the time, except that the problems of the greater Glasgow area were imprinted on the whole of Scotland, which was then classified as a depressed area. On the eve of war one of the best of these studies could be taken as representative in its forceful conclusion: '. . . now that the state increasingly intervenes in business, and is regulating and controlling economic life in many directions, the necessity for the specific considerations of differences becomes more acute precisely at the time when the Parliament of Westminster has less and less time or inclination to take account of them. All this I believe to be true, and to my mind it constitutes an unanswerable argument for a greater measure of responsibility and autonomy for Scotland.'[24]

The leading non-political organisation was the Scottish Development Council, set up in 1931 to encourage industrial development, followed in 1936 by the Scottish Economic Committee, set up by the Development Council in consultation with the Secretary of State. Neither body sought a cure for Scotland's economic ills by nationalist political solutions and many of those who were actively involved in them joined in a wholesale condemnation of any form of home rule.[25] But, whether they were effective or not, these organisations supplemented and encouraged any tendency in the Scottish administration to seek a separate solution for Scotland. The secretary of the Scottish Economic Committee explained the Committee's existence because 'It is undoubtedly true that Scotland's national economy tends to pass unnoticed in the hands of the Ministry of Labour and the Board of Trade',[26] probably justifying the view of the Commissioner for the Special Areas that his views were 'somewhat nationalist' and that 'a secretary of English birth and experience would be more likely to get things in their proper perspective'.[27] Given the nature of its remit — 'to examine the possibilities of improving economic conditions in Scotland'[28] — it was almost inevitable that some of the Committee's activities and publications should be grist to the economic case for nationalism.[29]

The limited but growing extent of government intervention in the economy in the 1930s strengthened the criticism that it was not necessarily in Scotland's interest, but many of the economic problems then facing Scotland were little different from those facing other parts of the United Kingdom. Some government departments thought Scotland already received preferential treatment or failed to take up all the aid available.[30] But, as has so often been the case, the existence of a separate legal and administrative structure was ready to hand and any agitation for specific treatment could be directed into it. Its importance grew between the wars as increasing legislation required more Scottish statutes and particularly when much of the Scottish administration moved physically from London to Edinburgh immediately before the war.[31] The replacement of the Calton Jail with St Andrew's House may have done more to focus the economic case for nationalism than the institution of the modern Scottish Office in 1885 because of the time when it took place, but it was not enough. While welcoming the planned move late in 1937, Walter Elliot, the then Secretary of State, feared the changes 'will not in themselves dispose of the problems upon whose solution a general improvement in Scottish social and economic conditions depends . . . It is the consciousness of their existence which is reflected, not in the small and unimportant Nationalist Party, but in the dissatisfaction and uneasiness amongst moderate and reasonable people of every view or rank — a dissatisfaction expressed in every book published about Scotland now for several years.'[32] Elliot had identified the source of discontent in the 1930s. As government began to play an increasingly interventionist role in the economy it became easy to advocate a nationalist remedy to ensure that it was in whatever was deemed Scotland's interest.

III

Between the wars the economic issue which led to increasing disquiet was less the poor performance of the Scottish economy compared with its past achievements and more its relatively poor performance compared with other parts of the United Kingdom. Geographical comparisons became more important after 1945 as a generation grew up which knew not the supremacy and security of Edwardian days, but which was aware of economic achievements elsewhere which Scotland lacked. Even the popular indices of comparative economic performance changed. Unemployment rates were less pertinent when the numbers out of work were dramatically reduced — around 60,000 in the first decade after the war against 100,000 to 400,000 in the inter-war years — even though Scotland still had a higher proportion out of work than in the United Kingdom as a whole. More relevant in the more prosperous conditions of the post-war years were comparisons which had become possible only through the wartime development of national income accounting and which could be used to show, for example, that real income per head, even though rising in most years from the depression of 1932, was still lower and more variable than in the United Kingdom.[33] Though such relative comparisons showed a continuing need to improve Scotland's apparently disadvantaged position, the incentive to act was counterbalanced by the improvement in Scotland's own economic plight after the inter-war years. Opportunities were lost to improve the productivity of old industries and to develop the new but, as before 1914, the easy conditions of world trade after 1945 enabled the need for drastic action to be postponed until the later 1950s when Scotland's economic progress deteriorated and some of the one-time giants in shipbuilding and heavy engineering were forced into liquidation.

If the economic problems of the Scottish economy could be side-stepped for almost fifteen years after 1945, government's responsibility and perhaps even its ability to tackle them was accepted as never before in peacetime, and so increased the contribution to the economic case for nationalism of the almost accidental way in which a legal and administrative system, maintained and developed separately in Scotland for quite different purposes, had ensured that even the minor government intervention of the 1930s had been assessed in a specifically Scottish context. After 1945 an extended Scottish administration played an increasingly more active and well-orchestrated role in a nationally more active consideration of economic policy, which it evaluated in a Scottish context, and which it enabled the public to do likewise by an extended official Scottish statistical service.[34] The desire to bring greater precision to Scottish economic issues is evident in the reports of the departmental committee on Scottish Financial and Trade Statistics of 1952 and of the Royal Commission on Scottish Affairs of 1954, as well as in a series of academic publications of the same years.[35] After 1945 even those who were not sympathetic to nationalism — even those who were actively hostile — considered economic issues in an increasingly Scottish context, none more effectively than the Scottish Council (Development and Industry) which was formed after the war through the merger of the pre-war Scottish Development Council and the wartime Scottish Council on Industry. Such bodies devised an economic policy, specifically for Scotland, not because of a new, or even a newly recognised, economic problem, but because the enhanced economic function of governments everywhere was grafted into the Scottish legal and administrative structure which had survived the Union of Parliaments and which had its status increased from the later nineteenth century,[36] long before an economic role had been found for it. Created and expanded for reasons of political expediency, it lay ready to hand to give focus to the possibility that its further growth could solve the economic problem when it was recognised and taken to fall within the ambit of government. In 1754 Lord Hardwicke told Lord Kames that without a common system of law in the two kingdoms 'an incorporating Union must be very defective'.[37] Two hundred years later he was proved right.

The post-1945 desire for such action increased with a renewed awareness of a regional economic problem from the late 1950s.[38] Later statistical studies were to show that the growth of the Scottish Gross Domestic Product (GDP) lagged behind that of the United Kingdom from 1954 and seriously by 1958, but in the late 1950s ample indicators were readily available pointing to the deteriorating regional achievement. It was tackled by a new industrial policy, beginning in 1960, and expounded in the publication in November 1963 of a white paper[39] as one of concentrating aid on those areas deemed to have the greatest potential for economic growth and so breaking from the older approach, which had been criticised as too concerned with the relief of unemployment to the possible detriment of tackling the fundamental problem of changing the industrial structure.[40] The new policy was developed more generally by the publication in January 1966, this time by a Labour administration, of a master plan for the whole Scottish economy.[41] Legislative changes throughout the 1960s increased the aid to industry in Scotland and lay behind its sharp rise from £18.4 million in 1961-2 to £96.3 million in 1969-70.[42] Scotland's share fell in those years from 55.8 per cent but was still 34.9 per cent in the latter year,[43] but government expenditure ran at such a high level that, whether judged by its relative population or by its relative income, Scotland was not contributing its financial share to common United Kingdom services.[44] The increased expenditure probably helped improve Scotland's comparative economic performance in the 1960s. Once again income per head approximated the British average and both GDP and personal income per head in the north of England were below the Scottish average later in the decade. The reversal of the adverse economic trends of the late 1950s meant that the greatly increased governmental intervention and expenditure took place within the framework of the United Kingdom, and there is no evidence of any other political change being envisaged even in some of the schemes most directly concerned with the economic problems of the time. The Scottish Council's *Inquiry into the Scottish Economy 1960-1961* was specific: 'The proposal for a Scottish Parliament ... implies constitutional changes of a kind that place it beyond our remit although it is fair to say that we do not regard it as a solution',[45] and *The Scottish Economy, 1965 to 1970* planned for expansion within an undevolved political framework.

The plethora of statistical material could be used to show success; it could also be used to show continued economic problems. Success in the fundamental task of changing the economic structure was evident in the growth of industrial production in the 1960s but was not matched by a comparable growth of employment because of the different labour requirements of the old and new industries, while the way in which even the success was based on government aid was evident in the relatively low GDP in Scotland ensuring that the higher Gross Domestic Expenditure (GDE) per head came not from high consumers' expenditure but from the expenditure of public authorities and from Gross Domestic Fixed Capital Formation. More speculatively, but more seriously, the relatively high GDE and the relatively low GDP may be taken to indicate that Scotland's balance of trade was adverse after 1968.[46] Even the massive financial injection of the 1960s was changing the Scottish economy only with qualifications, and any indigenous and sustained ability to transform itself was lacking, but, whatever the success or lack of it, both Conservative and Labour administrations could be held to have reached a valid diagnosis of the economic problem in the 1960s and to be applying the appropriate remedy, but that the measures 'had nothing to do with devolution. A Scottish Government might enable decisions on industrial grants to be taken more quickly, as in the case of Ulster, and make regional planning more effective. But, valuable though this is, it is marginal as far as the solution of Scotland's economic problems are concerned.'[47]

Others reached different conclusions, and the increasingly independent Scottish administration continued to give point to the discussion in a way which never applied in areas with similar economic problems, as in the north of England or even in Wales. Any failure to improve the relative position of Scotland led in the collectivism of the time — somewhat paradoxically — to demands for more action or for politically different action. Though the measures to deal with Scotland's economic problems could rightly be said to have nothing to do with devolution, it was easy in a Scottish context to think that devolution, or even independence, would make them more effective. An added boost to those who felt the way forward lay in an alternative political arrangement came with the belief that Scotland had resources adequate to deal with her own problems and that they were, or might be, exploited by others. So it could be alleged about schemes for hydro-electricity after 1945. When oil was discovered in the North Sea the economic case for nationalism was given an added dimension.[48] Then the way to economic plenty seemed easy, provided that its use was restricted for Scots by an independent Scottish administration. The economic case for nationalism was complete, even though academic studies always stressed that the way ahead could never be easy.[49] If the move of the Scottish Office to St Andrew's House in 1939 paved the way to the economic case for nationalism, it was completed by the electoral slogan of the 1970s that 'It's Scotland's Oil'.[50]

IV

It is now possible to attempt some generalisations on the three phases. The economic case must be assessed in its two facets. The case can be substantiated in the first place only by demonstrating recognition of a relatively disadvantaged economic position for Scotland by comparison with its own earlier achievements or with performances elsewhere. That emerged in the experiences of the inter-war years. It is also necessary to demonstrate a general belief at least in the responsibility of government to tackle the problem and preferably in its ability to do so. That did not emerge until after 1945, and in many cases the belief in the ability did not come until the discovery of oil resources seemed to ensure the ability to do so if the resources were used appropriately. Any analysis of the economic factor is bound to emphasise — perhaps to overemphasise — its significance, but it does offer a possible explanation of the rise of nationalism in Scotland, or at least an essential ingredient which must be incorporated into any explanation. Nationalist aspirations may have many causes but possibly widespread support in Scotland is based on economic considerations. Widespread interest grew first of all only in the austere conditions after 1945, but the Scottish Covenant movement faded with immediate post-war discontent and perhaps the most interesting political achievement in post-war Scotland was before the difficulties of the later 1950s, in the General Election of 1955, which produced a Conservative majority in Scotland. Although — a sign of things to come — the majority was lost in 1959, even while it increased in the United Kingdom, nationalist aspirations revived only in the mid-1960s with the renewed faith in the competence of government economic intervention and rose to a peak when the intervention seemed to be strengthened by the possession of oil resources which might benefit others. The stress on the economic issues and on government's responsibility to deal with them is confirmed by the emphasis on economic factors in all elections and by the vital arguments concerning the extent to which economic powers should be devolved in the passage of recent legislation.[51] There is little evidence that Scots were generally interested in nationalism other than for the economic benefits it might bring. They have certainly shown little inclination to risk the loss of economic benefits for any other advantage nationalism might have offered. In that case it is necessary to try to determine how far political nationalism might be able to guarantee the anticipated benefits. In short, how real is the imagined economic case for nationalism? The question must be tackled at two levels. The first is to show that a political change would lead to more effective government intervention in the context of the existing devolved administration. Unfortunately much of the discussion, whether from economists or political scientists, stops at that level, which is of relatively little importance. The more fundamental task is to show that any kind of government intervention can transform the Scottish economy. That is less easily done, with one obvious qualification.

The decline of the Scottish economy has been deep-seated. Its success in the years before 1914 may be attributed to a mixture of favourable endowments of the coal then needed for power and of a tradition of skilled heavy engineering production. The coal faded and the engineering tradition proved inflexible and not adaptable to new requirements and techniques. The partial exception to the generalisation is that the supplies of coal have been replaced by those of oil, and that is why its discovery is so vital to the nationalist case in Scotland. It must be Scotland's oil or there is no reality to the economic case which is so fundamental to its general acceptance. Whether it should be Scotland's oil, whether the Scots would adopt a policy which should ensure its exploitation, and what will happen when it is exhausted are questions of morality or law and of the future, which need not concern the historian, but even a historian must raise one question over the future. If the economic case is fundamental to any general acceptance of nationalist sentiment in Scotland, then political change, advocated and accepted ostensibly to achieve an economic transformation, will lead to severe dissatisfaction with the political change if it fails. An awkward, unstable political situation will then emerge. If the thesis that the economic case has led to general support for nationalism in Scotland is accepted, the country's future political stability requires that the imagined economic problem can really be tackled by government intervention. To that discussion the historian can make no contribution, but the intractable nature of Scotland's economic problems, and the many failures to tackle them, must raise doubt. The crisis of nationalism may yet have to be faced and the inability of any political solution to provide the economic transformation so desired be recognised.

NOTES

1. M. Hechter, *Internal Colonialism* (London, 1975), 161.

2. The best recent account of the modern Scottish economy is in A. Slaven, *The Development of the West of Scotland, 1750-1960* (London, 1975).

3. A. J. Robertson, 'The Decline of the Scottish Cotton Industry 1860-1914', *Business History*, 12 (1970), 127.

4. C. A. Oakley, *The Second City* (Glasgow, 1946); M. S. Moss and J. R. Hume, *Workshop of the British Empire* (London, 1977); S. G. Checkland, *The Upas Tree* (Glasgow, 1976).

5. E. H. Whetham, 'Prices and Production in Scottish Farming, 1850-1870', *Scottish Journal of Political Economy*, IX (1962), 233.

6. M. Flinn, *et al.*, *Scottish Population History* (Cambridge, 1977), 441.

7. An attitude which was evident as early as the 1850s in the National Association for the Vindication of Scottish Rights, and even more so in the Scottish Home Rule Association of 1886.

8. Cf. the effects of the findings of the Royal Commission on Physical Training (Scotland) 1903, Cd. 1507, BPP. 1903. XXX with those of the Interdepartmental Committee on Physical Deterioration, 1904, Cd. 2175, BPP. 1904. XXXII, which was appointed in September 1903 after the Royal Commission had reported.

9. *Municipal Glasgow: its evolution and enterprises* (Glasgow, 1915), 7-8.

10. J. Hunter, 'The Politics of Highland Land Reform, 1873-1895', *Scottish Historical Review*, liii (1974), 54-5 and *The Making of the Crofting Community* (Edinburgh, 1976), 136-7, 143.

11. Royal Commission on Mining Royalties. Second Report and Evidence. British Parliamentary Papers, 1890-91. XLI. Evidence of William Small. Q.7067.

12. A. Slaven, 'A Shipyard in Depression: John Brown's of Clydebank 1919-1938', *Business History*, xix (1977), 192 and R. H. Campbell, 'The North British Locomotive Company between the Wars', *Business History*, xx (1978), 201.

13. N. K. Buxton, 'The Scottish Shipbuilding Industry between the Wars: a Comparative Study', *Business History*, x (1968), 101; P. L. Payne, 'Rationality and Personality: a Study of Mergers in the Scottish Iron and Steel Industry, 1916-1936', *Business History*, xix (1977), 162.

14. Scottish Economic Committee, *Light Industries in Scotland* (1938); C. A. Oakley, *Scottish Industry Today* (Edinburgh, 1937).

15. Board of Trade, *An Industrial Survey of the West of Scotland 1932*. (Prepared for the Board of Trade by the University of Glasgow) para. 543.

16. 'No conceivable expansion of these industries [the heavy industries] is likely to absorb all the surplus labour which remains.' Sir Steven Bilsland in *The Glasgow Herald Trade Review*, 1937.

17. The resentment continued against the wartime direction of single women to work in England.

18. Scottish Office. Development Department (DD). Thomas Johnston to Lord Reith, 24 September 1941. Scottish Record Office (SRO) DD 12/41.

19. G. McCrone, *Regional Policy in Britain* (London, 1969); D. E. Pitfield, 'The Quest for an Effective Regional Policy, 1934-37', *Regional Studies*, 12 (1978), 429.

20. Scottish Office. T. Johnston to M. Burnett, 3 November 1930. SRO. DD10/208 (1930) (Closure of Shipyards).

21. R. K. Middlemas, *The Clydesiders* (London, 1965), 116.

22. Cf. a modern statement of the same position: '... the real opportunity which present events offer is of course something more. It is the challenge to force the pace towards socialism in Britain as a whole ...' G. Brown, 'Introduction: The Socialist Challenge' in G. Brown (ed.), *The Red Paper on Scotland* (Edinburgh, 1975), 19.

23. R. H. Campbell, 'The Scottish Office and the Special Areas in the 1930's', *Historical Journal*, 22 (1979), 167.

24. J. A. Bowie, *The Future of Scotland* (Edinburgh, 1939), 218-9. See also Sir Alexander MacEwen, *The Thistle and the Rose* (Edinburgh, 1932), 49 and G. M. Thomson, *Scotland, that Distressed Area* (Edinburgh, 1935), 97.

25. Information on the opposition of leading industrialists in the early 1930s is in the records of Upper Clyde Shipbuilders (UCS 1/9/22) in the University of Glasgow Archives. Full reports are in *The Glasgow Herald*, 15 November 1932.

26.   Scottish Office. Home and Health Department (HH). Sir William Goodchild to the Under Secretary of State, 3 September 1937. SRO HH 36/117 (1937-8). Scottish Economic Committee.

27.   Scottish Office. Note of meeting between Secretary of State and Commissioner for Special Areas on 2 March 1939. SRO DD 10/178 (1938-9). Future of Special Areas.

28.   Scottish Office. DD 10/84 (1936-39). Scottish Economic Committee.

29.   Notably in *Scotland's Industrial Future: The Case for Planned Development* (1939).

30.   As in grants from the Unemployment Grants Committee. SRO DD 10/201 (1929). Slum Clearance and Unemployment.

31.   Following the Report of the Committee on Scottish Administration (Gilmour Committee) in 1937, Cmd. 5563.

32.   Scottish Office. Memorandum on The State of Scotland 18 December 1937. SRO DD 10/175 (1938). Special Areas Inter-Departmental Committee.

33.   A. D. Campbell, 'Income' in A. K. Cairncross (ed.), *The Scottish Economy* (Cambridge, 1954), 50-1.

34.   Especially *Industry and Employment in Scotland*, which began in 1947 with Cmd. 7125 as a Scottish supplement to the *Economic Survey* and the *Scottish Digest of Statistics* for 1953.

35.   *Report of the Committee on Scottish Financial and Trade Statistics, 1952* (Catto Committee) Cmd. 8609; *Report of the Royal Commission on Scottish Affairs, 1952-54* (Balfour Commission) Cmd. 9212; the most important academic publication was A. K. Cairncross (ed.), *The Scottish Economy* (Cambridge, 1954).

36.   See Sir David Milne, *The Scottish Office* (London, 1957), 15-17.

37.   Letter dated 17 October 1754 in Abercairney MSS. SRO GD 24/1/557.

38.   The condition of the Scottish economy after 1945 is well discussed in A. D. Campbell, 'Changes in Scottish Incomes', *Economic Journal*, 65 (1955), 225; G. McCrone, *Scotland's Economic Progress, 1951-1960* (London, 1965) and *Scotland's Future: the Economics of Nationalism* (Oxford, 1969); I.G. Stewart, 'Statistics on Expenditure in Scotland', in J. N. Wolfe (ed.), *Government and Nationalism in Scotland* (Edinburgh, 1969); H.M. Begg, C. M. Lythe, R. Sorley, *Expenditure in Scotland 1961-1971* (Edinburgh, 1975).

39.   *Central Scotland. A Programme for Development and Growth*. Cmnd. 2188. Shortly before the Scottish Council had published a Report of an Inquiry into the Scottish Economy by the Toothill Committee which had pointed in the same direction.

40.   Scottish Council. *Report of the Committee on Local Development in Scotland* (Cairncross Committee) (Edinburgh, 1952).

41.   *The Scottish Economy 1965 to 1970, a Plan for Expansion*. Cmnd. 2864.

42.   H. M. Begg, C. M. Lythe, D. R. Macdonald and R. Scrley, *Special Regional Assistance in Scotland* (Glasgow, 1976), Fraser of Allander Institute (University of Strathclyde) Research Monograph No. 3, Table 1. See also, 'Regional Assistance in Scotland since 1960', *Scottish Economic Bulletin*, 9 (Winter 1976).

43.   Begg, *et al.*, *op.cit.*, Table 2.

44.   McCrone, *Economics of Nationalism*, 96-7; for an alternative view see David Simpson, 'Independence: the Economic Issues' in N. MacCormick (ed.), *The Scottish Debate* (Oxford, 1970), 123-4.

45.   Para. 22.08.

46.   These admittedly speculative points are based on Begg, *et al.*, 159-166. See also McCrone, *Economics of Nationalism*, 64.

47.   *Ibid.*, 98.

48.   As in the scholarly exposition of D. I. MacKay and G. A. Mackay, *The Political*

Economy of North Sea Oil (London, 1975): 'Independence would provide Scotland with major benefits for the forseeable future' (p. 178), and more popularly D. I. MacKay's Rejoinder in M. G. Clarke and H. M. Drucker, *Our Changing Scotland* (Edinburgh, 1976), 162-5.

49.   As in D. Mackay (ed.), *Scotland 1980: the economics of self-government* (Edinburgh, 1977).

50.   Cf. 'The SNP are far from unwilling to use the North Sea bonanza for propaganda purposes . . . All can be paid for from the North Sea oil revenues once Scotland is free. Oil in the context of independence is the panacea of all of Scotland's problems . . . There are now relatively few constraints on the expression of nationalist utopianism.' K. Webb, *The Growth of Nationalism in Scotland* (Glasgow, 1977), 120. At other levels of discussion oil and its consequences began to dominate all economic discussion. See J. Evans, 'The Outlook for Industry' in R. Underwood (ed.), *The Future of Scotland* (London, 1977), 119-127; D. Turnock, *The New Scotland* (Newton Abbot, 1979), chapter 5.

51.   The dilemma facing the government on what economic powers to devolve, if any, is stated clearly in V. Bogdanor, *Devolution* (Oxford, 1979), 185-9.

Some Conclusions

Rosalind Mitchison

THIS chapter is written as a personal expression resulting from the preceding papers and the discussions which they elicited. It does not necessarily express the opinions of the contributors, though it is based on ideas and information derived from them.

These essays on nationalism show that there is no simple typology which can be used to explain its growth in these various countries. Still less is there a simple explanation of why in some countries nationalism has led to a demand for independence and in others remained simply a cultural expression. In all these countries nationalism took a 'separating' rather than a 'uniting' form, except that in the complex story of Denmark and Schleswig it had both forms. There is also a common negative feature of the absence of an important role for force. The emphasis of the studies might be very different if they had included the story of Germany or of parts of Mediterranean Europe. Only in Ireland was there likelihood of fighting for independence, and this may well be because only in the case of Ireland was the strategic safety of the dominant power involved. Though Danish popular nationalism has sometimes been attributed to the defeat of 1864 its emergence was much more complex than simple reaction to military failure, and in its early stages nationalism had a part to play in forcing the separation of Schleswig from Denmark. The relationship of Denmark to Germany and Ireland to Britain should remind us that nationalism in its search for independence has not developed in a vacuum: the priorities and pressures of the dominant power and the politics of an area, the intrusion of external economic forces, have all had important parts to play. In varying ways in Scandinavia and in Scotland nationalism was aided by the existence of specific political or governmental institutions of a separate nature. In Scotland a separate legal system prevented cultural assimilation. Norway was practically independent of Sweden long before 1905. Separate institutions have clearly been constant reminders of an independent past as well as foci for current sentiments.

At first glance religion might not seem to be a causal factor in nationalism, if only because the universalist claims of the various churches have meant that the boundaries of nation and church have not coincided. Indeed in Ireland national sentiment for part of the island and for much of the nineteenth century could transcend religious differences, while at the same time there was an important one-way link between Catholicism and nationalism. But as nineteenth century nationalism came to focus on concepts of race, Gaelic culture, language and literature, the Protestant areas in the north came to build a coherent resistance to

159

Irish nationalism which has now almost become another nationalism. The twentieth century added sport to the strands of cultural separatism. In Wales non-conformity did not meet a barrier at the ancient frontier with England, though the manner in which it was adopted in the Principality, and particularly its use of Welsh as a vehicle for expression, made it a powerful element in national identity. Another reason for scepticism of the religious source of nationalism has been the fact that nationalism has grown in geographical terms and in the intensity of support in many countries at the same time as the hold of religious observance has slackened.

But case after case of these individual studies has shown religion and the organised churches playing parts of unexpected significance in the growth of nationalism. The common Lutheranism of the Scandinavian countries made it impossible for religion alone to be a separating feature, but Lutheranism was closely tied to the governments of these countries and linked with a number of government functions. It helped therefore to promote the recognition of the activities of an 'alien' government. More importantly, in the ethnic characteristics of all these peoples religion was woven into every strand of daily life and into the literary culture. Literature, particularly printed literature, brought the Bible to the fore in Protestant cultures, and even in Scotland, where the churches were bitterly divided as organisations, and had their strength in different economic groups, the common nature of doctrinal belief and of interpretation of the Bible held culture together. Protestant emphasis on the authority of the Bible, and the need of all to be able to read it, was a strong element in the creation or development of primary schooling, and primary schooling was the instrument by which middle class ideas were imposed on, or accepted by, the masses. The way in which religion was tied not only to education, but also to other governmental functions, particularly in the limited administrative structure of early nineteenth century Britain, meant that these functions drew on the emotional strength of religion. Religion has always been too important for governments to leave entirely to the church, or for the churches to keep in isolation.

Language has had a part even more subtle to play in the promotion of nationalism. There is striking contrast between its important role in the sense of Welsh identity in the past and its non-existence as an issue in Scottish, but at least in these countries its role has been a natural one. The Welsh language has covered both middle class and working class, and was retained through the dislocations caused by the Industrial Revolution, but the achievement, through the school system, of bilingualism in the Welsh speaking population is an illustration of the way in which English culture was not held as antipathetic to Welsh identity. Both Scots and Welsh could accept a common British culture without disturbing the sense of Scottishness or Welshness, a fact which is particularly remarkable for Wales since there was no alternative aid to national identity in the survival of formal historic separate political and governmental institutions. Wales, before conquest and absorption by England, had not created institutions which could continue into a modern state, and her independence had ended early. In Scandinavia, except for Iceland, linguistic frontiers have not coincided, and still do not coincide, with ethnic or political boundaries. For the most part nordic languages do not have marked differences one from another. It is, of course, possible to have a national literature in a language which is not specific to that nation. There are today various such literatures using English but using it in distinctive ways. It is even possible to have a national literature which is expressed in a 'foreign' language: it was pointed out in discussion that Ibsen's writings are not the less culturally Norwegian from having used Danish as their medium. Yet the popular nineteenth century theories of ethnicity which are shown to have played an important part in the birth of nationalism, have associated a 'people' with a language.

The development of state education made language a nationalist issue. Schoolchildren had to receive instruction in some defined language, and powerful sentiments could be involved in the selection of the medium of instruction. Less obvious is the contribution here of the whole expansion of the role of the state, which raised the linked questions of the language in which the paperwork of government was written, and the language by which the public had access to the services of the government, one an elitist, the other a popular issue. In the educational and the elitist governmental role language has mattered not simply as a means of natural expression but in more formal ways, and the various national stories here suggest that language is only of real significance in the growth of nationalism when it has become accepted as a written, eventually a printed, medium. This conclusion, however, reduces the significance of language in the form of a recognised ethnic identity.

Even after a successful movement for independence the Finns have not attained linguistic unity, and some Norwegians, dissatisfied with a speech shared with 'foreigners', have been promoting the minority dialect of *Landsmål* to the status of a national tongue. This artificial linguistic *persona* could be brought forward in this way only because in practice it and *Bokmål* are very similar, sufficiently so to be mutually intelligible. In Iceland linguistic purity has been a tailpiece to the successful assertion of national identity.

The development of modern media, starting with the newspaper in the nineteenth century, has brought a new emphasis to language, and given new scope for linguistic imperialism. The historic accidents which in Britain created a newspaper dominance by London have not been found elsewhere, and the more dispersed pattern of output in other countries has reduced the seriousness of dominance by one dialect. Even so, through the scope of modern propaganda, language has perhaps been of greater significance in confirming nationalism in the twentieth century than in creating it in the nineteenth. In Wales it has been to such a degree the area of chosen conflict by extremists that it is enforcing a junction of the English monoglot Welsh with the intruding English in some matters.

There seems to be less ambiguity on the issue of an economic basis for nationalism. Economic success, notably in nineteenth century Norway, can give confidence and promote assertion, but is hardly a direct source of nationalism. The histories of several of these countries show either no valid economic grievance, or no sense of one — the two things should not be identified. Indeed it needs some sophisticated arguing to produce an economic grievance for Wales or Scotland since in terms of the standard of living and the opportunities of employment they clearly benefited from association with England. Ireland, where the rise of modern nationalism did go in conjunction with the collapse of the economy, and where at least some part of that collapse was attributable to Union, was content to remain in the position of economic colonialism for some time after independence. Yet the increasingly apparent strain in the economy may well have played a role in the marked way in the nineteenth century in Ireland all cultural features and expressions tended to promote nationalism. The formal issue that forced the separation of Norway from Sweden, the control of the consular service, was indeed economic in its base, since it mattered to the Norwegian ship owners. It forced the completion of Norwegian independence, but the nationalism which thus gained its aims had existed long before there was this economic issue, and, for much of the time, of the diverging national economies it was the Norwegian rather than the Swedish which was profiting by state policy. For most of the nineteenth century, if there was to be a sense of economic grievance between Russians and Finns it was the Russians who might have expressed it, since the policy of the joint monarchy favoured Finnish interests.

This lack of a valid sense of economic repression or disadvantage is the more striking in that there are economic advantages for a small nation in independence which could be seen operating in the nineteenth century. Most such nations have economies which are unbalanced and do not show the same mixture as the dominant power. They have a strong emphasis on one sector or other. Such economies can benefit from an independent government pursuing a trade policy designed to benefit the dominant sectors.

The small part that economic grievance appears to have played in at least the early stages of the creation of nationalism — a developed and articulate nationalism will create its own grievances if it cannot accentuate those that do exist — is the more surprising since it was during and after the great economic changes of industrialisation that these nationalist movements got under way. Clearly, even if not in the form of grievance, economic change has been of great significance in the nineteenth century. These essays show that this was mainly by means of the social and cultural consequences of such change.

In the twentieth century economic stress and economic grievance have played a larger part in various ways in feeding existing nationalism, though they do not seem to have founded such sentiment. They have been aided by greater sophistication in analysis, in particular by theories of economic colonialism. Also, economic issues can create problems within nationalist sentiment, and promote regional demands. Norway has poured subsidies into the northern part of the country and may thereby develop resistance in the south. In Wales the demands of the industrial areas of the south may have weakened sentiments of cultural nationalism. The Common Market has altered the economic climate for many states, whether they belong or not, and this can create new issues. In Scotland the economic troubles of the inter-war period and the relative weakness of the economy after 1945 led to the expanding, or creation, of governmental functions and this has meant a new emphasis on the organs of the Scottish administration. Depression forced forward theories of state intervention, and these made in Scotland and Wales for an intellectual approach to economic matters similar to that found in the Scandinavian countries in the nineteenth century.

A further element common to some of these stories is failure. Irish economic failure and the Danish military defeat, as already mentioned, have had complicated repercussions within the national movement. So, it is arguable, may the Scottish religious and cultural stagnation of the nineteenth century. It is not clear that nationalism would have been thwarted in its development if these failures had not occurred but the development would have been slower. A sense of success or relative well-being may make the status quo attractive. In particular the weakening of the Irish economy had much to do with mass emigration, and the existence of a large émigré population clinging to a traditional, and in this instance if not always, erroneous picture of Ireland has fed back into the home country an accentuation of the aggressive form of nationalism.

The crucial question that the study of these different case histories promotes is, why was the nineteenth century the turning point to nationalist development in so many different cultures? This brings out the significance of general economic change. In political and in cultural terms these societies had had very different experiences. Some could look back to a historic, separate past, some could not; some were easily identifiable and separate in ethnic terms, some were not; some felt politically or culturally oppressed, others not; some had in use historic institutions or linguistic and literary practices which emphasised their separate identities, others had not. But all experienced the penetration of market forces that stemmed from industrialised countries, all saw shifts of the economy to industry, or to supplying the industries of others, and shifts of population to urban centres, though the scale of such changes varied greatly. In all, the new economic forces, and the social changes that sprang from them, led to an enlarged role for the state, and into all these states there intruded the demands of particular groups for political expression. Once it was admitted that a government should be responsible to public opinion, then the issue of the location of that opinion could make latent nationalism conscious. Icelanders who had not demanded separation from an autocratic Danish monarchy might demand it from a Danish democratic state. Scots might feel a new need to control their own affairs when the government started to enter into areas of life hitherto left to private or local initiatives.

In some countries, notably Denmark and Ireland, there had been a patriotic eighteenth century movement among the better educated. In Denmark this appears as a manifestation of the Enlightenment, in Ireland as a response to the political demoralisation produced by British failure in America. The French Revolution added a more precise concept of representation of the people, but also began the process by which the relatively disorganised and therefore weak, even if autocratic, governments of the eighteenth century were replaced by coherent administrations and a stronger concept of governmental function. In Britain this reorganisation was delayed until the 1820s, but even there the period of the

Napoleonic wars put pressure on the country for men and money which made it necessary to introduce some limited reforms into a ramshackle administration, to enable more effective use to be made of the existing power structure. For Norway and Finland the long wars ended with a new political relationship. Danish patriotism had been called out by the vicissitudes of war, and Denmark was also susceptible to the influence of the new German patriotism also produced by the war. The issue of the Duchies was to generate conflict between Danish and German patriotism, sharpening both, and this issue could not be dodged once either country began to experience demand for representative government. From Denmark new influences spread through shared languages to much of Norway, and to some degree to Iceland. In one way or another all these countries received an irrevocable push towards stronger and more representative governments through the stages of political event which followed the American Revolution. This hothouse development was most marked in Denmark where an already culturally sophisticated society was contributing to international literature.

Denmark was particularly receptive of German intellectual movements, since the governing elite of Denmark used German as its instrument of communication. It is noticeable that Danish ideas of ethnicity had a close resemblance to German theories. Both spread across frontiers. Grundtvig's concepts had an influence outwith Denmark. If Iceland gathered a new emphasis on the folk from Herder, Norway gathered it from Grundtvig, as well as from her own scholars. Finland was culturally open to Swedish literature and so could share in the general European interest in the historic nature of separate ethnic groups and the concept of a distinct people and its language. It is symptomatic of this that the Finnish literary world should at the same time have been concerned with gathering together Finnish folklore, translating Finnish literature and clearing up basic problems of Finnish grammar.

To say that this movement was elitist is not to deny it considerable force. In particular it led to the creation of Folk High Schools, and through this pattern of secondary education it eventually penetrated to the future teachers of the primary sector. In the relatively undeveloped culture of Finland any movement was bound to be of significance, but in Iceland where there was a large body of distinguished ancient literature still, because of linguistic conservatism, popularly accessible, the movement also carried great force.

In the discussion of these various papers a considerable amount of time was spent on drawing the distinction between the sense, found often early in the nineteenth century, of ethnicity, of a distinct people with its own culture, and nationalism. Recognition of ethnicity was usually confined to intellectuals, did not necessarily promote any political programme or demand, and in particular did not stress popular political sovereignty. But it was patriotic, laid stress on separate histories and investigated them in many cases. Even if the 'history' so stressed was largely imaginary it was of significance. History gave respectability to the separate features of a 'folk' and stress on history meant a stress on those historic institutions which survived from an independent past. One such institution might well be language: another might be religion. The ethnic approach would permeate higher education and encourage learned and semi-learned publications, often in the 'national' language. Even in Scotland, where most Scots evaded serious study of their own history, the people as a whole were aware that it had different features from that of England, held to a different mythology, and sought prestige in different periods and aspects. They could not escape noticing the different institutions that survived. In Finland the patriotic national consciousness included a more definitely nationalist hostility to the Swedish government, and was for that reason attached to the Russian monarchy. It was the Revolution within Russia that forced the issue of independence. It had taken some time for Finnish culture to become acceptable to the governing group. Finns for long were apparently content with a system in which higher education, and the jobs to which it led, meant the use of the Swedish language. By contrast in North Schleswig the Germanising of the school system had a great deal to do with fostering nationalism. Obviously a patriotic elitist cultural sentiment does not become what we can recognise as a movement of nationalism until it makes an impact in the popular press and the primary school system, and until it can find issues on which to gather heat. In some mysterious way the theories of 'folk', which involved a particular respect for a religious peasant society and its traditions, turned into nationalism and took root in urban and secular groups in the nineteenth and early twentieth centuries.

This transformation of patriotic ethnicity into nationalism was worked in societies experiencing the effects of the industrial revolution, either within their own bounds, or elsewhere, and of governmental response to it. The new economic forces might take the form of full-scale industrialisation, the harnessing of sources of power, the building of factories and the creation of large towns, or at the other extreme simply a suddenly increased demand for some primary product, grain, timber, fish etc. In the latter situation there would be little in the way of sophisticated economic development, but the intrusion of cash dealings into new areas was bound to involve new social relationships and to dissolve old ones. The successful export of a commodity on a large scale meant a transformation of transport services. In all these cases people found their old livelihoods closely linked to the fluctuations of distant markets, whether within or outwith the area governed by the state of which they were a part. These changes might appear beneficial in their effect on standards of living, but they made people more susceptible to economic movements elsewhere over which they might have no control. Very often they opened a community to new types of people and to the pervasive influence of newspapers.

All these types of economic change were likely to promote individualism. Choice in occupation, and perhaps in the location of settlement, new skills which weakened the aristocracy of old ones, new contacts of a personal kind, all loosened the authority of existing institutions, of village or kinship group. Particularly they were likely to remove the assumptions which sustained any one pattern of family formation and family authority. This would be attractive to many. New jobs or untraditional sources of money would change the distribution of power within the family, alter the questions of consent and opportunity in marriage or involve people cutting their links with their past homes. Direct urbanisation forced on couples or on individuals the need to remake a structure of social links, but even a more limited intrusion of the cash economy could have a solvent effect on family and village life. In this period of social change people seem to have shed the authority of family, local group or landowner more readily than that of the church. And in the actual movement to new places and employments, while language might or might not be retained for another generation at least — the stories of the industrialised Highlander or Irishman and the industrialised Welshman make an interesting contrast here — the religious denomination again was usually a persistent feature. People took their churches with them.

Added to the direct effects of economic change were the tremendous changes in the role of government. Urban society needed a new structure of local government, more active trading communities needed policing, often new law and new channels of political communication, sometimes protective tariffs, industrialised sectors needed government regulation of terms of employment, working conditions, the effects of industry on the environment. For both secular and religious reasons there were demands for schooling which in the end had to be met by the state. For reasons of health there had to be regulation of housing and of industrial processes. But at the same time the power of mass armies, first revealed in the early days of the French Revolution and accentuated by the creation of railway systems which could move large bodies of men swiftly, drew many states into policies of partial or total conscription of young men. Powers that did not participate in the build-up of military forces were made nervous and their nervousness became another ingredient in the issue of the identity of peoples within the state. Patriotism or nominal allegiance of whatever type was likely to be put to the test some day, and in the century after 1850 was, in most of the small countries of Europe. This was again a means of forcing the issue of to which basic society a man's allegiance really belonged. The increase in availability of newsprint meant that these concepts could not be ignored.

It is against these social and institutional changes, themselves based on the new type of coordinated economic change that, in many areas the cultural discoveries and enthusiasm of the nineteenth century were deployed. Even in areas such as Finland where the economy was still backward it was in thrall to the pressures of developed economies. People needing new links to replace those dissolved by these changes were also under pressure from more intrusive governments, and at the same time they could glimpse the theories of linguistic, ethnic, historic or religious unity. Those who had had no objection to government by a distant and ineffective elite found it replaced by intervention by a powerful bureaucracy. The concept of a people was seized on by those lacking other ties, or was forced into their consciousness by the dual instruments of the popular press and compulsory schooling. Social and economic change had made the masses open to the ideas generated in an elite or borrowed from abroad, but usually these ideas could be spread widely only in crude form. It is the protean strength of nationalism, as Dr Butt Philip has shown, that it can take many forms. It can appear religious or secular, literary, martial, historic, racist, internationalist, intellectual or philistine.

It can appeal to a sense of injury or to one of achievement. It can link to other forms of political ideology or social theory. Given the shock of economic change, these various societies were open to one or other form of the new infection of nationalism.

M

Index